THE GO[OD]
THE MA[D]
&THE
UGLY

... not to mention
Jeremy Clarkson

The GOLDEN years of
motoring journalism?

Peter Dron

A selection of books from Veloce:

Biographies

A Chequered Life – Graham Warner and the Chequered Flag (Hesletine)
A Life Awheel – The 'auto' biography of W de Forte (Skelton)
Amédée Gordini ... a true racing legend (Smith)
André Lefebvre, and the cars he created at Voisin and Citroën (Beck)
Chris Carter at Large – Stories from a lifetime in motorcycle racing (Carter & Skelton)
Cliff Allison, The Official Biography of – From the Fells to Ferrari (Gauld)
Edward Turner – The Man Behind the Motorcycles (Clew)
Driven by Desire – The Desiré Wilson Story
First Principles – The Official Biography of Keith Duckworth (Burr)
Inspired to Design – F1 cars, Indycars & racing tyres: the autobiography of Nigel Bennett (Bennett)
Jack Sears, The Official Biography of – Gentleman Jack (Gauld)
Jim Redman – 6 Times World Motorcycle Champion: The Autobiography (Redman)
John Chatham – 'Mr Big Healey' – The Official Biography (Burr)
The Lee Noble Story (Wilkins)
Mason's Motoring Mayhem – Tony Mason's hectic life in motorsport and television (Mason)
Raymond Mays' Magnificent Obsession (Apps)
Pat Moss Carlsson Story, The – Harnessing Horsepower (Turner)
'Sox' – Gary Hocking – the forgotten World Motorcycle Champion (Hughes)
Tony Robinson – The biography of a race mechanic (Wagstaff)
Virgil Exner – Visioneer: The Official Biography of Virgil M Exner Designer Extraordinaire (Grist)

General

1½-litre GP Racing 1961-1965 (Whitelock)
AC Two-litre Saloons & Buckland Sportscars (Archibald)
Alfa Romeo 155/156/147 Competition Touring Cars (Collins)
Alfa Romeo Giulia Coupé GT & GTA (Tipler)
Alfa Romeo Montreal – The dream car that came true (Taylor)
Alfa Romeo Montreal – The Essential Companion (Classic Reprint of 500 copies) (Taylor)
Alfa Tipo 33 (McDonough & Collins)
Alpine & Renault – The Development of the Revolutionary Turbo F1 Car 1968 to 1979 (Smith)
Alpine & Renault – The Sports Prototypes 1963 to 1969 (Smith)
Alpine & Renault – The Sports Prototypes 1973 to 1978 (Smith)
An Austin Anthology (Stringer)
An Incredible Journey (Falls & Reisch)
Anatomy of the Classic Mini (Huthert & Ely)
Anatomy of the Works Minis (Moylan)
Armstrong-Siddeley (Smith)
Art Deco and British Car Design (Down)
Austin Cars 1948 to 1990 – a pictorial history (Rowe)
Autodrome (Collins & Ireland)
Automotive A-Z, Lane's Dictionary of Automotive Terms (Lane)
Automotive Mascots (Kay & Springate)
Bahamas Speed Weeks, The (O'Neil)
Bentley Continental, Corniche and Azure (Bennett)
Bentley MkVI, Rolls-Royce Silver Wraith, Dawn & Cloud/Bentley R & S-Series (Nutland)
Bluebird CN7 (Stevens)
BMC Competitions Department Secrets (Turner, Chambers & Browning)
BMW 5-Series (Cranswick)
BMW Z-Cars (Taylor)
BMW – The Power of M (Vivian)
British at Indianapolis, The (Wagstaff)
British Cars, The Complete Catalogue of, 1895-1975 (Culshaw & Horrobin)
BRM – A Mechanic's Tale (Salmon)
BRM V16 (Ludvigsen)
Bugatti – The 8-cylinder Touring Cars 1920-34 (Price & Arbey)
Bugatti Type 40 (Price)
Bugatti 46/50 Updated Edition (Price & Arbey)
Bugatti T44 & T49 (Price & Arbey)
Bugatti 57 2nd Edition (Price)
Bugatti Type 57 Grand Prix – A Celebration (Tomlinson)
Caravan, Improve & Modify Your (Porter)
Caravans, The Illustrated History 1919-1959 (Jenkinson)
Caravans, The Illustrated History From 1960 (Jenkinson)
Carrera Panamericana, La (Tipler)
Car-tastrophes – 80 automotive atrocities from the past 20 years (Honest John, Fowler)
Chrysler 300 – America's Most Powerful Car 2nd Edition (Ackerson)
Chrysler PT Cruiser (Ackerson)
Citroën DS (Bobbitt)
Classic British Car Electrical Systems (Astley)
Cobra – The Real Thing! (Legate)
Competition Car Aerodynamics 3rd Edition (McBeath)
Competition Car Composites A Practical Handbook (Revised 2nd Edition) (McBeath)
Concept Cars, How to illustrate and design – New 2nd Edition (Dewey)
Cortina – Ford's Bestseller (Robson)
Cosworth – The Search for Power (6th edition) (Robson)
Coventry Climax Racing Engines (Hammill)
Daily Mirror 1970 World Cup Rally 40, The (Robson)
Daimler SP250 New Edition (Long)
Datsun Fairlady Roadster to 280ZX – The Z-Car Story (Long)
Dino – The V6 Ferrari (Long)
Dodge Challenger & Plymouth Barracuda (Grist)
Dodge Charger – Enduring Thunder (Ackerson)
Dodge Dynamite! (Grist)
Dorset from the Sea – The Jurassic Coast from Lyme Regis to Old Harry Rocks photographed from its best viewpoint (also Souvenir Edition) (Belasco)
Draw & Paint Cars – How to (Gardiner)
Drive on the Wild Side, A – 20 Extreme Driving Adventures From Around the World (Weaver)
Ducati 750 Bible, The (Falloon)
Ducati 750 SS 'round-case' 1974, The Book of the (Falloon)
Ducati 860, 900 and Mille Bible, The (Falloon)
Ducati Monster Bible (New Updated & Revised Edition), The (Falloon)
Ducati Story, The - 6th Edition (Falloon)
Ducati 916 (updated edition) (Falloon)
Dune Buggy, Building A – The Essential Manual (Shakespeare)
Dune Buggy Files (Hale)
Dune Buggy Handbook (Hale)
East German Motor Vehicles in Pictures (Suhr/Weinreich)
Fast Ladies – Female Racing Drivers 1888 to 1970 (Bouzanquet)
Fate of the Sleeping Beauties, The (op de Weegh/Hottendorff/op de Weegh)
Ferrari 288 GTO, The Book of the (Sackey)
Ferrari 333 SP (O'Neil)
Fiat & Abarth 124 Spider & Coupé (Tipler)
Fiat & Abarth 500 & 600 – 2nd Edition (Bobbitt)
Fiats, Great Small (Ward)
Ford Cleveland 335-Series V8 engine 1970 to 1982 – The Essential Source Book (Hammill)
Ford F100/F150 Pick-up 1948-1996 (Ackerson)
Ford F150 Pick-up 1997-2005 (Ackerson)
Ford Focus WRC (Robson)
Ford GT – Then, and Now (Streather)
Ford GT40 (Legate)
Ford Midsize Muscle – Fairlane, Torino & Ranchero (Cranswick)
Ford Model Y (Roberts)
Ford Small Block V8 Racing Engines 1962-1970 – The Essential Source Book (Hammill)
Ford Thunderbird From 1954, The Book of the (Long)
Formula One - The Real Score? (Harvey)
Formula 5000 Motor Racing, Back then ... and back now (Lawson)
Forza Minardi! (Vigar)
France: the essential guide for car enthusiasts – 200 things for the car enthusiast to see and do (Parish)
The Good, the Mad and the Ugly ... not to mention Jeremy Clarkson (Dron)
Grand Prix Ferrari – The Years of Enzo Ferrari's Power, 1948-1980 (Pritchard)
Grand Prix Ford – DFV-powered Formula 1 Cars (Robson)
GT – The World's Best GT Cars 1953-73 (Dawson)
Hillclimbing & Sprinting – The Essential Manual (Short & Wilkinson)
Honda NSX (Long)
How to Restore & Improve Classic Car Suspension, Steering & Wheels (Parish, translator)
Immortal Austin Seven (Morgan)
Inside the Rolls-Royce & Bentley Styling Department – 1971 to 2001 (Hull)
Intermeccanica – The Story of the Prancing Bull (McCredie & Reisner)
Jaguar E-type Racing Cars (Griffiths)
Jaguar, The Rise of (Price)
Jaguar XJ 220 – The Inside Story (Moreton)
Jaguar XJ-S, The Book of the (Long)
Jeep CJ (Ackerson)
Jeep Wrangler (Ackerson)
The Jowett Jupiter – The car that leaped to fame (Nankivell)
Karmann-Ghia Coupé & Convertible (Bobbitt)
Kris Meeke – Intercontinental Rally Challenge Champion (McBride)
Lancia 037 (Collins)
Lancia Delta HF Integrale (Blaettel & Wagner)
Lancia Delta Integrale (Collins)
Land Rover Series III Reborn (Porter)
Land Rover, The Half-ton Military (Cook)
Lea-Francis Story, The (Price)
Le Mans Panoramic (Ireland)
Lexus Story, The (Long)
Lola – The Illustrated History (1957-1977) (Starkey)
Lola – All the Sports Racing & Single-seater Racing Cars 1978-1997 (Starkey)
Lola T70 – The Racing History & Individual Chassis Record – 4th Edition (Starkey)
Lotus 18 Colin Chapman's U-turn (Whitelock)
Lotus 49 (Oliver)
Marketingmobiles, The Wonderful Wacky World of (Hale)
Maserati 250F In Focus (Pritchard)
Mazda MX-5/Miata 1.6 Enthusiast's Workshop Manual (Grainger & Shoemark)
Mazda MX-5/Miata 1.8 Enthusiast's Workshop Manual (Grainger & Shoemark)
Mazda MX-5 Miata, The book of the – The 'Mk1' NA-series 1988 to 1997 (Long)
Mazda MX-5 Miata Roadster (Long)
Mazda Rotary-engined Cars (Cranswick)
Maximum Mini (Booij)
Meet the English (Bowie)
Mercedes-Benz SL – R230 series 2001 to 2011 (Long)
Mercedes-Benz SL – W113-series 1963-1971 (Long)
Mercedes-Benz SL & SLC – 107-series 1971-1989 (Long)
Mercedes-Benz SLK – R170 series 1996-2004 (Long)
Mercedes-Benz SLK – R171 series 2004-2011 (Long)
Mercedes-Benz W123-series – All models 1976 to 1986 (Long)
Mercedes G-Wagen (Long)
MGA (Price Williams)
MGB & MGB GT– Expert Guide (Auto-doc Series) (Williams)
MGB Electrical Systems Updated & Revised Edition (Astley)
Micro Caravans (Jenkinson)
Micro Trucks (Mort)
Microcars at Large! (Quellin)
Mini Cooper – The Real Thing! (Tipler)
Mini Minor to Asia Minor (West)
Mitsubishi Lancer Evo, The Road Car & WRC Story (Long)
Montlhéry, The Story of the Paris Autodrome (Boddy)
MOPAR Muscle - Barracuda, Dart & Valiant 1960-1980 (Cranswick)
Morgan Maverick (Lawrence)
Morgan 3 Wheeler – back to the future!, The (Dron)
Morris Minor, 60 Years on the Road (Newell)
Motor Movies – The Posters! (Veysey)
Motor Racing – Reflections of a Lost Era (Carter)
Motor Racing – The Pursuit of Victory 1930-1962 (Carter)
Motor Racing – The Pursuit of Victory 1963-1972 (Wyatt/Sears)
Motor Racing Heroes – The Stories of 100 Greats (Newman)
Motorhomes, The Illustrated History (Jenkinson)
Motorsport In colour, 1950s (Wainwright)
MV Agusta Fours, The book of the classic (Falloon)
N.A.R.T. – A concise history of the North American Racing Team 1957 to 1983 (O'Neil)
Nissan 300ZX & 350Z – The Z-Car Story (Long)
Nissan GT-R Supercar: Born to race (Gorodji)
Northeast American Sports Car Races 1950-1959 (O'Neil)
Nothing Runs – Misadventures in the Classic, Collectable & Exotic Car Biz (Slutsky)
Pass the Theory and Practical Driving Tests (Gibson & Hoole)
Peking to Paris 2007 (Young)
Pontiac Firebird – New 3rd Edition (Cranswick)
Porsche 356 (2nd Edition) (Long)
Porsche 908 (Födisch, Neßhöver, Roßbach, Schwarz & Roßbach)
Porsche 911 Carrera – The Last of the Evolution (Corlett)
Porsche 911R, RS & RSR, 4th Edition (Starkey)
Porsche 911, The Book of the (Long)
Porsche 911 – The Definitive History 2004-2012 (Long)
Porsche – The Racing 914s (Smith)
Porsche 911SC 'Super Carrera' – The Essential Companion (Streather)
Porsche 914 & 914-6: The Definitive History of the Road & Competition Cars (Long)
Porsche 924 (Long)
The Porsche 924 Carreras – evolution to excellence (Smith)
Porsche 928 (Long)
Porsche 944 (Long)
Porsche 964, 993 & 996 Data Plate Code Breaker (Streather)
Porsche 993 'King Of Porsche' – The Essential Companion (Streather)
Porsche 996 'Supreme Porsche' – The Essential Companion (Streather)
Porsche 997 2004-2012 – Porsche Excellence (Streather)
Porsche Boxster – The 986 series 1996-2004 (Long)
Porsche Boxster & Cayman – The 987 series (2004-2013) (Long)
Porsche Racing Cars – 1953 to 1975 (Long)
Porsche Racing Cars – 1976 to 2005 (Long)
Porsche – The Rally Story (Meredith)
Porsche: Three Generations of Genius (Meredith)
Powered by Porsche (Smith)
Preston Tucker & Others (Linde)
RAC Rally Action! (Gardiner)
Racing Colours – Motor Racing Compositions 1908-2009 (Newman)
Racing Line – British motorcycle racing in the golden age of the big single (Guntrip)
Rallye Sport Fords: The Inside Story (Moreton)
Renewable Energy Home Handbook, The (Porter)
Roads with a View – England's greatest views and how to find them by road (Corfield)
Rolls-Royce Silver Shadow/Bentley T Series Corniche & Camargue – Revised & Enlarged Edition (Bobbitt)
Rolls-Royce Silver Spirit, Silver Spur & Bentley Mulsanne 2nd Edition (Bobbitt)
Rootes Cars of the 50s, 60s & 70s – Hillman, Humber, Singer, Sunbeam & Talbot (Rowe)
Rover P4 (Bobbitt)
Runways & Racers (O'Neil)
Russian Motor Vehicles – Soviet Limousines 1930-2003 (Kelly)
Russian Motor Vehicles – The Czarist Period 1784 to 1917 (Kelly)
RX-7 – Mazda's Rotary Engine Sportscar (Updated & Revised New Edition) (Long)
Singer Story: Cars, Commercial Vehicles, Bicycles & Motorcycle (Atkinson)
Sleeping Beauties USA – abandoned classic cars & trucks (Marek)
SM – Citroën's Maserati-engined Supercar (Long & Claverol)
Speedway – Auto racing's ghost tracks (Collins & Ireland)
Sprite Caravans, The Story of (Jenkinson)
Standard Motor Company, The Book of the (Robson)
Steve Hole's Kit Car Cornucopia – Cars, Companies, Stories, Facts & Figures: the UK's kit car scene since 1949 (Hole)
Subaru Impreza: The Road Car And WRC Story (Long)
Supercar, How to Build your own (Thompson)
Tales from the Toolbox (Oliver)
Tatra – The Legacy of Hans Ledwinka, Updated & Enlarged Collector's Edition of 1500 copies (Margolius & Henry)
Taxi! The Story of the 'London' Taxicab (Bobbitt)
This Day in Automotive History (Corey)
To Boldly Go – twenty six vehicle designs that dared to be different (Hull)
Toleman Story, The (Hilton)
Toyota Celica & Supra, The Book of Toyota's Sports Coupés (Long)
Toyota MR2 Coupés & Spyders (Long)
Triumph & Standard Cars 1945 to 1984 (Warrington)
Triumph Speed Twin & Thunderbird Bible (Woolridge)
Triumph TR6 (Kimberley)
Two Summers – The Mercedes-Benz W196R Racing Car (Ackerson)
TWR Story, The – Group A (Hughes & Scott)
Unraced (Collins)
Volkswagen Bus Book, The (Bobbitt)
Volkswagen Bus or Van to Camper, How to Convert (Porter)
Volkswagens of the World (Glen)
VW Beetle Cabriolet – The full story of the convertible Beetle (Bobbitt)
VW Beetle – The Car of the 20th Century (Copping)
VW Bus – 40 Years of Splitties, Bays & Wedges (Copping)
VW Bus Book, The (Bobbitt)
VW Golf: Five Generations of Fun (Copping & Cservenka)
VW – The Air-cooled Era (Copping)
VW T5 Camper Conversion Manual (Porter)
VW Campers (Copping)
Volkswagen Type 3, The book of the – Concept, Design, International Production Models & Development (Glen)
Volvo Estate, The (Hollebone)
You & Your Jaguar XK8/XKR – Buying, Enjoying, Maintaining, Modifying – New Edition (Thorley)
Which Oil? – Choosing the right oils & greases for your antique, vintage, veteran, classic or collector car (Michell)
Wolseley Cars 1948 to 1975 (Rowe)
Works Minis, The Last (Purves & Brenchley)
Works Rally Mechanic (Moylan)

Also available Apps Download now from www.digital.veloce.co.uk

Also available ... eBook Download now from www.digital.veloce.co.uk

Hubble & Hattie www.hubbleandhattie.com

Belvedere

www.veloce.co.uk

First published in February 2018 by Veloce Publishing Limited, Veloce House, Parkway Farm Business Park, Middle Farm Way, Poundbury, Dorchester DT1 3AR, England. Tel 01305 260068 / Fax 01305 268864 / e-mail info@veloce.co.uk / web www.veloce.co.uk or www.velocebooks.com.
ISBN: 978-1-787111-84-4; UPC: 6-36847-01184-0.

© 2018 Peter Dron and Veloce Publishing. All rights reserved. With the exception of quoting brief passages for the purpose of review, no part of this publication may be recorded, reproduced or transmitted by any means, including photocopying, without the written permission of Veloce Publishing Ltd. Throughout this book logos, model names and designations, etc, have been used for the purposes of identification, illustration and decoration. Such names are the property of the trademark holder as this is not an official publication. Readers with ideas for automotive books, or books on other transport or related hobby subjects, are invited to write to the editorial director of Veloce Publishing at the above address.

British Library Cataloguing in Publication Data – A catalogue record for this book is available from the British Library.
Typesetting, design and page make-up all by Veloce Publishing Ltd on Apple Mac. Printed in India by Replika Press.

Cover illustration: Don Grant

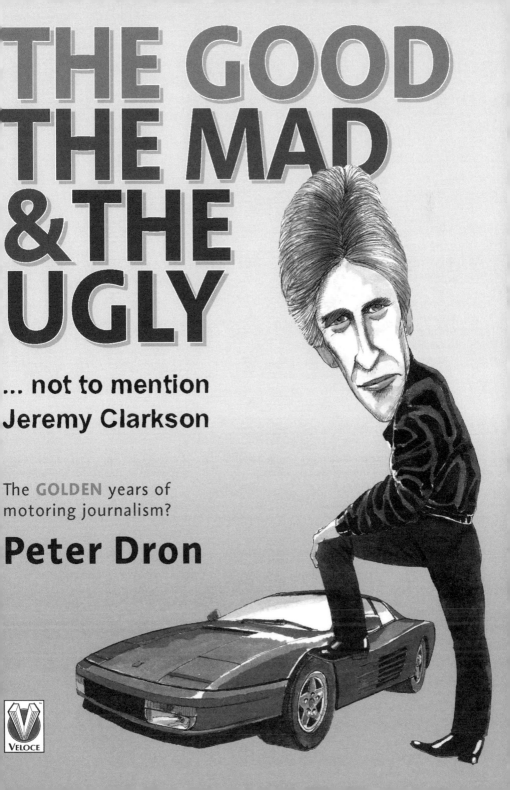

THE GOOD THE MAD & THE UGLY

... not to mention
Jeremy Clarkson

The **GOLDEN** years of
motoring journalism?

Peter Dron

VELOCE

Contents

Dedicated to Jeremy Clarkson, whose decision to ignore me led directly to major textual alterations in order to avoid the possibility of bankruptcy.

Introduction

IT WOULD BE A good idea as a starter, perhaps, to explain who I am, as far as anyone can. At least I can describe briefly some of the respectable things I have done in return for money. A momentous day in my life was when I joined the staff of *Motor*†, which then had the highest circulation of any British weekly motoring magazine, on Monday 4 October 1976.

What happened before then is essentially none of your damned business, though if this book becomes a blockbuster I intend to follow up with a second volume which will purportedly tell all, though of course it will leave a few things out and mildly exaggerate others. Autobiographies are mainly works of fiction.

I began on *Motor* as a road tester and, during my seven years on the magazine, I drove about 100 different cars each year. I had various job titles during this period, the strangest of which was Deputy Assistant Editor. I would willingly have deputised for the Assistant Editor, a charming old cove named Tony Kyd (see Chapters 8 and 9), but the occasion never arose. I would have eaten sheep's eyes or pig's testicles rather than assist the Deputy Editor of that period, whose nickname was Jabba the Hutt (see Chapter 29). My final title was Features Editor.

In 1983, the Publishing Director of *Motor* suggested that I should become the launch Editor of a new monthly motoring magazine. After considerable hesitation, because I foresaw that editing a magazine entailed a lot of hassle (and I was not wrong), I agreed. In retrospect, I think that one reason for my acceptance was that I suspected that there was a possibility that I might be in line to be Editor of *Motor* and I was not at all keen on the idea. Running a monthly magazine rather than a weekly seemed like slightly less of a nerve-jangling grind, though creating a brand-new magazine from scratch was a somewhat daunting prospect. The first issue of *Fast Lane*† appeared the following spring.

In 1991, IPC, having stupidly thrown away its domination of Britain's motoring magazine market, sold *Fast Lane* to a big and significant German publisher operating through a small and insignificant British publisher. I foolishly agreed to stay, before having read the small print in the new contract and before having even met the small and insignificant British publishing director. Regrets? I have a few. After six acrimonious months, I was fired (see Chapter 32).

Then I was freelance. My major outlet for 15 years was *The Daily Telegraph*, with which I had a contract. For seven of those years I contributed a weekly column. Over the decades, my byline and/or my words have appeared in other newspapers (such as *The Independent* and *The Sunday Times*), in most of the major British motoring magazines – *CAR*, *EVO*, *Performance Car*†, *Autocar* – and in various foreign magazines, among them *Car & Driver* (USA). Despite that, many of these publications survive. My words have also appeared in some crap publications, such as *Auto Express*, that I shall not dwell upon.

* * *

I started making notes for this book about 20 years ago, adding bits here and there, but never really deciding what it was, or what to do with it. Suddenly, in the early winter of 2012, a bizarre and inexplicable urge to complete it came over me like a fever.

I found, to my surprise, that I had over 100,000 words in the computer. I then asked myself that question: what is it? This was pertinent in the circumstances, though it would perhaps have been more intelligent to have asked it earlier. I realized, with mild alarm, that I had written my autobiography, with a few inventions, embellishments, deletions and exaggerations (as in all autobiographies, as previously suggested). Almost immediately, it was obvious that this was an absurd idea. I mean, who am I?

You need particular qualifications, as well as terminal vanity, to have an autobiography published, unless you do it as a vanity publishing project, in which case you need only vanity and cash. The principal qualification is that your name must already be well-known to the general public. A glance at the list of best-selling autobiographies, most of which end up as unwanted Christmas presents and are rarely read by anyone, proves this to be so. I intend to buck the trend, by becoming famous *because of* my autobiography, not that this is it. Volume 2, if there is one, will be … up to a point.

All of this would be simpler if I had played Hamlet at the Old Vic, been overpaid to kick a ball about, undergone a sex-change, murdered someone famous, invented the nuclear toothbrush, and then robbed The Bank of England. With even three out of five of these, I might have had the basis in the fast-moving modern world for a plausible sales pitch for an autobiography, and then I could have underpaid some desperate loser to write it for me, while I lurked in drag, armed to the teeth, within a boring luxury villa in a gated community on the Costa Brava.

However, I have no desire to live in Spain and I have never done even one of those things, let alone the full set, and have no intention to attempt any of them, especially the sex change. I am not even a television 'personality,' so I am obliged to write this stuff myself. Publishers have patiently explained to me that one cannot charge extra for that, which seems grossly unfair.

In fact, I did make a cameo appearance on 'nationwide' television on one occasion. I was standing directly behind the Chief Constable of Kent[1], who was speaking earnestly to camera about the problem of drinking and driving, and what should be done about it, in his opinion. I removed his fancy braided hat, exposing his shiny bald bonce for the benefit of BBC viewers, put it on my own head, and stared over his right shoulder with what somebody later described as "a rather manic expression." Then I shifted to the other side, and stared over his left shoulder. I expect that anyone removing the braided hat of a Chief Constable these days would be tasered, or shot dead within ten seconds.

In my defence, I was exceedingly drunk at the time, and I did not recall anything about the incident until I watched it on (pre-Clarkson) *Top Gear*. Even then, it was like watching a video recording of someone else's dream. I was impressed that the removal of his hat did not put the Chief Constable off his stroke. He continued to bumble along as if nothing untoward had occurred. Unfortunately, I did not keep the hat. I should have run off into the woods and crawled on all fours to the nearest railway station, but this would have taken a long time for various reasons, the least of which was that I had no idea which was the nearest railway station to the circuit. This was neither the first, nor the last, missed opportunity in my life. So it goes.

For a long time, I abandoned that literary project, if one could so describe it. Perhaps subconsciously deciding that I did not have sufficient problems in my life, I bought a new Morgan 3 Wheeler in 2013. The following year, to complicate things further, I wrote the definitive book about it[2], on the basis that nobody else was likely to do so. This was simultaneously absurd and accurate, a combination that is less rare than some people imagine.

In May 2015, I sold the 3 Wheeler to an Italian banker, and the next day ordered a new Morgan 4/4[3], possibly a sign of late-blossoming maturity, but who am I to judge? Having done that, I paused again, and eventually went back to the rambling manuscript that languished on my computer.

I chopped it into themed sections. The one that evolved into what you are reading is almost entirely about cars in general, and, in particular, about motoring journalism, but do not be put off, if you are not even slightly interested in cars – they feature mostly in the background.

I cut out all the other stuff (mostly from before the autumn of 1976, and after the spring of 2009), and put it into a separate folder, to which, as I have mentioned, I may return at a later stage, when I am rich and famous, and still, perhaps, more or less compos mentis. Thus, for the time being at least, you are spared a lengthy section entitled 'An exciting childhood near Watford, among other Oxhey morons,' though there is a hint of that period of my life in Chapter 62. Nor will you read, here, about how I served spaghetti[4] to Clint Eastwood in Rome, or about how I briefly discovered The Meaning of Life, after consuming D-Lysergic acid in Belsize Park in the summer of 1972[5].

So, what is this, the sharp-minded reader will be asking, if not an autobiography? It is a celebration of what, in retrospect, I consider to have been a golden era for motoring journalists, the 1980s and the 1990s, of which I was privileged to be a part. Technology was making cars better and better. Car launches and Motor Shows were hard work, but they were fun, as well. Also, it is a lament that all the best things of that era have gone for ever. Now, for example, covering a Motor Show is nothing but what Philip Larkin described as "the toad, work."

Among those mentioned in this book whom I have actually met over the years are, in alphabetic surname order: Chris Bangle, Raymond Baxter, Derek Bell, George Bishop, Steve Cropley, Jean-Martin Folz, Gavin Green, Roy Harry, Alexander Hesketh, James Hunt, Eberhard von Kuenheim, Brian Laban, José Ignacio Lopez, Hannu Mikkola, John Miles, Charles Morgan, Ferdinand Piëch, Bernd Pischetsrieder, Frank M Rinderknecht, Leonard Setright, Donald Stokes, Amherst Villiers and Peter Wheeler. Also, there are memorable encounters with Frank the Yard Man (surname unknown), and the Duke of Edinburgh. And I almost met Jeremy Beadle.

Various other characters lurk in the background, among them, in no particular order, King Edward VII, Piers Morgan, Professor Joseph Stiglitz, Leonardo da Vinci, Tom Stoppard, Jean Genet, Jean-Charles de Castelbajac, and Horst Pinschewer, the man who, for no obvious reason, shot Lord Haw-Haw twice in the buttocks.

I spent 30-plus years as a motoring hack. It was almost like having a job, in some respects, only far more fun than most jobs. In the final chapters, I explain why that was a golden era, and also make some characteristically gloomy predictions.

The essential elements of what I did consisted of testing new cars, reporting on international Motor Shows, interviewing industry bigwigs, general reporting of this and that, and filling opinionated columns with finely-chiselled prose. All of this you will discover if you read on, and thank you, if you do. I am sorry that there is not a chapter explaining how I guided a young and impressionable Jeremy Clarkson onto the path which led to international stardom. However, there is a chapter explaining why there is not such a chapter.

Now read on, if you wish. I hope you enjoy this collection of yarns. There are 99 of them[6].

[1] The unfortunately-named Barry Pain, who succeeded the you-could-not-make-it-up Richard Dawnay Lemon as Kent's Chief Constable in 1974. For a detailed account of this episode, you may jump to

Chapter 69, if you wish, but, if you have bought this book, rather than nicked it or had it passed on by a dyspeptic relation, please carry on reading and get your full value for money, if that is not an exaggeration.

[2] *MORGAN 3 WHEELER – Back to the future*, published by Veloce. If you enjoy reading this book, you will want to buy it, even if you think three-wheelers are mad.

[3] As I explain in Chapter 95, this was, at least, a logical progression ...

[4] In reality it was pizza, but spaghetti improves the yarn.

[5] Alas, I did not write it down, and almost immediately forgot what it was. It was obviously nothing of importance.

[6] Why not a round hundred? I have followed the principle, 'Leave them wanting more.'

[†] Deceased.

1 The not-about-Jeremy-Clarkson chapter

IN MY ORIGINAL PLAN, as mentioned, the first chapter of this book concerned Jeremy Charles Robert Clarkson, the world-famous televisual person, who may not be the most complex character ever to have walked upon this strange planet, but who is far less simple than some people might imagine.

Jeremy was also mentioned in the title, and was to appear, in an amusing caricature, dressed as Paddington Bear, on the cover. Of course, this was all a cynical ploy to boost sales. I imagined that it would not bother him in the slightest and that his skin was like that of a rhinoceros. I was mistaken.

When my publisher read my text, he was worried about libel. I assured him that most of those mentioned in this book, such as Leonard Setright and George Bishop (plus a few less famous freaks), were now in a place from which one cannot sue anybody for anything, which from our point of view was certainly a better place. That left only one problem case. Mr Grainger homed in on that, and Mr Clarkson was, indeed, the metaphorical elephant in the room.

It was felt, though not by me, that the chapter, and even the proposed title, might be libellous. I thought the whole thing was nothing more than waspishly satirical – if that, but one must always consider what might happen if someone with no shortage of funds takes umbrage and a different view.

In my opinion, as I have implied, the original chapter was not defamatory either. However, there was a risk. Even if we had not all ended up in front of Mr Justice Cocklecarrot in the High Court, which might have been simultaneously amusing and ruinous for us as defendants, lawyers for both sides would be ordering new Bentleys and booking their holidays in the Bahamas, or wherever slimy, over-paid silks go in summer, and I would be in hiding.

JCRC could certainly afford to go to court even if he were not awarded costs, indeed even if he did not win the case … and he might have done that just for the hell of it. I doubted that he would, but you never know. My publisher informed me that *he* could not afford that risk. I certainly could not.

The only way to resolve this, I decided, was a direct approach to the man himself. So I e-mailed Jeremy, attaching the mildly offensive chapter in question. Here is that e-mail, minus the possibly libellous attachment:

Hello Jeremy,

How would you react if a book with this title and this first chapter (see attached) were published? I assure you that this is the only chapter in which you are featured.

Pistols at dawn.
Hit squad.
A shrug.
Sue me for all I'm worth.

Please choose only one. Number 4 seems to be the only one that bothers my potential publisher.

With best wishes,
Peter D

Jeremy e-mailed back. He was evidently not amused, which was no big surprise. He did not state that he would take legal action, but, crucially and to my dismay, neither did he undertake *not* to do so.

I sent him another e-mail, explaining that I was not seeking literary criticism. I offered him the opportunity to write a foreword in which he could be as rude as he wished. He did not reply to that, so I then proposed that I should buy him a high-quality 44in-long scale model of the Hindenburg (hydrogen not included), if he would undertake not to sue in the event of publication. I was confident that this would be a clincher, but alas there was still no reply.

Then I read in the newspapers that he had blown up an old farmhouse to make way for a larger mansion, slightly smaller than Blenheim Palace, in the Cotswold Palladian style. Although the farmhouse looked quite attractive in photos, I have to admit that the proposed replacement is rather magnificent. By way of congratulation for Jeremy's architectural taste, I sent him another e-mail in which I wrote that he had obviously undertaken this drastic demolition in order to have higher ceilings, which would provide adequate space for a scale model of the Hindenburg. In view of this, I offered him the even more expensive 65in version[1]. Answer came there none, but soon after there was an unexpected development.

Ahead of the first edition of their new show, *The Grand Tour*, Clarkson, along with his sidekicks Worzel Gummidge and Little Noddy, appeared in a short video in which they answered some apparently pointless questions about their portable telephones. However, this turned out to be more interesting than I had imagined.

One of the questions was "How many unread e-mails do you have?" JC replied, "Here is my Inbox. *All* of them are unread. If you are watching this, Peter Dron … [he mentioned a few other names] … Jeff Bezos – Unread!"

I am fairly sure that this was the first time that anyone has mentioned Jeff Bezos in the same sentence as me. Bravo, Jeff. I sent Jeremy a further e-mail:

Hello Jeremy,

My old pal Jeff Bezos tells me that he is deeply upset that you keep ignoring the e-mails he sends you.

Best as ever,
Peter D

I found out that Bezos has a public e-mail address, so I sent him a message, suggesting that it would be amusing if he were to ask Clarkson why he does not reply to my e-mails. There was no reply to that either. Well, we are a bit funny, us superstars.

Jeremy Clarkson and I go back a long way. Some time in the mid-1990s, I was walking through a Motor Show hall on Press Day. On a stand that I was passing, a film crew was setting up its equipment. And there was Jeremy. He pointed at me and bellowed to his crew, "Hey, look! There goes the grand old man of British motoring journalism."

I already had grey hair, but I thought that was a bit cheeky. Of course, he was still developing his persona in those days. I bellowed back, "Well, it's probably better than being the Simon Dee[2] of the 1990s." Jeremy looked mildly vexed, but his crew fell about laughing.

Clarkson is a misunderstood man, to some extent. He is really somewhat like Steve Coogan playing the role of Alan Partridge, or possibly vice versa. He does not generally take himself too seriously when hot pies are not involved. In my experience, he tends not to punch people unless they stand between him and his dinner, or have a face like that of Mr Piers Morgan, either of which would surely be regarded by any reasonable jury as mitigating circumstances, at the very least.

When my Morgan 3 Wheeler book came out in March 2015, I sent him an e-mail, beginning, "Dear Jeremy, Elvis Presley would be 80 years old next Thursday and for some reason this made me think of you ..." I added, "It occurred to me that you, the thinking man's Roger Melly, would leap at the opportunity of promoting my forthcoming book."

In those days, before he began to trouser some of Mr Bezos' billions, he did take the trouble to answer e-mails. To my astonishment, he replied that he would "do something big." I was hoping for a sarcastic plug on prime-time television, while he sat around the low table swapping scripted witticisms with his funny little pals ...

A mutual friend, lunching with Jeremy a few days later, handed him a copy of my book. JC took a snap of it with his expensive telephonic apparatus and promptly tweeted it, whatever that means, with the message, "An old friend of mine has written this book," which was nice, as they used to say on *The Fast Show*. He did that before even checking the index, though I had informed him in my e-mail that he was mentioned in the book. That was not as good as a plug on the haunted fishtank, but helpful nevertheless.

I continue to believe that Clarkson is a good sport, but evidently, this time, I had stretched his good-sportiveness factor beyond the point where the elastic snaps. Therefore, this is not a chapter about his early years when he was struggling for recognition. The title that did not amuse Clarkson has also had to be altered.

So there is nothing about Jeremy Clarkson here – and certainly nothing libellous. If you have bought this book thinking that there might be, I apologize for having raised false expectations. You may sue me on the basis of expectations unmet if you wish, and good luck to you. Let us move on to slightly more serious topics.

[1] By a curious coincidence, this is approximately the height of Richard Hammond.
[2] Cyril Nicholas Henty-Dodd, stage-name Simon Dee (1935-2009), was, for a short period in the 1960s, the highest-paid presenter on British television. He later appeared periodically on 'Where are they now?' programmes, and where he was then was mostly living rough.

2 A conspicuously successful man

IN 1976, BMW WAS still struggling to be considered on the same level as mighty Daimler-Benz. But it was in much better shape than it had been only a few years earlier, and was already regarded, except in Stuttgart, as a serious contender. One of my earliest assignments after joining the staff of *Motor* magazine in October of that year was a visit to Munich to discover how this had been achieved.

In desperation in the 1950s, BMW had bought the rights to the Isetta bubble-car, and fitted it with a modified version of its motorcycle engine. During this period, its only real car had been the 507, an elegant low-volume sporty roadster, which, these days, fetches seven figures at auction in the currency of your choice, but which barely turned a profit when in production. The company was only just ticking over ... and then the bubble-car bubble burst, as the German economy began to take off. At the same time, motorcycle sales had declined severely. In 1958, the company, which had begun as an aero engine manufacturer during the First World War, was on the edge of total financial collapse.

BMW was almost absorbed into Daimler-Benz, which would probably have simply liquidated its assets and taken on a few key people. Instead, the group was acquired by the stupendously wealthy Quandt family of industrialists. With new investment and the hiring of some talented engineers, the company had been re-invented during the 1960s, and it went from strength to strength. It had a new and expanding range of cars that people wanted to buy.

After a hectic schedule, photographer Maurice Rowe[1] and I arrived at the famous four-cylinder headquarters building. That morning had been spent touring production facilities and the small test track to the east of the city. The previous afternoon, we had inspected the then fledgling Motorsport department. The grand finale was a meeting with top brass.

The contrast with a British car company's headquarters in that era was marked. There was an air of vibrant urgency. Everyone bustled about doing things, as if their lives depended upon taking action *now,* rather than tomorrow or next week. Telephones rang and people answered them. Nobody appeared to be even slightly drunk, though it was well after lunchtime.

Uncle Maurice and I, issued with special passes, were taken to the very top of the building, the 22nd floor. While waiting, we had time to enjoy the magnificent views in every direction. After about 20 minutes, a severe-looking secretary instructed us to follow her into the boardroom.

Eberhard von Kuenheim[2] was then approaching 50. He and his acolytes sat at one end of a long modern table. They looked, in their expensively tailored suits and brightly shining black brogues, like the officers of an elite regiment, in civilian clothes yet by no means off-duty: von K was their General. While Maurice prepared his camera gear, I sat in my allocated place, alone at the other end of the table, wearing a dark suit, white shirt with dark tie and black Oxfords. I had shaved that morning. Yet somehow I felt scruffy in this company and also increasingly nervous, though I had prepared carefully for the interview. It was as if I were a non-commissioned officer facing a court martial, obliged to provide his own defence.

The German officers stared intently. I switched on my tape recorder. Nobody said anything for a while. Then von K briefly introduced his team, and delivered a short

14

oration, explaining how brilliantly the company had been managed since he had been appointed executive director six years earlier. This was one of his favourite speeches and he did not need notes.

"You may now ask questions," he said with cool generosity. His answers were terse and humourless, as were those of his colleagues, to whom the General directed some questions for extra detail or clarification.

Half an hour passed. Suddenly I felt hot and in difficulty. My throat was parched. My mind had gone entirely blank. I had asked my original questions and my supplementary questions, having scribbled numerous extra notes for this purpose.

Half a dozen pairs of beady eyes stared at me. To me, it seemed that they were like vultures observing an injured kudu in the Masai Mara. Pouring myself a glass of water, I took a large gulp, said, "Excuse me a moment," walked to the windows and stared out at Behnisch and Otto's spectacular Olympic Stadium, far below and several hundred yards away. I noted the absence of hinges or latches on the building's windows, which were angled, like the rear window of the Ford Anglia, or, indeed, that of the most hideous car of all time, the Citroën Ami 6 saloon. I wondered how Bertoni[3] could have designed *that*. Then I became aware of some murmuring.

I turned to von K and his team and said, "I see that it is impossible to open these windows." They stared at me, all looking puzzled. I explained: "That must reduce the suicide rate, I suppose."

Returning to my seat in a better frame of mind, I fired off a series of questions. Did they *really* believe that their engineering quality yet matched that of Mercedes-Benz? I mentioned that this was not the view in Stuttgart. How might Motorsport develop? Were they worried that, one day, Japanese manufacturers might provide Germany with serious competition? How did they plan to tackle North America? Finally, I thanked them for their cooperation and said that we had a flight to catch.

Back at base, I described how the trip had gone. My Editor, Roger Bell, laughed and said, "Oh, you find von Kuenheim scary, do you? In that case, I'll send you to interview Ferdinand Piëch[4] ..."

Perhaps von Kuenheim's most remarkable achievement was to fire both the men vying to succeed him at BMW ... simultaneously.

[1] Maurice Rowe (1929-2016), an excellent photographer, a much-appreciated colleague, and one of the nicest people ever to have walked on this planet.
[2] Eberhard von Kuenheim (born East Prussia, 2 October 1928). This is a modest tribute he wrote concerning himself for insertion in a British annual publication after he had been appointed Chairman of the BMW Supervisory Board:
    "1970 Chairman of BMW AG's Managing Board; stood down after 23 years of conspicuous success – in May 1993 – to take up present position."
[3] Flaminio Bertoni (1903-1964) was also responsible for the Traction Avant, the Deux Chevaux, the DS and the Type H van. Every top-class designer has an off-day, though, oddly, the man himself considered the Ami 6 his finest creation.
[4] Ferdinand Piëch (born Vienna, 17 April 1937). Possibly Europe's leading megalomaniac of the second half of the 20th century. Scion of the Porsche dynasty through his mother Louise. During World War II, his father Anton Piëch, a lawyer, managed the Wolfsburg factory where slave labour was used. Created, in aggressive collaboration with his equally talented cousin, Ferdinand Alexander 'Butzi' Porsche (1935-2012), the original 911. Turned the Volkswagen group into an international force. Father of at least 12 children with four different women. Detests air conditioning (and carries with him a special toolkit to ensure that hotel windows can be opened). Legend suggests that he can render goldfish unconscious by staring at them.

3 The Rollerball corporation

ONE OF THE MOST memorable features of *Rollerball*, an almost entirely unintelligible 1975 film starring an almost entirely unintelligible James Caan, is a building in the shape of four cylinders. It is among the most extraordinary buildings of the 20th century[1].

In the film, the corporation that occupies this tower is the organizing body of the popular and lethally dangerous game of rollerball. The corporation is presented as unusually evil and cynical, but it has always struck me as being essentially similar to any reputable sporting authority, such as, for example, the *Fédération Internationale de l'Automobile*, which supposedly controls Formula 1 motor racing[2].

It is not hard to imagine three successive Presidents of the FIA, Messrs Balestre, Mosley and Todt, in charge of the *Fédération Internationale de Rollerball*. A fine job they would make of it, too, I am sure.

Many filmgoers outside Germany will not have recognized that four-cylinder building and perhaps imagined it was in Chicago or Singapore. In fact, it is the BMW AG headquarters in Munich, mentioned in the previous chapter.

Therein lies a puzzle. BMW has never made a square-four engine, and I doubt that such a configuration has been considered by the company, either for its cars or motorcycles. I can only suppose that the Quandt family, which owns BMW, wanted a straight-six building, but the plot of land was unsuited to that. A V8 might fit but would, of course, be impractical, unless escalators were adopted instead of lifts. Even then, if horizontal floors and work surfaces were required, it would be hugely wasteful of space, though this would probably not deter an ambitious architect seeking an international award.

When Bernd Pischetsrieder and Wolfgang Reitzle, two of Germany's leading motor industry leaders of the period, left that building on February 5, 1999, both having been sacked after a long and acrimonious board meeting, they would perhaps have agreed, though they rarely agreed about anything, including facial furniture, with the late Leslie Halliwell's review of *Rollerball*:

> "A one-point parable, and an obvious point at that, is stretched out over more than two hours of violence in which the rules of the game are not even explained. A distinctly unlikeable film."

From what I have heard, most German board meetings are very much like that, except that they usually last several hours longer and contain more dialogue, some of which would not have got past the censors in a less permissive era. They also contain what LJK Setright[3] might have described, without translation or explanation, as *Furor Teutonicus*[4].

Pischetsrieder had been BMW's chairman since 1993. His feud with Reitzle, who was more than mildly disappointed at being passed over for that post, was too virulent to be considered credible for a Hollywood script. One of the biggest bones of contention was BMW's acquisition of, and plans for, Rover.

Of similar age (both then around 50), Pischetsrieder and Reitzle had followed closely parallel careers: both studied mechanical engineering at Munich Technical University, and both joined BMW in the 1970s. I have always wondered whether they left the building via the same lift, manufactured perhaps by the Swiss group Schindler[5].

Herr Reitzle had film-star looks, uncannily resembling Vincent Price in Hammer House of Horror productions, including the sinister eyes and pencil-thin moustache, though he appeared to lack that actor's jollier characteristics. Reitzle allegedly received five million Dm (about £1.8 million) for walking out of the door, but must have kicked himself for turning down the chairmanship of Porsche, which had been offered to him in 1993. In addition to a substantial annual salary, he had been promised five per cent of the company, which by 1999 would have been worth £145 million. He could have bought Rover from BMW and run it as a hobby, not that he would have considered anything as frivolous as that; though Pischetsrieder, who was fascinated by old English marques, even including Wolseley, might have done.

The feud between these two high fliers was somewhat like a Shakespearean tragedy and, in a more sporting era, they would no doubt have ended up sorting out their differences with pistols or swords at dawn. The man who ordered them out of the building was the chairman of the Board of Management, Eberhard von Kuenheim, who also featured in the preceding chapter.

Pischetsrieder was later hired in 2002 by Ferdinand Piëch[6] to run the Volkswagen group. Shortly after this (18 January 2003), I wrote in *The Daily Telegraph* a paragraph that turned out to be unfortunately prophetic: "With Germany in recession, Pischetsrieder has a tough assignment: if he cannot rapidly clear up the mess left by his autocratic predecessor [Piëch], he may become the first Chairman to have been fired by two German car manufacturing groups."

And so it came to pass. Most observers thought Pischetsrieder was doing the demanding job more than adequately and were astonished when he was fired. He seems to have given Dr Piëch a funny look in 2006. Reitzle, in contrast, ended up in charge of a group producing gas and forklift trucks. There is possibly a moral to be drawn from that, though I have no idea what it might be.

Whatever one thinks of people like von Kuenheim, Piëch, Reitzle and Pischetsrieder, and various other engineer/managers from across the Rhine, there is no denying that their dynamism drove the German motor industry to set worldwide standards. Britain, on the other hand, had Donald Stokes and Sparky Edwards … and later the 'Phoenix Four'[7].

[1] The architect was Karl Schwanzer (b. Vienna 1918; d. Vienna 1975). His former pupil, the amusingly-named Wolf D Prix, was architect of the adjacent BMW museum, another interesting structure. With Helmut Swiczinsky, Prix created the Vodöl, possibly the most ludicrous armchair in recorded history.
[2] Sometimes one gets the impression that it is now run by the World Wide Motor Racing Federation, a branch of the same group that organizes wrestling matches.
[3] Leonardo Jehovah Kingpin Setright, known as Leonard. See Chapter 7.
[4] If the late Setright could get away with that kind of thing, I might as well follow his example.
[5] While interviewing engineers at Porsche's Weissach research centre, I was told that one of the firm's clients was an elevator manufacturer. I asked which one and was told that it was Schindler. "Ah," I said, "Schindler's lift." There was an uncomfortable silence. Then they all laughed. Well, you had to be there, perhaps.
[6] The motor industry's mogul of moguls in the second half of the 20th century. I once began a report of the Paris Motor Show in *The Daily Telegraph* as follows: "When Dr Piëch cracks a joke, his colleagues are unsure whether to laugh or to bite into their cyanide pills." This clipping, I later learned, was pinned up on the notice board in the Volkswagen Press Office in Wolfsburg, but hidden in a drawer every time the great man paid a visit.
[7] Who says that crime does not pay?

4 Public Enemy Number One

A FAVOURITE BUGBEAR OF British motor industry watchers in the 1980s was Lord Stokes[1]. He was the boss of British Leyland between 1968 and 1975, which are not generally looked back upon as the company's golden years[2]. However, a great many things happened both before and after that seven-year stretch, so anyone who points at him as The Man Who Destroyed British Car Manufacturing should get a job on *The Sun*[3], where facts are less important than snappy headlines.

I had been among those to cast aspersions about Stokes in print, so it was very sporting of him, when, in the 1990s, he agreed to interrupt his then semi-retirement, mostly spent sailing in Poole Bay, to defend his role. I had not previously met him, but I must say that he came across as an agreeably feisty old cove.

By coincidence, the driver of the cab I took to meet him started rabbiting about Rover, which was then going through one of its periodic crises before it finally evaporated as if it had never been there.

"Funny you should mention that," I said, and told him with whom I was going to have lunch.

"Oh yeah, I remember 'im," said the taxi driver. "He and Lady Stokes used to go around in a gold-plated Rolls-Royce, right?"

"Er, no," I replied. "That was Lord and Lady Docker ... and it was a Daimler[4]."

Stokes found this anecdote extremely amusing. He was not in the least like the snobbish, pretentious, avaricious coxcomb Bernard Docker. When Stokes was planning his maiden speech (traditionally non-controversial) in the House of Lords, someone advised him to talk about industrial relations.

"I was terribly nervous," he recalled, "so I invited a number of trade unionists down to lunch and to sit in the public gallery. At the end of my impassioned speech, they all stood and clapped. They were thrown out. Afterwards, I asked them why they had clapped, because surely they didn't agree with what I had said. One of them replied, 'No, we just felt sorry for you, with that dozy lot of buggers down there'."

Donald Stokes may not have been the right man in the right place at the right time, but the meltdown of the indigenous British motor industry was not his fault. He was a salesman rather than an engineer or a factory manager. But which industrial superman could have sorted out all the problems of BL? When the Germans had a crack at it in the 1990s, they made an almighty balls-up of the job.

From the late 1950s onwards, everything that *could* be wrong about the British car industry *was* wrong: cynical and/or ineffectual management, bolshy union leaders such as 'Red Robbo'[5], worn-out manufacturing facilities, unhelpful governmental pressure, a suicidal 'Just shift the metal' culture, and so on.

Despite having several engineers and managers of great talent and integrity, who created some cars, such as the Rover SD1, which in slightly different circumstances might have turned things around, the cards were stacked unfavourably.

One thing that Stokes mentioned in our interview was the Longbridge problem. His analysis was faultless: the plant was ancient, outdated, with an ageing workforce. It needed to be pulled down and rebuilt, probably transferred elsewhere, so that a large profit could be drawn from the sale of the site[7] and invested in new model development. But governments of both parties did not dare, terrified of the consequences of the short-term unemployment that this would cause and of losing important marginal parliamentary seats. As often happens in such cases, the end result was far worse than if a courageous blood-letting decision had been taken.

So BL, after changing logos and names a few times, went down the plughole[6], having consumed enormous wads of taxpayers' money, and the whole structure of the British motor industry altered radically, with the unsurprising disappearance of Rootes/Chrysler, the closure of Peugeot's Ryton plant (which had been built by Rootes in 1940), and the gradual downscaling of the operations of Ford and GM.

Ryton's demise was a sad tale. When Chrysler acquired the Rootes Group, it sent executives on investigative missions to all the factories. During a tour of the Hillman Imp factory at Linwood, near Glasgow, one of the Chrysler men asked how many people worked there. "Oh, about 30 per cent of them," replied a Rootes manager drily.

Ryton was different. It was an outdated plant in most respects, and there was a higher manual content than in more-modern factories, but the management and workforce together had cleverly managed to make it remarkably efficient. Predictably, when PSA (Peugeot-Citroën) decided that it had one factory too many, it was the British plant that got the chop rather than a French one.

Somehow, the French and Italian manufacturers, who also made crap cars in outdated factories, who also had serious union problems, and who also had some third-rate managers, managed to survive into the 21st century.

It would have surprised Sir John Harvey-Jones[8] that Morgan ended up as the biggest independent British-owned car maker in Blighty. However, life is increasingly tough for the smaller car makers, too.

Nevertheless, the factories built by Nissan, Toyota and Honda, combined with the operations of BMW (Mini) and the luxury sector, have ensured that the volume of cars produced in the UK has not diminished[9], though the French, to coin a phrase, pulled out.

[1] Donald Gresham Stokes (1914-2008), who spent his entire working life with Leyland Motors and its successors, taking a break between 1939 and 1945 (becoming a Lieutenant-Colonel).

[2] But when *were* BL's golden years?

[3] Or on any other 'newspaper,' these days.

[4] Bernard Docker was a British industrialist (or rather, the privileged son of an industrialist, whose progression to the top was assured by birth), not nearly as clever as Lord Stokes. His second wife, Norah (oddly enough, her middle name was Royce), a former 'showgirl' and serial widow of luxury-goods manufacturers, was well ahead of her time, the prototype celebrity dimwit.

[5] Even Lord Stokes' fiercest critics usually had a good word to say about him. The same was not so of Communist union convenor Derek Robinson.

[6] How prophetic that British Leyland logo with the large L in the centre of the swirling plughole was; I have often thought that the designer presented it as a urinal joke, and that his bosses were either so thick that they didn't get it, or so cynical that they didn't care ...

[7] But one could say the same about Wolfsburg, and somehow VW has survived that, among other problems.

[8] Forerunner of the generic TV entrepreneur, far more jovial than Lord Sugar, which admittedly is not difficult. On his visit to the Morgan Motor Car Company for the programme *Troubleshooter*, he gave some harsh advice. It was not all wrong.

[9] People are often surprised to learn that Britain still has more going on, at the time of writing, than service industries.

5 An industry mogul follows my advice

IN EARLY 1997 JACQUES Calvet[1] was finally extracted, like a bad tooth with obstinate roots, after a 15-year tenure, from his post as President/Director General (more simply, Managing Director, in English) of PSA Peugeot-Citroën. I had the impertinence to offer his successor Jean-Martin Folz[2] some advice, in a column in *The Daily Telegraph*, published in March 1997.

This is one advantage of being a newspaper columnist: you can tell far more qualified people what they should do. It is a lot easier when you do not have the pressure of responsibility.

In my defence, the wise advice I offered to Monsieur Folz, whom I had not yet met, was not something that came out of my own head. Instead, I quoted an acknowledged business genius, Professor C Northcote Parkinson[3]. I knew a few things about the condition of the French group at that time, and there was certainly a job to be done, especially concerning its foreign subsidiaries. One of the esteemed Professor's remarks seemed particularly apposite.

His advice as usual was concise, to the point and bleeding obvious[4]. In expounding his third economic Law, he gave a list of essential actions for the incoming chief executive of his imaginary Stupendous Group, the object being to identify signs of decay within the organization.

He wrote: "Visit the most remote outpost of the Stupendic Empire, the experimental farm in Iceland or the research unit in Tasmania. Discover what they are doing and then ask them the crucial question: when were you last visited by a director of the firm? If the answer is 'Last year,' the situation is bad. If the answer is 'In 1958' [the book was published in 1962], the situation is worse. If the answer is 'Never,' the situation is almost beyond remedy."

Applying this analysis to PSA, I suggested that the situation was very serious indeed and that the nearest equivalent to the Icelandic farm or the Tasmanian research unit was its Chinese factories. In the 12 years from 1985 until 1987, Calvet had only once visited his group's furthest-flung output, where the elderly Peugeot 505 and the Citroën ZX[5] were built.

Calvet had described Britain as "a Japanese aircraft carrier moored off the north-west coast of Europe." However, I pointed out that in 1997, Peugeot was regarded, if at all, as a rotting tramp steamer, holed below the water line.

I wrote: "If I were Folz, I would book a flight to Beijing at the earliest opportunity. After some ritual grovelling before the charming politicians in that city, he might take the train south to Guangzhou to inspect the Peugeot factory, designed to make 50,000 cars a year. It is in disrepair and currently at a standstill. At Wuhan, in the middle of nowhere, they are supposed to make 600 Citroëns a day, but are struggling to turn out 50. Folz will seek in vain Citroën's Chinese managing director: he disappeared months ago, leaving no forwarding address."

A little more than a year later, in May 1998, I received a letter with an unusual oriental postmark, containing an interesting card. On the glossy side of the card, from the Beijing International Club Hotel, there was a reproduction of an abstract painting with some Chinese text. The work was *The Beginning of the Universe*[6] by Kiao Dayuan. On the other side, neatly hand-written with a blue ballpoint, was the following message:

Beijing, May 15

Dear Mr Dron,

I did not forget the advice you gave me in The Daily Telegraph in March (or April?) 97!! "Mieux tard que jamais" as the French saying goes …

Très cordialement à vous
Jean-Martin FOLZ

"Blimey!" was my first thought. Then I put in a request to interview Monsieur Folz for *The Daily Telegraph* during the Paris Motor Show later that year. This was granted, and we had a 45-minute chat on Press Day. Many high-flying moguls in the motor industry – and in industry in general – are at least slightly mad. It almost goes with the job. Folz struck me as among the most rational, as well as one of the most intelligent, people I have ever met, but also, by far, the most relaxed and friendly senior motor industry executive.

Ironically, PSA is now a partly Chinese-owned corporation. It is also, with the acquisition from General Motors of Opel, Europe's second-largest car maker. Whether this is a clever strategic move or a recipe for disaster is not clear.

Jean-Martin Folz did a lot of good things for PSA, and, for the first half of his ten-year tenure, he seemed to have halted the group's steady decline. In 2001, he was named as 'Manager of the Year' by a French business magazine. But then profits dipped sharply. He did not need to be removed forcibly like his predecessor: he announced his retirement. This was perhaps at the request of the PSA Board, but he left with dignity. It would be difficult to argue that his successors did any better at that very difficult job.

It occurs to me, if I may ramble, that a fascinating book might be created from an anthology of motor industry job references.

[1] A large pair of forceps was required for this operation. Calvet decided that the PSA age limit for senior executives did not apply to him. If the Board had wished, it could have waived the rule; but it did not wish. For a while after finally having been forced to clear his desk, Calvet, who had been a senior civil servant before his appointment to the Board of PSA, imagined that his next task would be as President of the Republic but almost nobody else shared this vision.

[2] Born in 1947, Folz, like Calvet, did not have a motor industry background. But he learned fast and hired clever people.

[3] Most famous for his first Law, which states with deceptive simplicity, "Work expands so as to fill the time available for its completion."

[4] Only those of exceptionally high intelligence can do all three in one shot, and things are often bleeding obvious only after someone perceptive has identified them as such.

[5] Known locally as the Fukang. Yes, really.

[6] This is possibly a less explicit version of Gustave Courbet's figurative work *The Origin of the World*. In this instance, it is impossible to determine which way is up.

6 Reference points

WHEN AN EMPLOYER IS asked to supply references for an employee seeking a job elsewhere, there may be conflicting sentiments. The whole truth, whatever that may be, is, of course, rarely attempted, either at work or at home. We do not necessarily tell fibs, but the whole truth is a rare commodity, wisely sidestepped in most cases.

The employer, giving a glowing reference, may be suggesting, "Good wishes to a fine colleague. We are sincerely sorry to lose you." Or it may be, "Good riddance, you useless bastard." Often it is difficult to tell. Sometimes there may be an overlap between the two. Human relations are complex.

I first met my late good friend Brian Laban (1948-2016) in the Belsize Tavern, which was at the time the best pub in NW3, probably the best pub in London, and possibly the best pub in Britain, in which case it was undoubtedly the best pub in the world[1]. Brian and I pursued slightly different careers. I tried to persuade him to join the staff of *Motor* a couple of times when there was a vacancy, and once, later, at *Fast Lane*, but he preferred either to be an Editor or to remain independent. He was the fastest journalist I ever shared a car with on a press launch, apart from John Miles, but John was an ex-Grand Prix driver.

Brian had a dry wit. When he was Editor of *On Four Wheels*, a part-work publication, he was asked, about 18 months after I had joined *Motor*, to write a reference for David Vivian[2], who worked for him. The reference he supplied was simultaneously concise and gnomic: "I have known David Vivian for two years. During that time he has been consistently 5ft 9in tall." Editor Tony Curtis[3] was bewildered. Rex Greenslade and I laughed but were unable to supply a convincing explanation. 'Vivid' got the job. He became a valued member of the team and, on at least one occasion, I was present when he bought a round of drinks.

That was one of the two most amusing references I saw for a job applicant on *Motor*. The person involved in the other vacancy shall remain nameless. The standard IPC reference form had been sent to his then employers. A senior member of the management of that company responded with a typed two-page eulogy.

The job candidate, he wrote, was fluent in several languages, his command of English was impeccable, he knew everyone in the field in which he was involved, his knowledge of the history of his particular speciality was second to none, and so on and so forth. And then, either having reflected or having planned it right from the start – and my money would be on the latter – he took a broad-tipped red felt pen and wrote neatly over all this in approximately 288-point capitals: YOU'LL REGRET IT. I thought the subtlest part of that was the lack of an exclamation mark.

When I became an Editor, the part of the job that I disliked the most was hiring people, or perhaps I should rephrase that as "*not* hiring people." Almost always, it came down to a choice between two, three or four people with a variety of abilities, all of whom seemed entirely suitable in different ways … and always, of course, it was necessary to reject two or three of them.

Whenever someone left, that was a nuisance. Not only was one losing a member of the small, close-knit team, but one had to begin the whole damned process of hiring again. However, one can value someone's work without necessarily becoming friends. On one occasion, I very soon found an excellent replacement for someone who had given notice, though, as usual, there had been one or two who seemed almost as good. So it was good all round. My soon-to-be-ex-employee was moving on to a better-paid job, the vacant post had been satisfactorily filled, and I certainly did not have the feeling that I was losing a close friend from my workplace.

One morning I received a phone call from the leaver's new employer, whom I had known for a few years. "Sorry to steal your star performer," he said, not sounding remotely sorry.

"Oh, that's all right," I replied. "I wish X … all the best."

"Oh, I thought you'd be upset." He now sounded slightly upset that I did not seem to be upset, which I wasn't.

"No, not at all. No hard feelings."

"Are you trying to tell me something, Peter?" he asked.

"No. I am sure X … will go far. He's very ambitious."

"OK, out with it: what do you mean exactly?"

I laughed and said, "Oh, nothing really … Just watch your back."

About a year later, this chap called me again, out of the blue. After the usual initial small talk, he got to the point. "Do you remember that conversation we had when X … was about to start working here?" Well, of course I remembered.

"Er, no," I replied. "Remind me." He reminded me, and then said, "You were absolutely right!" One encountered an eclectic mix of people in the business.

[1] Alas, like Brian (1948-2016), it also is no more.
[2] David later became one of Britain's most successful freelance motoring journalists.
[3] Nicknamed 'Bernie Schwartz.'

7 The good, the mad and the ugly

CAR MAGAZINE WAS LAUNCHED in London in the 1960s. Although it did not begin specifically as an Australian magazine, it developed as such and was based for some years in that most northerly province of Oz, Earls Court, in what had previously been a brothel of some repute[1].

CAR really took off in the 1970s, with quality production and photography that set new standards, under the art direction of the gifted Wendy Harrop. There were also some good contributing writers.

One of the features of the magazine was a trio of columnists: Ronald 'Steady' Barker, LJK Setright, and George Bishop. Only one of these, LJKS, was of Australian origin.

Steady was a wonderful chap, a talented engineer, a bon viveur, and one of the smuttiest raconteurs ever to have walked the planet. His columns were always fascinating and erudite, though curiously he somewhat disliked writing, and stopped doing it as soon as he could.

The most famous of the eccentric trio was LJKS, son of a clever engineer. If you have ever travelled on a bus, just about anywhere in the world but especially in Britain[2] and western Europe, it is possible that you have held a slip of paper with serrated edges at each end that was snapped out of a Setright machine.

There were, broadly speaking, two views of Leonard Setright. The first view, which he shared enthusiastically, was that he was almost omniscient, the world's leading expert on all things automotive, the greatest analyst that there had ever been or ever would be of vehicle ride and handling, and quite possibly the fastest driver in the world. The second was that he suffered from an advanced form of what the shrinks call Narcissistic Personality Disorder.

Every few years, rather like David Bowie, Leonard would completely re-invent his entire persona. In one of these periods, he was renowned for sartorial elegance and it was widely assumed that he had his suits made to measure at enormous cost by tailors such as Gieves & Hawkes or Henry Poole & Co. In fact, it is possible that Leonard never set foot in Savile Row in his entire life; he certainly never bought a suit there.

Instead, he bought dead men's tailored suits at knockdown prices from a market stall in the World's End, Chelsea, then had them altered by a Jewish tailor in the backstreets of Islington. Likewise, his brogues may have originated from Lobb's, but he was their second owner.

During this dandy period, Setright had regular haircuts and a neatly-trimmed beard. He often wore a fedora and for a while even affected a monocle, with clear glass of course. It is surprising that he did not, as far as I am aware, attempt to reintroduce the fashion for spats[3].

LJKS became progressively weirder. In the latter part of his career, he impersonated an Old Testament prophet, complete with yarmulke and flowing robes, long grey hair and shaggy beard. The only obvious carry-over from the era in which he had re-interpreted Beau Brummel for the 20th century was the chain-smoking of Sobranie Black Russian cigarettes, which was anachronistic for an OT prophet[4].

He was renowned internationally as a reckless driver who barely slowed down while passing through villages, and once boasted in a column that he had spun a test car through 360 degrees downhill "without losing control at any point during the manoeuvre."

Someone on *Motor* warned me about Setright's driving, and I took care never to share a car with him. In fact, it was this that led me to compile a list of suitable driving partners on car launches. One colleague who shared driving with LJKS once (few of those who underwent the experience signed up for a repeat) told me that, at least on that particular occasion, there was another unpleasant aspect apart from the flat-out through villages tendency.

Flat-out and silently flatulent, apparently. I understand from my informant that kosher farts are every bit as pungent as the Gentile variety. After they had been driving for a while, my colleague began to observe a pattern. While driving along a straight stretch of road, the illuminated bearded weirdo would shift slightly in his seat. Then he would open the window an inch or two and light one of his aromatic Russian cigarettes, but not soon enough to overcome the other odour.

Leonard apparently believed that Jehovah took a personal interest in his case, which is always a worrying trait. This did not prevent him from colliding with a London bus while riding a BMW motorcycle, which disappeared under the Routemaster while he suffered only bruises.

A crowd gathered. "Good heavens!" said someone as the groggy motorcyclist removed his helmet and struggled to his feet. "Setright!"

"Nah," said the bus conductor. "We use Gibsons."[5]

Setright's writing style, revered by some, did not please everyone; his insistence on using untranslated Latin phrases infuriated many readers, especially Americans. One editor instructed him to desist from this forthwith. The first paragraph of the next (and final) column that Setright sent was entirely in Latin.

At his best, he could be an exceptionally witty writer. He contributed to *Motor* for a while before I joined the magazine, and he had evidently had a disagreement with Tony Curtis, then Technical Editor and later Editor: he asserted in one article that everyone agreed with such-and-such a theory "except Mr Technical Editor Curtis, who retires nightly in binary form to his computer bank in Potters Bar."

On a car launch in the south of France, I was standing on the terrace of a swanky hotel owned by the Italian Mafia (which is perhaps classified as 'old money' these days) enjoying a pre-dinner drink. Setright installed himself a short distance away. We both smiled and nodded in the formally polite manner of people who dislike each other. Gorgeous George, the motoring correspondent of *The Daily Star*, came out of the 18th century chateau and walked over to LJKS.

"Good evening, Mr Setright," he began nervously, "... or may I call you Leonard?"

"By all means, my dear fellow," replied the Sage of Surbiton magnanimously.

"Or should that be Len?" inquired the rat-faced hack. I nearly choked on my gin and tonic. Setright's face contorted into an expression that would have curdled milk.

The third of CAR's early columnists was George Bishop. He had been the launch editor of a magazine with the inspiring and imaginative title, *Small Car & Mini Owner (Incorporating Sporting Driver)*, before being sacked for gross incompetence. This magazine was then relaunched as *SMALL CAR* which soon dropped the adjective to expand its potential. George would claim years later that he had been the founding editor of *CAR*, which is what even we non-Australians call 'total bollocks.'

George was among the most obnoxious people one could hope to meet, a really nasty drunkard with a habit of picking on inexperienced waitresses and reducing them to tears. His columns in *CAR* were almost exclusively about the hospitality provided by car manufacturers.

Some people used to defend Bishop, saying that he was really quite a nice chap when sober. The same was said of *The Guardian*'s ghastly motoring correspondent, Roy Harry[6]. To this, I say: RATS! If you behave like a shit when you have had a few shots of alcohol, that means you are a shit. The alcohol has merely released your shitty id from its habitual restraints. Although Bishop was by far the least interesting and least talented of *CAR*'s trio of columnists, he would have merited an entry in *Brewer's Book of Rogues, Villains and Eccentrics* by the late William Donaldson (alias Henry Root), so I have devoted two chapters to his dastardly exploits[7].

[1] Ian Fraser, one of the major figures in *CAR*'s success, told me that there were still two-way mirrors in the building when the magazine moved in.

[2] London Transport used the equally excellent Gibson machine.

[3] A contemporary of mine at school claimed that his grandfather had been the last 'City gent' to commute every day to London wearing spats, up until about 1956.

[4] "By Gad sir, you are a character!"

[5] See Note 2.

[6] Mr Harry (1933-2002) was finally required to clear his desk after being found plastered and slumped over the steering wheel, his forehead pressing the horn button, at a set of traffic lights in central London. A remark in *The Guardian*'s obituary of its former employee, Royston Haydn Harry (yes, really) said all you need to know about the man. He was "… when he was in the right mood, very entertaining company."

[7] We cherish and honour the good, and we forgive and/or forget the mad. Try as we might to erase the ugly from our memory banks, they stubbornly live forever.

8 Cardinal Sin

GEORGE BISHOP WAS A humorous writer, or at least that was how he believed he should be classified, and some people evidently agreed sufficiently for him to scratch a reasonably comfortable living from it. Others took the northern clubman's view: *"'e's all right if tha' likes laffing."*

The surprising thing is that any of the motor industry's Press Officers put up with George. Some of them did not. As Chris Willows, former Public Affairs Manager at BMW GB, told me, "Early into my tenure as PR boss after Raymond [Playfoot], Mr Bishop called me and said, 'Your predecessor never invited me on your events. What is your policy?' I replied 'The same.' Never spoke to the man again."

CAR, then Britain's most stylish monthly motoring magazine, continued to employ Bishop even after The Big Scandal of 1987[1]. He was widely thought of as a colourful rebel by those who had never had any personal contact with him, and as an ill-mannered, unprincipled oaf by most of those who had.

Why or how Bishop, alias Cardinal Sin, had drifted into motoring journalism was lost in the fogs of memory, and not only his own. He had no technical knowledge and he was certainly not an expert driver: he did not even enjoy driving and, by the 1970s, he did not really write about cars any more. Why he stayed in motoring journalism was easier to pinpoint. He was not just a freeloader, he was the freeloader's freeloader: the uncrowned king of blagging.

His columnar ramblings were rarely connected directly to the cars he had driven. Instead, he wrote about the food and wine that he had consumed at the expense of car makers while staying in swanky hotels in exotic locations. Above all, he wrote about The Blag ...

Usually, The Blag was a small but pleasing object of little value, though occasionally manufacturers were absurdly generous. Even then, it was piddling stuff compared with barrow-boy bankers' bonuses, golden parachutes and golden handshakes, or the fiddled expenses of politicians, with or without duck ponds.

Back in the 1970s and 1980s, for some third-rate hacks and especially for George Bishop, The Blag was the thing. Italian car makers were renowned as the most consistently extravagant blag-providers. On one occasion, Bishop was waiting in Terminal 3 at Heathrow to board a flight when he noticed the brand-new black leather briefcase of a young journalist sitting next to him.

"Where did you get that?" he asked in his harsh, nasal voice. He was told that it was from a recent Fiat launch. Fiat's British HQ was then in Brentford, so a conveniently short detour for Bishop on the return trip. The following afternoon, Bishop walked through the swing doors and up to the reception desk.

"I wish to see Mr Thorold-Palmer," he announced to the Italian receptionist.

"Do you have an appointment?" she asked.

"No, but he'll see me. Tell him it's George Bishop."

"One moment, please." She picked up the telephone, tapped in a number, and said that there was a man in reception who wanted to see Mr Thorold-Palmer. "'e says 'is name is ..." She paused and looked at George Bishop. "... What you say your name was?" she asked.

"George Bishop," said George Bishop tetchily.

After a long pause, the receptionist said, "Mr Thorold-Palmer will be down in a moment." She pointed at a settee where he might sit and wait patiently while she filed her nails.

Several minutes later, the Fiat Auto UK's Head of Press Relations came down the stairs and asked, "To what do I owe the unexpected honour of this visit, George?"

Bishop said that he had heard that on a recent press launch a rather fine black leather briefcase had been presented to journalists. He added, "I wondered if by chance you might have one left over that you could give me?"

Unblinking, Thorold-Palmer stared at George Bishop for ten seconds, then said, "Wait here."

Bishop was kept waiting in reception for more than 20 minutes. Then three people came slowly down the wide staircase – the short, bespectacled, Italian Managing Director, the tall Thorold-Palmer, and his secretary, who was holding a large, shiny carrier bag bearing the FIAT logo. Inside this was a black leather briefcase made by Schedoni of Modena[2]. The party of three drew up in line in front of George. The secretary handed the bag to Mr Thorold-Palmer. Mr Thorold-Palmer handed the bag to the MD, and the MD handed the bag to George. Then, without a word, all three turned on their heels and went back upstairs, leaving the impressively unembarrassable George with his new briefcase.

This could be generously classified as bad behaviour, but it was a surprise, even to those who knew him well and detested him (the overlap was not quite 100 per cent), when George committed the crime of the year in Reigate, Surrey.

[1] See next chapter. I personally ensured that he never worked for *Motor* again.
[2] Originally a shoemaker (founded 1880) and now, still under the control of the family, one of the world's finest manufacturers of leather goods, famous for its fitted luggage for Ferraris.

9 Bargain of the week!!!

JA 'TONY' KYD HAD a dry wit and a terrible stammer, which miraculously disappeared whenever he was interviewed about cars on Radio Four. In my early days on *Motor* magazine, my desk was near the door of the main editorial room. At four o'clock one afternoon, Tony, putting on his coat, said with a slight smile, "I m-m-m-might g-g-g-get in late … b-b-b-but I leave early."

Tony had been on the staff of *Motor* for over 30 years and he had gradually turned his job into a sinecure. He got away with it because everyone liked him. He had the nominal title of Assistant Editor. At one stage, after a promotion, I became 'Deputy Assistant Editor,' though I never had occasion to deputize for Tony and I never knowingly assisted the Deputy Editor (see Chapter 23).

Tony Kyd's greatest eccentricity was his friendship with his neighbour in Reigate, George Bishop, to whom the reader has already been introduced. That was until Tony and his wife returned from holiday to find that Mrs Kyd's Metro was no longer in their garage. It was like Piglet and Pooh: the more they looked, the more it wasn't there.

While the Kyds had been away, Bishop had been entrusted with the keys of the house, including the garage key, and requested to keep an eye on the property. He expressed surprise at the disappearance of the Metro. "It was there when I checked the other day," he said, expertly feigning bewilderment.

Tony informed the local police, who took down details in the standard disengaged manner. Several days later, Tony spotted an ad in his local rag, placed by the town's Austin Rover dealer. Within this was a box with the headline 'BARGAIN OF THE WEEK!!!' That week's bargain (!!!) was a year-old Metro, under 5000 miles on the clock, British Racing Green. Tony, not having a strong belief in coincidence, rushed to the dealership.

Sure enough, there was Mrs Kyd's Metro on a dais. The Sales Manager soon dropped his sales pitch and was embarrassed to discover that he had been attempting to sell stolen property to its rightful owner. He explained that the car had been bought in good faith from the recent car auction at Blackbushe.

"Who was the s-s-s-seller?" asked Tony.

The Sales Manager opened a filing cabinet and pulled out the dossier. "Ah yes, here we are. A Mr Bishop … George Bishop." He assured Tony that the car would be removed from the showroom immediately and kept in the workshop until the police authorized its release.

Tony went straight to the police station and explained the circumstances to the thick Desk Sergeant[1], who seemed to think that Mr Kyd must be part of some kind of big-time car-stealing conspiracy, though how that would work was not clear, especially the detail about why the kingpin in such a conspiracy would then complain to the police.

Why did George Bishop do this? It was never satisfactorily clarified. In court, he kept contradicting himself under cross-examination. At one point, he suggested that he had done it "for a laugh," at another that he was working on a journalistic exposé of how easy it was to carry out such thefts.

One of The Cardinal's Editors testified under oath that George Bishop was a man of previously good character[2]. The chairman of the magistrates said that the court took a very grave view of this kind of thing, but that, on this occasion, it would be lenient, considering the defendant's previously unblemished record, "even though," he emphasized, "Mr Bishop's evidence has been, to put it mildly, highly unreliable[3]." Bishop was fined £300 with costs, and given a six-month suspended prison sentence.

Outside the courthouse, Bishop found Tony Kyd barring the way to his car.

"Hello George," said Tony.

"Hello, Tony," said Bishop nervously.

"You are going to s-s-sell your house at the earliest opportunity, and m-m-m-move at least 100 miles from here." Then Tony Kyd turned and walked to his own car. George Bishop obeyed the instruction and moved to the West Country. Nobody in the business saw or heard of him for a couple of years. He was not widely missed, except perhaps by people who had never met him.

He reappeared at the Geneva Motor Show, turning up at the reception held by the SMMT (Society of Motor Manufacturers and Traders) at the beautiful Parc des Eaux Vives, an 18th century palazzo on the southern shore of the lake. I was in conversation with Michael Schimpke, then BMW's foreign press officer. Bishop, evidently nine parts drunk, lurched over and grabbed my lapel.

"Ah, you're wearing a suit," he slurred. "I didn't know you had a suit."

"I didn't, George," I replied quietly with a smile, while twisting his thumb until he grimaced. "But I heard that Tony Kyd was away on holiday, so I broke into his house and stole his. Now why don't you fuck off and stop bothering me?"

"Who is that awful man?" asked Michael Schimpke.

"That's George Bishop," I replied. "The famous humorist."

At some point after this, an inexperienced press officer loaned George Bishop a test car and then had considerable difficulty getting it back. And then, as we all must one day, George Bishop died. Those who never met the man, and those of an exceptionally tolerant and forgiving nature, might say, "Rest In Peace."

---

[1] "It w-w-w-was the Sergeant who was th-th-th-thick," explained Tony, "not the d-d-d-desk."
[2] He was not charged with perjury for this astonishing remark, which is odd, to say the least.
[3] Had I been the chairman of the magistrates, I would have added, "He is, in the view of this court, a vexatious cockwomble," but perhaps I am unsuited to such a role.

10 Geneva as it was

I ARRIVED IN GENEVA for my first visit on Monday 14 March 1977 and I thought it was a magical place. It may have been the most expensive city in Europe, but it was also the cleanest, and it was lots of fun, especially at Motor Show time, despite the appalling traffic, and the world's slowest-changing traffic lights.

For many years, its annual Motor Show was an essential entry in the diaries of a large proportion of the world's motoring journalists.

It has always been a mystery why there is a Geneva Motor Show at all as there have never been any Swiss car manufacturers apart from a few small operators. There was Frank M Rinderknecht (whose business continues after his retirement), a visionary showman and entrepreneur, rather than a car manufacturer, as mentioned in other chapters. There was Franco Sbarro, who did some interesting stuff, such as the hubless wheel[1], before founding his car school. He never produced anything in volume; anyway, he is of Italian origin. And there were a few other coachbuilders and tuners scratching at the edges. Yet the Geneva show became, and remains, one of the major annual international Motor Shows.

The Geneva show dates from 1905, but it was in 1924, the first year that the show was based at Plainpalais, near the old city centre and almost within a stone's throw of the banks of the Rhone, where the great river continues its long journey to the Mediterranean after the artificial interruption of Lac Leman, that things really took off.

The first European Motor Show after World War II was in Geneva, in 1947. Perhaps the famous neutrality of Switzerland was the key to its success, which, of course resulted, in the short term, in Swiss cities not being flattened by carpet bombing, and Swiss businessmen not being unduly inconvenienced by the strife between neighbouring nations.

In the longer term, while the French and then the Germans cut costs by making their Motor Shows biennial, and the British and once-splendid Italian shows fell off their perches with differing degrees of resounding thuds, the Geneva show somehow carried on unperturbed, like the annual arrival of the cuckoo.

As the show was on the southern side of the Rhone, the best plan was to stay in a hotel there, so that one could do everything except the SMMT reception on foot. The show was compact but all the major manufacturers were there, many of them unveiling new models or concepts, and the Italian coachbuilders took the show just as seriously as their home event in Turin, which had become biennial.

At the edge of Plainpalais there were several excellent restaurants. Each was taken over by one of the car manufacturers, and one had no shortage of invitations to lunch. *Motor* had two or three reporters and a photographer at the show, so we would head off in different directions, to enjoy the hospitality of, for example, Fiat, Renault, Mercedes-Benz and British Leyland. Then we would meet up in the show hall and compare notes. In the evening, we might variously have been entertained by BMW, PSA (Peugeot-Citroën), Volkswagen and Volvo.

Then we hacks would hammer copy onto sheets of A4 with our portable typewriters. By the Wednesday morning, we usually had everything covered, and we would set off for the Col de la Faucille and points north, dropping off the photographer at the airport for him to fly home with rolls of film and our copy.

Since 1982 it has been possible to go to the Geneva show without going to Geneva.

You land at the airport, go through customs, leave the terminal and cross the bridge, and you are in Palexpo, a sprawling exhibition centre. Then, a few hours later, you return to the terminal and fly home. Apart from the splendid alpine view as you walk from airport to exhibition centre (and perhaps back if the sun has not set), and having to pay for stuff with Swiss francs and later euros (for a while), you might just as well be at the NEC in Birmingham in the era when it held a Motor Show. Or anywhere.

The airport and Palexpo are just a few miles north of the city, but, of course, the move immediately lost the annual event its feeling of intimacy. The logistics of covering the Motor Show obviously became more complex. But one adapts.

After the move to Palexpo, the centre of Geneva continued to be the focal point for Motor Show professionals after hours, though to get from point A (the show halls) to point B (the city centre) no longer entailed an easy stroll but a tedious traffic jam² that became tediouser as the years passed.

The Monday evening during my coverage of the show (I missed only one between 1977 and 2007) evolved into a routine. First event was the SMMT (Society of Motor Manufacturers and Traders) reception at the Parc des Eaux-Vives (see Chapter 9), and, after that, the VW UK dinner at the Hotel Métropole, near the southern end of the Pont du Mont-Blanc. These two events were always useful for gathering information.

On Tuesday evening, after one had spent the day plodding around the show, there were invitations from manufacturers to receptions, press conferences and/or dinners.

There were excellent restaurants, among them the Café de Paris, and then there was the Fiat Boat (see Chapter 11). There was just fun everywhere, and one always had a good laugh with the gang of drunken car designers.

Saab held a dinner every Tuesday evening at La Reserve, a large hotel midway between Palexpo and the centre of Geneva. All the 'Fleet Street' crowd would be there, along with journalists from all over the world. The event coincided nearly, and occasionally exactly, with the birthday of Erik Carlsson, a huge bear of a man who had been a top rally driver in his day and who had become Saab's international 'ambassador'.

Then there was the Bataclan, a sophisticated strip club in the old part of the city. While sitting in the Bataclan one evening, I asked BMW's suave UK Press Relations Director Raymond Playfoot what sort of budget he had for that kind of thing. He replied casually, "Oh I try to keep it below a thousand pounds for the evening, old boy." This was in about 1985.

Gradually, things changed. My charming little hotel on the south side of the Rhone near the centre of the old city, occupied one quarter of its block when I first stayed in it in 1978. Over several years, it steadily expanded, until it eventually filled the entire block. At the same time, floor by floor, the interior was gutted and remodelled; the rooms became smaller while the prices rose in inverse proportion. The staff remained the same in one sense – they were the same people – but they became unpleasantly arrogant, to the edge of rudeness, for no obvious reason. They had previously been pleasant, helpful and welcoming, and, I presume, less well paid.

In about 1985, I decided the price was too high and left my place to motor industry representatives, who were not at that time under severe cost restraints. Besides, while the hotel was convenient for various evening events, it made the morning journey to the show an ordeal; it took ages just to cross the Pont du Mont-Blanc. Those who worked in the centre of the city selfishly refused to take a week off to leave room for visiting journalists and motor industry people to go about their business.

From then on, my team and I stayed in hotels in the area between the station and the north bank of the lake. Then that went upmarket, too. By that time, I was a freelance, and I picked the scruffiest dump I could find. My friend and colleague Atomic Underpants called it the Hotel Scrofuloso. That eventually got tarted up sufficiently for its prices to become unacceptable.

By now, I did not enjoy the Motor Show, the Fiat Boat[3] was no more, and Volkswagen UK had pulled the plug on its annual dinner for British motoring hacks. Oh, and I did not like Geneva itself any more, either. My favourite restaurants had closed or become absurdly expensive. The streets, no longer impeccably clean, harboured scruffy hookers, beggars, junkies, and other lurking ne'er-do-wells of an evening.

Some colleagues responded by adopting the one-day in-and-out procedure. I decided to stop going. I had had enough. I miss numerous things about Geneva that no longer exist. Only one of those is the Fiat Boat. The Bataclan closed down long ago. Now, the city is just a drab, dirty place, though still very expensive. Bankers, hookers and malevolent-looking beggars lurk everywhere.

[1] Beautifully engineered, these wheels never progressed beyond the prototype stage. The theoretical technical advantages were marginal, especially when manufacturing costs were taken into account. There was also a major problem of high wear rates because of the difficulty of keeping dirt out of the bearings.
[2] Aggravated by the world's slowest-changing traffic lights.
[3] See next chapter.

11 Fiatboating

ONE OF THE HIGHLIGHTS of the Geneva show in the 1980s was the Fiat Boat. This was one of Lac Leman's vintage paddle-steamers, moored alongside the Quai du Mont-Blanc, close to the spot where Princess Elisabeth ('Sisi') of Austria was assassinated by a deranged Italian anarchist in 1898. Many Italians are deranged, but not all are anarchists … and vice versa.

Fiat hired the boat primarily to entertain business guests, but also, prompted by PR men who had spotted an opportunity, invited journalists aboard. On the evenings following press days, the boat was always packed with journalists of all nationalities, plus half the PR men in the international motor industry, all unwinding enthusiastically. Soon, the car designers got to hear about it; they all turned up and, in my experience, no group of people in the 1980s unwound as enthusiastically as a bunch of car designers.

There was plenty of careless talk, especially after a few glasses of the notoriously awful red wine, which tasted like a mixture of Ribena and surgical spirit, spiced up with a shot of diesel fuel.

The expression 'Fiatboat' passed into the language as a verbed compound noun, as in "Are you Fiatboating tonight?" or the next morning (generally from behind dark glasses), "I feel severely Fiatboated."

This jollity continued for about ten years and then there was the shocking news before the show in 1994: there would be no Fiat boat. The Italian corporation's car division was going through one of its periodic crises, and began to do something which goes against the grain for Italian car manufacturers: it closely scrutinized its entertainment expenditure. My friend Gadzooks[1] told me that the final straw came when, in 1993, a senior Fiat executive spotted a crass British PR 'entertaining' three journalists on the Fiat boat, at Fiat's expense.

So in 1994, where one expected to see a lovely old paddle-steamer, there was an empty quayside. As with Piglet and Pooh, the more one looked, the more it wasn't there[2].

The following year, Volkswagen, having noted the popularity of the Fiat Boat, took up the challenge. And we had the same magnificent, elderly boat, with exposed man-sized con-rods, now sporting different flags. Volkswagen decided that the Italians did not have the faintest clue about fun: they expect it to happen spontaneously, without any market research and without a series of planning meetings using flip-charts and pie-charts and all sorts of other charts, and without hired entertainers and without everything carefully timed to the nearest minute. The Germans, on the other hand, understood that fun had to be meticulously planned several months in advance, down to the last detail. Otherwise, how could it be fun?

In particular, they decided to control the number of boarders with maximum severity. You could not get in without an official invitation. I was amused and impressed when I found the usual full complement of car designers on board, revelling away at VW's expense, as they had at Fiat's. I have no idea how they managed that, but they are exceptionally clever and inventive people who at that time operated like the Mafia or the Freemasons, accustomed to taking shortcuts and generally getting the better of bean counters and middle management.

In 1996 Volkswagen expanded the fun concept with a troupe of half-naked and highly athletic black dancers, all female and some of them seriously fruity. Guests jostled to obtain a better view of this artistic cabaret act, which involved a lot of vigorous jumping about. There were fears, almost certainly unjustified, that the boat might turn turtle. As a result, in 1997 a modern boat replaced the venerable paddle-steamer. It was spacious, solidly built, fully equipped and spotlessly clean. I thought it had probably been Type-Approved, crash-tested and perhaps even put through a wind tunnel. VW is the world leader in passing exams of that kind ...

One could choose between a first-rate Burgundy and a tolerable Bordeaux. A troupe of weirdly-dressed 'performance artists' enacted a weird dance to weird, atonal music, keeping all their clothes on, and being careful not to jump about. At the other end of the boat, there was the alternative of booming heavy-metal music that young Germans seem to like so much, and older Germans pretend to like so as not to cause offence to younger Germans. After a couple of glasses of Burgundy, with a break in-between for a glass of Bordeaux, I retired early, before a mildly-famous French *chanteuse*, whose style was not to my taste, did her stuff. My fun had been thoroughly organized and one can have too much of a good thing[3].

[1] See Chapter 34.
[2] Apologies for repeating that joke.
[3] Volkswagen pulled the plug on its Geneva boating activity after several years.

12 Whiteout en Provence

AFTER SEVERAL SUCCESSIVE MILD winters, the clever burghers charged with protecting the city of Geneva against wintry elements decided that most of their snow-clearing equipment was an unsustainable overhead, so, during the 1990s, they ignored Sod's Law and sold a load of snowploughs and other stuff to the highest bidder. The inevitable happened: the very next winter snow fell as if in a morality tale, and the streets of Geneva were impassable for days on end. Profits from the sale of snow-clearing equipment evaporated faster than the snow.

Well, everyone makes mistakes, and, concerning snowy weather, I made a few. I commuted to Geneva for the annual Motor Show every year between 1977 and 1995 from England, and after that until 2007 from France. I was generally lucky with road conditions, but, at that time of year (end of February/early March), the weather can fluctuate, especially in mountainous regions, between winter and spring with alarming rapidity.

This pilgrimage almost went pear-shaped in 2001. The outward journey was in bright sunshine, on dry roads. The return was fine until, after lunch near Monestiers, we got into the high Alps, on the Route Napoleon. South of Barrème, an illuminated sign stated that 'special equipment'[1] was required on the RN85, which we were on. I did not point this out to my wife, who had not seen it, and pressed on with a veneer of nonchalance covering deep apprehension, as I had to write my show report and send it by e-mail to *The Daily Telegraph* first thing next morning.

Despite occasional packed snow and icy patches, the RN85 was driveable, my car's summer tyres working adequately. We got to Le Logis du Pin without drama and the D21 towards Draguignan had been cleared. Then I made the mistake of turning off on to the D25, which had not …

It was all right initially, though I had to switch off the ASC[2], which would otherwise have brought us to an earlier halt. At the ghost village of Brovès[3], conditions worsened suddenly, the road ahead disappeared, and I stopped. But I stopped just a few yards too late. Despite digging frantically with my folding spade, I could not make the car go either forwards or backwards. The sun was shining pleasantly, but preparing to take his hat off and dip below the horizon. I thought we were stuck for the night, a mere 13km from home by road (only eight in a direct line). A hired A-class arrived and stopped behind us. The driver turned out to be an obnoxious young Englishman; he and his mousey little wife[4] were on their way to Fayence.

He did not offer to help, barely acknowledging my presence. He got back in his car and attempted to turn round; he also got stuck. Well, fuck you, too, I thought, as one does. Then, miraculously, two 4x4s appeared from the south, driving along the invisible road towards us. They stopped and a pair of jovial peasants emerged, one a chunky, rosy-faced chap, the famous Monsieur Philippe Fabre. There was a little lamb on the passenger seat of his battered vehicle, and he had a marvellous dog, a large Bas-Rouge cross with fine eyes.

I said to the rosy-faced one that I thought I had seen his bearded colleague on television, in a programme about sheep farming on the Canjuers plateau. Yes, he said, but that's not my colleague, that's my brother. They were members of the Fabre family of La Roque Esclapon, near La Bastide, where they had a restaurant during the summer.

After gently taking the piss, they pushed us around, then we pushed the shithead's A-class to get it going, and we came back via a long detour on cleared roads. I was following matey in the A-class, who seemed to be driving quite competently at first, and as I was tired I couldn't be bothered to overtake. But then he overtook two pompier vehicles very dangerously. Why do people risk themselves and others so stupidly? This was nothing to do with excessive speed, with which authorities everywhere are obsessed.

He must have gone straight on towards Draguignan after Montferrat (either not knowing the military road or wrongly imagining that it would be impassable), because I was not far behind him when I turned off towards Figanières and I would undoubtedly have caught him, as I went over the col rapidly, anger having fully woken me up. I hope the selfish berk became utterly lost. There was hardly any snow in Bargemon, though the descent of our icy drive was scary even after we had brushed it. Half a bottle of Aberlour got me nicely through my show report.

About six months later, I was watching the local early-evening news on France 3 – and there was Monsieur Fabre the shepherd. He was being interviewed about wolves attacking his sheep and about working as a shepherd on the high plateau of Canjuers. He mentioned that he had rescued numerous people, mostly foreigners, in winter, and added that nobody had taken the trouble to thank him in any way ... "except a tall Englishman with grey hair, with a French wife. They found where I lived and brought us a case of champagne." So I have done my bit for *l'Entente Cordiale*.

Did I learn from this mistake? Well, um, not really. By 2006, I had decided that the hotels in Geneva had all become far too expensive and that this would be the last time I would stay in the city. My hotel near the railway station, until then agreeably scruffy and acceptably inexpensive, had been completely done up, quite well, under new ownership and naturally the room rate had skyrocketed.

I found this out rather late in my preparations and I booked as usual for the Monday night but I had a clever plan for the Tuesday evening after I had finished my work: instead of getting stuck in the awful stop-start early-evening traffic heading back into Geneva, I would go north through the tunnel to Ferney-Voltaire, and then skirt the western side of the city and stop at La Bonne Auberge in Allonzier-la-Caille, on the road towards Annecy, that I had noticed over the years.

That way I would save money, and also get a head start on the journey home the next morning. I knew these twisty back roads, passing through a surprisingly rural area, from years past.

When I stepped out of Palexpo into a nascent blizzard at 6pm on the Tuesday, I should have aborted the plan and chugged through the centre of Geneva, but instead I pressed on in that dogged, rather foolhardy (perhaps 'ineffably stupid' is the phrase I am seeking) spirit that sometimes comes over me.

I got out of the traffic around Palexpo and the airport and through the tunnel into France in no time, and turned left, which was fine, and all seemed to be going well for a few minutes. However, after that the blizzard and the darkness made it increasingly hard and then impossible to read the road signs. It was whiteout and blackout all in one. Nothing was recognizable. I must have missed a sign and I became a bit lost for a while.

Well, actually, I was completely lost in the middle of nowhere for about 45 minutes. I was on snow-covered country lanes, with hills. My BMW would undoubtedly have got stuck, and even in the Focus I thought I was going to spend a miserable night inside the car, perhaps in a ditch. Then I had a stroke of luck, seeing a sign to Collonges, which was one of my reference points.

Immediately, I made another foolish decision and followed the first sign I saw to Cruseilles, rather than taking the safer option and going via St Julien-en-Genevois ... I was soon slithering along hilly country lanes covered in snow, in pitch darkness.

Eventually, I struggled onto the main road, which was then the RN (Route Nationale) 201, since been demoted to D (Départementale) 1201. It was clear of snow, though not of traffic, and there was a room left at the Auberge in Allonzier.

Phew! What a prat I can be sometimes. I had a delicious dinner, œuf en cocotte à l'estragon followed by Boeuf Bourguignon, washed down by a very pleasant red wine from Taradeau in the Var; Madame told me that her family owned the vineyard. Dinner and the room came to 55€, which was outstanding value. When I got home, I regretted that I had not noted down the address of the vineyard and resolved to check it out the next year. But I was in for an unpleasant surprise (See Chapter 17).

I reported on every Geneva show but one between 1977 and 2007. The single exception was 1981. On that occasion, I got within 20 miles of the city and then turned round and drove to Paris. It was frustrating but I was obeying orders: it was part of a plan, my Editor's plan. And it was the start of a bad week.

[1] Chains? Thermal underwear? A bible?
[2] Automatic Stability Control; not necessarily the answer to everything.
[3] The village is on the plateau de Canjuers, the biggest military exercise area in Europe. There is a long military history there – 'Canjuers' is a corruption of 'Camp de Jules' – Julius Caesar had his base camp there before deciding that "Gallia in tres partes divisa est." Canjuers is huge – about 350sqkm. It would have been simpler and cheaper and fairer, and all sorts of other things, if the military and the French State (not that they are two separate entities) had left Brovès and its inhabitants alone, and instead built a village somewhere using breeze blocks.
[4] Or vice versa (with acknowledgement to Edward Albee).

13 A memorably bad week

THIS IS A PERFECT topic for Chapter 13; my response to those who thought my job was an unending wallow in the lap of luxury. Some days of my work were tough. Some weeks were hellish. This was one of them.

We crossed the Channel on the first Saturday afternoon of March 1981, four of us in two cars, a BMW 735 (the first, E23 generation), and an Audi Quattro, the idea being to do a comparison test in various conditions.

Having stopped for the night at Chaumont in the Haute-Marne, on the Sunday we tackled le Ballon d'Alsace, a mountain to the north of Belfort with a ski resort at its summit. The ascent, on the north face, had patches of ice and snow and the BMW, which I was driving, struggled for traction out of the hairpin turns. I could not keep up with the Quattro, driven by Editor Curtis, who was out of the car and sporting a smug grin when I reached the ski resort at the 1200m peak.

A few minutes later, we descended the southern face, which was sunny and almost entirely dry. This time I was leading and the 735 had the advantage, thanks to its superior brakes. After three or four bends, I could no longer see the Audi in the rear-view mirror.

We then drove south, ending up close to the Col de la Faucille, from which Lac Leman is almost in view. Here, we were about 100 metres higher than we had been on the Ballon. The road had been well cleared, but there was a deep carpet of snow all around and, again, plenty of skiers.

We found a snowy, flat track and my Editor drove along it for about 100 yards or metres, turned round and drove back without difficulty. Then it was my turn to drive along the track as far as possible in the BMW. That turned out to be about 20 yards. Full stop, rear wheels spinning hopelessly. The idea then was to tow it out with the Audi.

The previous week, Editor Curtis had instructed me to buy a tow wire for this purpose. I had replied that it was not necessary because on a recent Fiat launch I had been given a splendid emergency kit, full of useful stuff, in a fancy plastic briefcase. The sturdy-looking tow wire had neat fittings at each end. I attached these to the rear tow hooks of both cars.

I sat in the BMW, keeping the auto trans in neutral, and looking in the rear-view mirror for the moment to select reverse. Editor Curtis put the Audi in first and gently eased forward to take up the strain. The wire immediately snapped. Some crook had sold Fiat a consignment of several hundred tow wires that were unfit for purpose; indeed, utter crap.

After we had stopped falling about laughing, we somehow coaxed the 735 back onto the road. Curtis and the other two crammed themselves and their luggage into the Quattro, and headed south to creep into Geneva because the car had begun to lose oil from a chafed oil pipe, which, in turn, caused an intermittent electrical fault. I drove in the opposite direction back through the Jura, joining the A6 at Chalon-sur-Saone.

Though disappointed not to be attending the Motor Show, I was looking forward to an evening in Paris, but I chose the wrong lunch stop and, while cruising up the autoroute, I began to have stomach pains, and realized that I had mild food poisoning[1]. Early in the evening I checked into my favoured scruffy hotel, at that time in a side street near l'Etoile, and shut myself in my room for a disturbed night.

After breakfast next morning, Tuesday, feeling somewhat better, I drove early to Renault HQ at Boulogne-Billancourt, to the west of the city, where I was to collect a

5 Turbo, the mid-engined model. I parked the BMW, took my luggage and walked into the press office, where I met a pompous, overweight ass with a silly waxed moustache who was at that time the head of Renault's Press Department. He behaved like a medium-level *fonctionnaire* (civil servant), which I suppose is what he was, as it was still the *Régie* Renault in those days.

He kept insisting that the car must at all costs be returned by 4pm the following Friday. I did not take much notice of this, as I was examining the paperwork he had provided for the car ... and I did not like what I saw.

I reminded him that we had been in contact over a period of several weeks, by telephone and fax, and that I had given him precise instructions on the paperwork that was required to take a French-registered car in and out of the UK. He made a dismissive gesture, said that it would be no problem and reminded me, again, that the car had to be returned by four o'clock that Friday, at the latest. I took the keys from him, gave him one of my withering looks, and left his office.

I set off for Calais in the certainty that I was going to land in deep shit in Dover with the R5 Turbo, the initial homologation version of Renault's rally car of that era. It was bright red, and it stood out like a sore big toe, resembling a gigantic surgical boot. Also, it had a garish red and blue interior. It was not going to pass through British Customs & Excise without touching the sides. I had on board slightly more than the strictly-permitted allowance of booze and cigarettes ... but I guessed correctly that the car was the greater problem.

Having disembarked, in the port of Dover, I chose the red channel and was immediately instructed to park in the special treatment spot. The first Customs chap seemed quite reasonable and I thought for a moment that, having examined the paperwork, and heard my explanation that the car was going to be in Britain for only three nights, he would let me through. But he decided he needed to bring in his superior. This fellow, of cadaverous appearance, turned out to be one of those bitter failures who rise to a certain level in what is sarcastically described as 'public service,' believing that they are officer material, whereas they are actually corporals who have somehow become sergeants. Where do they dig these people up?

He was pointlessly aggressive from the start. It was immediately clear that my unprovoked admission of the excess booze/tobacco was a trivial matter. He was more interested in why I should be committing the criminal act of driving a car with a French number plate while having a British passport and driving licence.

I explained carefully and calmly, at least twice, what the car was, who I was, who I worked for, and why I wanted to bring the car into Britain for two days. However, through stupidity or obstinacy, or probably genetically-transmitted unpleasantness, he appeared to favour other explanations. I had built the car myself and/or it was a one-off prototype. Undoubtedly, I planned to sell it the next day. Perhaps I was bringing it back into Britain after a short visit to France, for devious reasons unclear. In short, he wanted to believe anything, including anything stupid, except the plain truth that I had told him.

Whistling the whistle of a Master of the Inquisition with a new set of thumbscrews, he wandered off to tell someone in higher authority that he had caught a felon in the act of that most heinous of crimes, not having the correct paperwork when passing through Customs & Excise.

Half an hour later, he returned with a malicious grin on his pallid face. He instructed me to take the car to some hut in the middle of nowhere and to present there an unintelligible piece of paper he had handed to me, duly rubber-stamped.

The officers in this hut, when I finally found it, were not at all interested. They sent me to the next barrier. It turned out that in my manoeuvres across the tarmac, I had inadvertently 'left England' and I had to go through a second passport check. Next, I was told to park the car a couple of hundred yards further on and to go into an office hidden at the back of the compound to sort out the paperwork.

The place was full of lorry drivers. Most of them, it seemed, had the correct paperwork, but they were in a bad mood as they queued at various windows marked 'Dover Harbour Board' or 'Dover Control Services' or something else equally meaningless to outsiders.

After a long time in the queue, I was sent by the first of these to the second, where, after queuing again for ages, the man behind the Control Services window told me to go to Customs & Excise. The chap there said that I should go to DHB or DCS and was uninterested that they had sent me to him.

At this point, amazingly without displaying any loss of temper, I said that I did not wish to spend the rest of the night or the rest of my life being shunted from one long queue to another without resolving the problem.

"What you need is an agent," said the Excise man. This seemed like the first helpful remark anyone had made to me since I had disembarked. I asked "Where can I find an agent? No ... don't tell me – DHB or DCS?" He nodded helpfully.

I appointed an agent through DHB and the agent helped me to fill in a long and absurd Temporary Import (or was it Export?) form, for which he charged £35 – and £35 was worth more than £35 in those long-off days. Everything went smoothly after that. It took only a further three hours to be released from the compound.

I drove home and threw myself into bed. Before falling asleep, I reflected on how Britain's membership of the Common Market (as it was then called) had created a free trade area, and how grateful we should all be for our civil servants. Then the alarm rang. It was 6am, time to get up and out, and on the road to MIRA.

I met a colleague for breakfast at the Newport Pagnell services. From there, we drove in high-speed convoy to the test track, where we measured the car's performance. This included one of the fastest flat-out laps I ever did of the triangular high-speed circuit, at 123.8mph. The best quarter-mile along the straights was just over 126mph, so Renault's official top speed claim of 128mph was credible. I drove home, began writing the test, ate some cheese on toast and fell into a deep sleep.

The next morning, Thursday, was spent with a photographer, hooning about in the lanes of Sussex, and then I drove to the office, completed the test report and started making plans for the following week.

There was another early start on Friday, for the return journey to Paris. At Dover, it took only half an hour to sort through the papers, escape being always easier than invasion.

A small, surly slob of a Customs man in Calais refused to listen to my explanation of why a British passport-holder was driving a French-registered car. I was delayed an hour before an intelligent, friendly official was found, who explained to the idiot exactly what I had said. I thought for a while that he might box the ears of his thick colleague.

As I left the port of Calais, the sun was shining and I felt that all was well with the world. I was looking forward to dinner in Paris and this time I was not suffering from food poisoning.

An hour later, at around 2pm, very suddenly the sky turned dark and soon it was raining heavily. I was in the overtaking lane cruising at 100mph, headlights on and wipers on the highest setting. Suddenly, there was complete silence, the instrument display disappeared and there was no forward visibility. The Renault's electrical system had shut down completely. The engine had died, the wipers and the lights switched off, and I had to navigate out of this traffic without power and without being able to indicate my intentions. I could not even make hand signals, because it was impossible to lower the electric window.

Those who believe in childish concepts such as guardian angels would say that mine was on duty that day, though, after what had happened to me over the previous few days, I felt that if I had a guardian angel, he, she or it was taking the piss. Somehow I made it to the relative safety of the hard shoulder.

I rolled to a stop, breathed a sigh of relief and then walked to the emergency phone that I had spotted during my scary deceleration. The rain had now eased to a drizzle. After notifying the authorities of my plight, I walked back to the car. Then I wondered what to do. This was before the days of mobile phones. I looked at my watch. It was just after 2pm. I knew I was roughly an hour's drive from Boulogne-Billancourt. Theoretically I was well ahead of schedule, but the flying surgical boot had other plans.

In the distance, at the far side of a ploughed field, I could see a group of buildings. I walked across the field and found a school. For some reason it was closed, but there was a door open and there was a woman teacher. I explained my problem and asked if I could use a phone.

I dialled Monsieur Waxed Moustache's number. I explained to him that I would have delivered the car on time but that it had expired, somewhere near Roye in the Somme and that he would not have it back that day as arranged. He asked, in his fonctionnaire's haughty tone, "And what do you expect me to do?"

I replied, "Considering what you have done for me so far, I am very confident that you will do absolutely fuck all." I put the receiver down and thanked the schoolteacher, who laughed, evidently understanding English.

Then I picked my way back across the muddy field. The low loader had arrived and also some police or gendarmes. They were irritatingly keen to arrest me for abandoning the vehicle, which is nearly as serious as having the wrong paperwork. I talked them out of that, the R5 Turbo was winched onto the low loader, and we went to the nearest Renault garage, which turned out to be about 45 minutes away.

I found the manager and explained the situation. The garage was like a caricature of Renault's dealer network at the time. A group of grease monkeys in filthy overalls wheeled the stricken R5 Turbo into the workshop, which looked as if it had last been cleaned and tidied some time in the 1930s.

Of course, these chaps had never seen this model before. They examined it thoroughly. There was a faint chance of a loose connection somewhere, but after a few minutes, they gave up. The chief mechanic stated the obvious: "C'est la boîte électronique."

I gave the manager the name and phone number of Waxed Moustache and asked him where the nearest railway station was. I thought he might offer me a lift, but I ended up in a taxi and this was another 45-minute ride. I still had faint hopes of a tasty dinner in Paris, but I had just missed a train and the next one was not for an hour and a half. Fortunately, there was an excellent restaurant next to the station.

I arrived in Paris some time before midnight and collected the BMW from Boulogne-Billancourt the next morning. My fear that the whole administrative building would be closed on a Saturday morning turned out to be misplaced. I drove back to Calais, and then home and had a long sleep.

On Sunday, I drove to Chichester for lunch with my uncle and aunt. It was raining hard on the way there and the wipers of the 735 failed. I ended up driving with both front windows open, operating the wipers of BMW's flagship via a length of string. It was a fitting end to the week.

And now, a memorable journey to Turin, for the Motor Show, where Fiat, which then owned much of the city including all its best hotels, paid for the accommodation of selected journalists. On this occasion, a British Press Officer sorted out a serious problem for my colleagues.

[1] Not that it ever feels mild.

14 To Turin by Quattro – part 1

THE YEAR BEFORE THAT R5 turbo episode, I had been assigned the task by my Editor at *Motor* magazine to be the advance guard at the Turin Motor Show, which in those days was an important international event, even though it had, by then, become biennial.

For complicated reasons involving a partial strike by the National Union of Journalists, the rest of the team (Editor Curtis himself, Technical Editor Greenslade and Peter Burn, photographer) would not be able to get to the show before lunchtime on Tuesday, at the earliest. I left my home in Sussex on the Monday morning and boarded the Dover-Calais ferry in good time for lunch. A couple of hours later, I was possibly the first Audi Quattro driver on French soil.

There was hardly any traffic on the autoroute, so I kept up a high average speed, though rarely exceeding 135mph[1]. I had selected Beaune as a suitable spot to stop for the night. I had not booked a hotel, but cruised into the centre of town early in the evening, parked in what turned out to be Place Carnot, named after the assassinated President rather than his uncle the famous thermodynamicist, and began my accommodation recce, which was agreeably brief. Almost immediately, I found the Hotel Central at one corner of the pleasant square. This was reasonably priced, and it had what turned out to be a very good restaurant. It does not always work out so well when one is seeking accommodation and a decent meal on the hoof.

While I was having a pre-dinner drink in the bar near the reception desk, a couple of young men carrying rucksacks entered the hotel. I guessed from the big burly man's accent that they must both be Australians. It was evident that neither the big burly man nor the thin lugubrious one spoke any French and that the receptionist did not understand that they were trying to find out what time dinner was served, so I told them.

I had dinner and returned to the bar. The two of them were there already. I ordered a drink and asked where they were hitching to.

"You're Peter Dron, aren't you?" said the big burly man, who turned out to be Steve Cropley[2]. He was at that time Deputy Editor of *CAR* and soon the magazine's Editor, later moving to Haymarket after it bought *Autocar*. I knew the name, but it was the first time I had met him. The other chap was one of *CAR*'s first-rate photographers, Colin Curwood, who is not really lugubrious. He just has that kind of face[3]. Neither is he Australian. Cropley, on the other hand, is about as Australian as anyone can reasonably be, so I got that bit right. All a bit embarrassing, really.

Next morning was a new day, a Monday, as generally happens after Sunday. I decided to cruise at 90-95mph, just a touch above the 130km/h (80.778mph) autoroute limit, so as not to attract unwanted attention, having reasoned that the French police might be actively engaged in revenue collection on a working day.

I was right about the last part but wrong otherwise. They spotted me, just before the toll north of Lyon, and I had not spotted them. While I was paying my toll fee, I saw that a gendarme (in English, a bloke with a gun) was waiting to have a discussion, and I was fairly sure that he did not want to tell me how interested he was to see an Audi Quattro in France after he had seen it on *Turbo*, the French television motoring programme[4].

I was invited to park and then to walk into the gendarmerie, which contained a number of other blokes with guns. I accepted both invitations. I was instructed to produce my "papers" – passport, driving licence, insurance, registration document. There followed a tedious period of filling in of forms and then there was the standard tax demand, which was 900 francs in those pre-euro days, about £90 at the time.

I had gathered during this tiresome procedure that none of the officers spoke any English. The transaction completed, I was escorted to the door by one of them. I said, smiling, "Thank you. I hope that you and the next three generations of your family suffer from severe piles." The officer smiled, saluted and replied, "Merci, Monsieur! Et bonne route!"

A couple of years later, I was at the annual dinner of the Guild of Motoring Writers in the Royal Automobile Club in Pall Mall and the conversation turned to speeding fines, so I related this yarn to Derek Bell[5] who was at my table. He told me that he had been stopped at exactly the same place. While they were checking his papers, one of the gendarmes exclaimed, "Mais, alors, vous êtes le fameux Monsieur Bell qui cour au Mans avec le Monsieur Ickx, n'est-ce pas?"

Derek replied that, yes, he was, indeed, that Monsieur Bell. The gendarmes took lots of photos of themselves grinning in the company of the famous pilote Monsieur Bell and there was a long session of autograph signing. "And then," said Derek, outraged, "the captain smiled at me and said that I had to pay 900 francs." If he had driven a French car at Le Mans, they might have let him off with a caution.

[1] That was the Quattro's maximum speed on a flat road, but it was a little faster downhill with a following wind.

[2] Memorably lampooned some years ago by Richard Porter in his sniffpetrol website as 'Steve Crapley.' Mr Porter for some years earned substantial wads as a scriptwriter for *Top Gear* during the Jeremy Clarkson period. Then he resigned and said that he would never work with Clarkson again. Then he accepted a job writing scripts for *The Grand Tour*. No, they don't just make it up as they go along; all those feeble jokes are scripted in advance and all stunts carefully rehearsed, apart from the occasional biff on the nose. Porter was apparently not expecting to be headhunted by Haymarket Publishing (and if he was, he wasn't).

[3] When I discussed this with a former contributor to *CAR*, he shrugged and said that "all professional photographers have that kind of face," which got me thinking.

[4] This would have surprised me because the first edition of the programme was in 1987.

[5] Winner of the Le Mans 24 Hours on five occasions, usually but not always sharing with le Monsieur Ickx, who rarely makes it onto those lists of Famous Belgians, despite an illustrious racing career that included six Le Mans victories, eight Grand Prix wins, the CanAm Championship and the Dakar rally, from the time when it ended in Dakar.

15 To Turin by Quattro – part 2

NINE HUNDRED FRANCS LIGHTER, I got back in the Audi and negotiated the stop-start traffic jam through Lyon[1], then left the autoroute without regret, heading east towards Chambery, for the most enjoyable part of the journey.

The autoroute/autostrada between Chambery and Turin, including the Tunnel de Fréjus, had not yet been completed and the road through the mountains before the border with Italy offered an exceptional driving experience, though the succession of bends did expose the weakest point of the early Quattro, its brakes, which had a tendency to fade when given too much work.

After a few miles of fun, encountering virtually no other vehicles, I spotted something red and interesting-looking in the distance. I gradually reeled it in. It was a French-registered 365 GTB/4, known as the Daytona, one of Pininfarina's most beautiful creations, though not the easiest Ferrari to drive. This one would by then have been about ten years old. We travelled in convoy for a while, the Ferrari pulling away along the straights, while I could edge closer through the twisty sections, despite the naff brakes.

We passed a sign indicating the last petrol station before the border. The Audi had less than a gallon left and I knew that petrol was then a bit cheaper in France than in Italy. So when the Ferrari indicated to pull in, I followed and we stopped either side of the island. We got out and both laughed. I asked if he was heading for Turin for the show. He said he was. "Etes-vous journaliste?" asked the nosy-parker reporter. "Non," he replied, with an enigmatic smile. After a pause, he added, "Je m'appelle Peugeot."

I filled the Audi's tank first, paid and set off. Having passed the border, I found myself in some traffic. After a while, every time I pulled out to overtake, I could see in my door mirror the red Ferrari in the distance, doing likewise, gradually getting closer.

When we arrived at a long downhill straight, I dropped the Quattro's window to hear the Daytona's magnificent V12 growl as it went by, six twin-choke Weber carburettors delivering peak flow rate. Then there was some more traffic ahead and I was directly behind him. One needed to turn off this road, to the right and Monsieur Peugeot failed to do so, so I flashed my lights vigorously.

We both pulled over and I explained his error. I suggested that he should follow me to the start of the autostrada. From there, TORINO would be clearly signposted. We turned round and he followed me. After a few miles, we arrived at a long right-hand bend leading on to the E70 autostrada to Turin. I pushed the Quattro as hard as I could through the gently banked 180-degree curve, pulling out a couple of car lengths on the Ferrari, and kept my foot hard down on the straight, all the way up to maximum speed in fifth gear. By then, of course, the Daytona was so far ahead that I could barely see it as a speck on the horizon.

If Monsieur Peugeot has kept his Ferrari, it could now be converted into a useful pension fund, worth something like 50 times its original showroom price; and I'd bet my pension that he did not pay that much, if anything.

In those days, Italy was still not just the land of the free but the land of the non-combatant anarchist. You could smoke cigars in hotel bars and autostrada speed limits were considered advisory, if that. Many people thought all that would last forever, but of course, like nearly everything else, it did not. Cruising through the outskirts of Torino,

I was in a relaxed mood, which is an abnormal and always short interval in the human condition.

[1] A bypass, completed in the 1980s, has more or less maintained the status quo, but now one has to guess in advance whether the bypass or the direct route will be more fluid.

16 *Nobody* messed with The Electric Carrot

SHORTLY BEFORE LUNCHTIME, I left the Quattro in the safety[1] of the basement car park of the hotel near the centre of Turin and took my luggage, including a portable typewriter[2], to the reception desk. I checked in and mentioned that my colleagues, Messrs Curtis, Greenslade and Burn, had been delayed and would be arriving the next day, ie Tuesday, probably in the afternoon.

The chap behind the desk stared at me for a moment and said something casual and dismissive to the effect that what I was suggesting was not remotely possible. I told him that the rooms were booked in the names of Curtis, Greenslade and Burn and that this had been arranged through Fiat. He said, no, is not possible. He added that if my colleagues had not arrived "by 6 o'clock this evening," their bookings would be cancelled. I said that they would not. And so on.

We argued for a while and it nearly turned into a shouting match, but I could see that I might as well have been talking to the wall, so I took my key, picked up my luggage, went to my room and telephoned The Electric Carrot[3]. I related to him the circumstances and what the man at the desk had said.

"What?!" he exploded. "We'll soon see about that. Don't worry, I'll sort it out."

I changed into my formal outfit and went to the show, a 20-minute walk away. As expected, many of the stands were still being worked upon by an army of chippies and sparks, but I got a clear idea of the layout and had a few useful conversations with other early arrivals, journalists and press officers.

This was the first time that the show had been held inside Lingotto, the famous former factory with the rooftop test track; previously it had been put on in a hall a short distance to the north, in the Parco del Valentino[4] beside the River Po, but it had outgrown that.

The show had been hastily organized, and the interior had not yet been redecorated. The rough walls, patchy floors and improvised lighting equipment gave the whole event the look of a film set, which was rather charming. I thought they should have left it like that forever.

I had an invitation to dinner from a car manufacturer and that also gave me some ideas for the next day. When I arrived back at my hotel, the same man was at the desk. This time he smiled and said, "Good evening, Signor." I took my room key from him and asked about the rooms of my colleagues, Messrs Curtis, etc. He looked at me with the kind of astonishment that an innocent bystander[5] might consider to be sincere.

"Their rooms are waiting for their arrival, whenever they arrive. Where the problem, Signor?" I stared at him, eye to eye, for a few seconds, and then burst out laughing. Well, that's Italy, I thought. And *nobody* messed with The Electric Carrot.

I had a dreamlike Press Day. All the people I wanted to see were on their stands when I wanted to meet them. I covered all the stories that had previously been discussed and listed in the office, found several more and ended up with dozens of pages of notes.

I bumped into my friend Doug Nye[6] and his photographer Eeyore[7], and had a chat. Just in case the team failed to arrive, I took it upon myself to ask Eeyore, who occasionally worked for *Motor* as a freelance, if he could supply me with a roll of film of the vital stuff. He said that would be no problem, so we sat down for five minutes and I gave him a list, to which he and Doug added a couple of ideas.

During my tour of the show, I crossed the path of Monsieur Peugeot from the day before. He shook my hand, laughed and said, "That was fun!" I said, yes, it was, but thought of adding that if we had been stopped by the police, he, Monsieur Peugeot in a red Ferrari, would probably have been let off with a caution, if that, for exceeding 170mph, whereas I, an unknown Englishman in a German car travelling at 135mph …

I arrived back early to the hotel and went upstairs to hammer my notes onto sheets of A4, using my typewriter. By 10pm, I had it finished. I cannot recall a show report that was easier to write. I went downstairs for a snack and a drink or three.

I had just settled down in a relaxed and increasingly mellow mood when Schwartz, Greensalad and Scorch arrived. They all looked tired and stressed, but The Editor especially was hot and bothered, and started firing off a load of nervous questions. I raised my right hand like a Sioux in a 1950s Western saying 'How' and interrupted him.

"Tony," I said. "I have written the report." He stared at me, and his astonishment was sincere. I said, "Get yourself a drink. Relax. I'll be back in two minutes." I went to my room and returned with my evening's work. I did think of saying that, if he lost it, I would probably have to kill him. He had a quick flick through, and looked as if a big weight had been taken from his shoulders.

"What about photographs?" he asked. I took Geoff's roll of film from my pocket.

I never saw Tony C, a high-tension chap, as relaxed in all the time he was Editor of *Motor*. And I had redeemed myself from misdeeds of the past.

I cannot recall much about the Motor Show itself, except that Pininfarina exhibited a four-door concept car based on the Ferrari 400, which Enzo Ferrari wisely decided not to put into production.

The Germans made, and make, some very good cars and the Italians at that time made some excellent cars with lots of faults, but it's best to forget about most of the indigenous British mainstream motor industry post-1945[8]. However when good organization and planning was required for press events, the British were, I think it is fair to suggest, by far the best overall. But when things go pear-shaped, even the best can become sweaty in the brow.

[1] Press Days at the Turin Motor Show were notorious for car theft. Every day in Turin is notorious for car theft, but Motor Show Press Days provided a bumper harvest. Once, over 600 cars were stolen in a single day. Some Mercedes-Benz engineers arrived one year in a W123 saloon fitted with an experimental version of the five-link '*raum-lenken*' rear suspension that became standard on its successor, the W124, and other models. The car was not there the next morning, and was never, as far as I know, recovered.
[2] A 20th century writing instrument, not necessarily electrically powered. Mine was not. Younger readers will be gasping in astonishment.
[3] Richard Seth-Smith, for many years a PR man for Fiat.
[4] This park, between 1935 and 1955, contained a motor racing circuit. Major events were won there by such drivers as Tazio Nuvolari, Achille Varzi, Jean-Pierre Wimille and Alberto Ascari. Italy is full of fascinating history, some of it relatively modern.
[5] If such a person exists.
[6] Britain's leading motor racing historian. Prolific author and journalist and a funny man, despite being teetotal. A tiny but increasingly impatient segment of the world's population hopes that Volume 4 of his masterwork *BRM: The Saga of British Racing Motor* will one day be published.
[7] Geoffrey Goddard (1930-2006), one of the outstanding photographers of his era, specialising mainly in motor racing. Although to say that he had an Eeyore-style disposition would be a gross understatement, he was in fact very good company, with a marvellously pitiless sense of humour. He detested "the bloody frogs" so much, for reasons unclear (cherchez la femme?), that whenever he needed to urinate while travelling through France, he would stand on the sill of his car, avoiding direct contact with the hated foreign soil.
[8] And as for the French manufacturers …

17 The best laid plans[1]

THE PLAN WAS SIMPLE enough: hop on a flight to Lisbon, pick up a pre-booked rental car, stay in the same hotel as the Audi rally team in Figueira da Foz, and then, the next day, be driven by Hannu Mikkola in the new Quattro during its shake-down runs for its debut event, the Portugal Rally, a round of the World Rally Championship.

It was unusually convenient for me that the outward flight was on a Sunday at 1pm, from Gatwick, only 20 minutes' drive from where I lived in Sussex. On most occasions, for brief foreign escapades, I had to get to Thiefrow at about nine o'clock on a Monday morning, and, even then (in 1981), it was impossible to make an accurate estimate of the journey time.

There were four of us on the trip, three hacks and Tony Hill, who was at that time Press Relations Manager for VW Audi GB. Tony was renowned as one of the most efficient organizers in the business. But this trip probably gave him nightmares for years after.

Things started to go wrong from the start. There was a strike, of baggage handlers I think, as a consequence of which all flights were delayed, and, for hours, we had no idea when our aeroplane would take off. The terminal, normally quite quiet on a Sunday outside the holiday season, became steadily more overcrowded with frustrated would-be travellers.

Having all arrived in plenty of time before noon, we eventually took off more than eight hours later – and we were diverted to Faro, the southernmost point of Portugal. We were all travelling with only hand baggage, and we just managed to scramble onto the last connecting flight to the capital. By the time we arrived there, it was around midnight and the desk of the car hire company with the car that Tony had pre-arranged was closed. Only one car hire company remained open for business. Our luck seemed to be in.

Tony was visibly relieved. He handed his papers to the man at the desk, who filled in a form, using a typewriter[2]. He then casually produced his credit card for payment. The desk man went through the standard security procedure, which in those days involved making a telephone call. The payment was refused.

Tony Hill went back into nervous breakdown mode, or as close as he ever got to it. There was a period of arguing, but it was obviously impossible to solve the problem on the spot. It turned out that he was in dispute with the credit card company over some trivial sum, around £10. Even though thousands of pounds went through his account each month, they had temporarily blocked his card without prior warning, which was nice of them.

We three impoverished journalists had credit cards, but they were all at the edge of their limits, as usual, and would not cover the deposit for the 'excess.' So that was the end of our negotiations for a replacement hire car.

"Right," said Tony, trying not to look desperate. "Let's find a taxi." We went out into the warm night and there was a taxi rank, with a couple of cabs waiting. We were in luck, up to a point.

It was obvious almost immediately that there was something seriously wrong with the taxi's suspension: at least a worn-out damper, probably some suspension damage and/or a bent chassis. Within a short distance, this did not seem surprising in the least.

Our cab driver obviously felt that the gods had smiled upon him. He had expected merely the usual short ride into the centre of the city. Perhaps because of this, he was

50

even more annoyingly talkative than the average cabbie; also, he wanted to demonstrate how good his English was, in his opinion. This would have been only a minor irritation if he had not insisted on looking around to make eye contact with the person to whom he was speaking. Several times we nearly went off the road as he entered a bend while talking non-stop rubbish in his version of fluent English. Once I had to shout at him and we narrowly avoided a head-on collision.

After that incident, one of the others said firmly, "Please stop talking and concentrate on the road." Our pilot maintained a huffy silence after that and the rest of the journey was marginally less terrifying.

Finally, at around 3am, we arrived at our hotel in Figueira da Foz. We checked in and once again Tony looked relieved. But then he asked the man on the desk if the Audi rally people were there, as expected. "No," said the night man, after looking in the register, "they left yesterday morning." He had no idea where they had gone, but he said that the hotel manager, who would be in at 9am, might know.

I got up at 9.30, did my ablutions rapidly, and went looking for Tony Hill. He was in a bad state. The team had left no message and the hotel manager did not know where they were. Tony had been phoning Wolfsburg, Ingolstadt, Milton Keynes (base of VW/Audi GB), and so far he had come up with nothing.

He said that he was going to take a taxi to Lisbon to get a loan car from the VW dealer. "Maybe," he added, more in hope than expectation, "by the time I get back here someone will have located the team for us."

I had breakfast under a shade on the sunny terrace and wondered what to do. Then I realized that the answer was obvious. It was a hot, sunny day, the Atlantic Ocean was splashing gently onto the beach on the other side of the road ... and I had remembered to pack my trunks[3]. So I had a nice, refreshing swim, towelled off, put my shirt back on and strolled barefoot back towards the hotel. Then there was one of those miraculous strokes of luck that so rarely click in when they are most needed.

On the other side of the road, near the hotel, there was a chap about to get into a car. I immediately recognized him – it was Ari Vatanen[4], who was at that time a driver for the Ford works team. I ran over. We had met a couple of times before and he was naturally surprised to see me.

I explained why I was there and asked if he knew where the Audi people were. He said, "I think they are up in the hills ... a place called ..." – he churned his memory for a moment – "Bussaco."

Since my memory is sieve-like, I wrote that down as soon as I got back into the hotel and, with the help of the hotel manager, looked it up on a map. It was about 40 miles away. Tony Hill returned with the loan car that he had prised out of a reluctant dealer, still looking troubled. He asked if there had been any replies to his calls[5]. I said no, but gave him the good news and he brightened up and sprang into action.

Within half an hour he instructed the three of us to get ready to leave. We arrived at the Bussaco Palace Hotel, which is exactly what it says on the label, a former royal palace, a splendidly extravagant, late 19th century building in the gothic-romantic style[6].

---

[1] As the bard of Alloway noted, for rodents as well as *homo sapiens,* these "aft gang agley." In unfavourable conditions, as in the case considered in this chapter and the next two, this can result in what American military men colourfully describe as "a clusterfuck situation."

[2] See Chapter 16, Notes 2 and 7.

[3] I nearly always remembered to pack my trunks, but I think I had a swim only twice in 30 years of travelling about for work.

[4] In 1981 he won the World Rally Championship driving for Ford. He also won the Pike's Peak hillclimb in a Peugeot and the Paris-Dakar Rally four times, again driving for the French company.

[5] It should be remembered that this was before the era of mobiles, otherwise he might have been on the phone to Britain and Germany all the way to Lisbon and back, to no avail, though one call to someone in the rally team would probably have solved the problem earlier.

[6] The Battle of Bussaco (1810), in which an Anglo-Portuguese force of 50,000 men under the command of Viscount Wellington (later the Duke of) defeated a larger French army, was fought nearby.

18 Up the hill with Hannu

THERE WERE NINE OF us around the table and we started a delicious four-course dinner with a fine bottle of Bussaco red from 1921. Since Hannu Mikkola[1] was scheduled to drive later in the evening, he was drinking only water and not eating much, the poor chap, so there was just enough in the bottle for a glass each for the rest of us.

We then drank a Bussaco red from 1931. We enjoyed that, too, so we moved on to 1941, and then 1951, both equally excellent. Pleasantly mellowed, we were just savouring the 1961 vintage, also very nice, when we were informed that we had to be in the bus outside within ten minutes. So we never had the opportunity to try the 1971 red[2].

We boarded the bus on a moonless night and were transported to a clearing in the forest of Bussaco a couple of miles away, possibly standing above the bones of unfortunate Frenchmen, Englishmen and Portuguese. Here, under powerful day-for-night arc lights, mechanics were getting the Quattro ready with the usual calm-but-rapid efficiency of the professional men in motor sport.

"Who wants to go first?" asked Tony, and I was quickest on the draw. I reasoned that – especially with the way the trip had gone up to that point – the car might fail terminally on the first run and then I would have a limp story to tell about how I had *nearly* sat in the passenger seat of the works Audi Quattro during its shakedown for the Portugal Rally.

I clambered through the rollcage into the bucket seat, buckled myself in tightly and then pulled the shoulder straps even tighter, because that is what you have to do to remain anything close to comfortable when some Scandiwegian nutcase is in the other seat doing almost unimaginable things with the steering wheel and pedals, not to mention changing up a gear when most people would change down.

Hannu was already strapped in. While mechanics did some final checks, he casually remarked that he was still learning about how to drive the car[2]. He put on his helmet and then his gloves, and we set off gently to the start of a steep, uphill dirt road.

Then he floored the throttle in first gear and the Quattro leaped forward with impressive violence. The next four or five minutes flashed by, the four-wheel-drive car adopting less extreme angles in the bends than was usual in more conventional rally cars[3], but generating unprecedented lateral *g* force, even on the unmade surface.

The headlights on rally cars also give that day-for-night effect, but I was puzzled at first by flashes of light through my door window, as if we were being followed by another car, which seemed improbable to say the least. Then I realized that it was flames shooting from the open exhaust on the overrun. I also noticed as we ascended the steep track that there was an increasingly scary drop off the hill, on my side.

We arrived at the top of the hill and Hannu braked hard and slowed to walking pace at the edge of what seemed to be a deserted village.

"Where does the road go from here?" I asked.

"I have no idea," replied Hannu, grinning. "I have never been here before."

Mikkola failed to finish the 1981 Portugal Rally, though Michèle Mouton in the other Quattro took fourth place.

The Quattro ran perfectly throughout that evening of testing and the two other journalists had exciting runs up the hillside. So, all's well that ends well. Er, not quite …

The four of us took our leave of Hannu, the engineers and mechanics, and were transferred back to the splendour of the Bussaco Palace. If everything had gone to plan, we would already have been back in Blighty.

First thing next morning, Tuesday, Tony Hill was back in mild panic mode. We could not make it in time for that morning's flight from Lisbon to London. We could, perhaps, just make it to Oporto in the north for a flight at around noon. However, this introduced a new problem.

The Volkswagen dealer in Lisbon had been reluctant to loan a car to Tony and he wanted it back. There was no time to take it back and make the flight to Oporto. Tony took an executive decision. "Let's go!" he said.

We chucked our luggage in the boot. I was assigned the task of driving to Oporto Airport, some 90 miles away. These days, you could do the journey in well under two hours without even exceeding the speed limit. However, in the early 1980s, Portugal's motorway network was in the early stages of development, and the first half of the route was on a busy A-road.

I drove as hard as was reasonable, but there was a lot of traffic, including chugging lorries. When we got onto the motorway, we were seriously behind schedule. I drove flat out. I noticed that the fuel gauge was getting towards the danger zone. And then the orange warning light came on.

I felt that I should open up a debate about this when I saw a sign announcing that there was a fuel station 10km up the road. I asked our map reader how far we were from the destination. Tony Hill said, "I think we should stop." I said that, if we stopped, we would definitely miss our flight, but, if we continued, we stood a small chance of making it.

By a majority of three to one, we continued, flat out. We made it to the airport and I stopped right outside the terminal entrance. Tony Hill leapt out and ran in, while I found a parking space. Then we three hacks grabbed all the luggage and followed him as fast as we could.

The Law of Sod states that when you actually want a flight to be delayed by a strike or technical problem, or anything, it isn't, and that was the case in this instance.

Tony was engaged in a sharp discussion with a woman behind the desk who was telling him that it was far too late, because the BA 'plane was already taxiing towards the runway.

Then a man came out from an office at the back. "How many of you are there?" he asked. Tony said four, and the man got on the phone and spoke to Flight Control. We were rushed through Customs, onto a bus and right up to the BA Boeing 737. We had to wait for the boarding steps lorry, and then we felt obliged to apologize to the passengers we had delayed.

This was not as difficult as Tony Hill's task of apologizing to the Lisbon VW dealer for the fact that his car was 200 miles away, with a thimbleful of petrol in its tank, if that ... and the keys would be in the post.

Smaller car makers do not have in-house press officers, and when one undertakes any kind of exercise with them, things rarely follow the original plan, if there was one.

[1] Finnish World Rally Champion (1983, with Audi).
[2] At the time, all these wines, even including the earliest from 1921, were surprisingly inexpensive. Portugal produces some very fine wines, but this is no longer a big secret and some of them are no longer surprisingly inexpensive. I checked the cost of a bottle of Bussaco 1981 while writing this book and ... erk! If we had put wine at that price on VW/Audi's tab, Tony Hill's nightmares might have been far worse.
[3] An interesting point about the development of the Quattro is that before being hired by Audi, Mikkola had never rallied a front-wheel drive car, while Stig Blomqvist[4] had never rallied a rear-wheel drive car.

Stig (the one and only Stig; accept no substitutes) had the advantage because of this – the Quattro was like a powerful front-wheel-drive car without traction problems – and Hannu learned a lot about left-foot braking from him.

[4] Swedish World Rally Champion (1984, with Audi), one of the top five rally drivers of all time.

19 My ego is bigger than yours

IN 1969 A CALIFORNIAN 'performance artist' named Steve Paige produced a customized car called the Dickmobile, parodying the sexual nature of sports cars. Finished in a flesh tone[1], it had a long cylindrical bonnet and a bulbous radiator cowling. There was no mistaking what it represented, which explains why he was arrested when he took to the public highway in it.

The Rinspeed Mono Ego, which made its debut at the 1997 Geneva Motor Show, was more subtle, but not much. It was created by Swiss motoring performance artist Frank M Rinderknecht (Rin of Rinspeed), who had already been adding much-needed eccentricity to the annual salon for two decades[2].

Mono Ego went beyond egotism into solipsism[3]. It was a single-seater, described in the blurb as 'a fully-fledged sports car,' with enough feathers in its upholstery patterns to support this assertion. At a glance it seemed to have no mudguards, but its carbon-fibre cycle wings were imprinted with photographic images of the tyres.

According to Rinderknecht, the Mono Ego complied with EU regulations. The rubber-stamping inspector somehow missed the pedestrian-grater grille and the suicidal-looking steering wheel (though that was attached to the front wheels via a collapsible column).

Among Rinderknecht's greatest talents was extracting cash from partners to share in his bizarre projects. In the case of Mono Ego, the engine and gearbox were Korean, the suspension developed by Germans, the aluminium bodywork made in California, and the paintwork and interior styling created by the definitively pretentious French fashion designer, Jean-Charles de Castelbajac. This celebrated coxcomb had links with the Pommery champagne producers, which is why I went to Reims to drive Mono Ego. Things did not go exactly to plan.

As an exercise in packaging, Mono Ego lowered the bar: at 182in, it was 4in longer than a Renault Espace, yet provided room for only one ego. One's company, two's a crowd, and an extra four inches can make a crucial difference, especially when you are parking.

Rinderknecht boldly described the piece of carpet in the minimal luggage space in the tail section as 'the finest of all carpets,' an assertion that was never debated among our allegedly learned friends. On the floor beside the seat there was room for a squashy bag or even a specially-designed golf bag[4].

When one takes one's McLaren F1[5] out for an evening of sophisticated debauchery with two gorgeous pouting starlets, one should shower, shave and look one's best; and also make them sign an insurance waiver. It's all a bit of an effort, frankly. With the Mono Ego, there was no need to dress up … and perhaps you might engage with a better class of person.

It was advisable to wear goggles, however, or you could go blind: although the seat and pedals were offset (which would please Mr Bangle), the strange, forward-angled wind deflector was centrally-mounted and useless for anyone over 5ft 6in tall. Weather protection consisted of plastic sheathing over the seat.

Always a self-starter, I looked forward to a hands-on experience. I climbed into Mono Ego's cockpit (I use the term advisedly), which involved stepping in beside the seat[6], sliding one leg under the wheel, dropping into the seat, followed by a legover-gear-lever manoeuvre.

Buttons for adjusting the seat electrically did not work (fortunately there was a lever allowing fore/aft movement), nor did the adjuster for the external mirrors, or the radio/cassette player[7]. The screen of the sat-nav system remained blank. There was a socket for a telephone; I bet that was out of commission, too, just like the ignition security code system. But this was a show car, finished hastily to look right for Geneva, but not wired up. Most concept cars are not fully functional when the covers are pulled off in those tedious unveiling ceremonies; many of them never receive the finishing touches.

I grasped the gear lever, eight inches of firm steel, and thrust it vigorously into an available slot. So we – Mono Ego and me, not to mention my id – headed off into the sunset. Well, we didn't actually. It was the wrong time of day and raining a fine drizzle.

More to the point, although a PR man[8] had promised that the car would be registered and insured, it was not. Anyway, although I did not exceed 50mph while blasting up and down Pommery's driveway and never got above second gear, the chassis felt undeveloped, though its technical specification gave it the potential to handle well. The claimed 410bhp of its prototype Hyundai V8 seemed to me an exaggeration, by at least 25 per cent.

For some reason, Mono Ego, like all of Rinderknecht's Geneva concepts, never made it to series production. But did he care?

---

[1] A pinky flesh tone. One may speculate whether the offence would have been regarded as more or less serious if darker paint had been used.
[2] One of his less outlandish creations had been a VW Golf with gullwing doors. In later years, it got weirder than that. Mono Ego was a step on the way. See next chapter.
[3] The theory that self-existence is the only certainty. Personally, I'm not sure about even that.
[4] Golf, as I have previously mentioned, is a game in which you play with yourself.
[5] A dangerous big boy's toy with a central driver's seat and two totty seats behind.
[6] An exercise that would probably become difficult with the custom-built golf bag in situ.
[7] Remember, this was back in the 20th century.
[8] Not all of them are compulsive liars, but this one was.

20 Answering questions nobody asked

IN 1998 RINSPEED'S E-GO Rocket built on the Mono Ego concept. A single-seater with nearly identical running gear, it looked vaguely like a German racing car from the 1930s. It was considerably more sophisticated than its predecessor; for one thing, it did not have the capacity to carry golf clubs.

Frank M Rinderknecht's contributions to the Geneva show have often been amusing and clever. At the very least, he invariably filled the 'And also ...' slot.

The Presto (2002) was a 12ft long, four-seater cabriolet that, to facilitate parking, could be compressed electro-hydraulically into a nine-foot two-seater. It was advisable for insurance and other considerations to let rear-seat passengers out first. A minor inconvenience in inclement weather was the absence of a roof.

The Chopster (2004) was a Porsche Cayenne with two doors removed and the roof lowered, fitted with even bigger wheels and tyres than standard and the engine tuned for even more power and torque. It was finished in Candy Apple Tangerine.

The Senso (2005) was a 'futuristic' concept; here we go into that 'avant-garde' argument again. It was designed to analyse its driver's mood and behaviour via a pulse-rate monitor and a 'mobile eye' camera. The driver was then influenced by visual, acoustic and aromatic signals to behave with 'relaxed attentiveness'[1].

The Lotus Elise-based Squba (2008) was an electric submarine sportscar. The X-dream of 1999 seemed to be more of a nightmare. The Dock+Go (2011) was an electric Smart modified so that plug-in modules at the rear could convert it into a six-wheeler pickup or hatchback.

The work that went into this stuff was often impressive, in the same way as the sewing on some absurd *haute couture* offerings: you can see that amazingly skilled craftspersons have been at work. Rinderknecht is an artist. Some might say a bullshit artist for the way he talked about production plans he had for his concepts. There *never* was a production run. There did not have to be. Frank MR cleverly set himself up as a sophisticated publicity agent for his various partners, involved in all aspects of vehicle production. *That's* what it was all about.

Of all his creations, the one I would most like to have on my fleet is the exAsis (2007), a tandem two-seater with styling influenced (again) by the 1930s Auto Union grand prix cars. I could do without the transparent plastic bodywork and the bioethanol fuel, but this little two-seater with kerb weight of 750kg[2] and 150bhp[2] from its 750cc turbocharged engine would surely be fun to drive.

Rinspeed's most amusing concept was undoubtedly the Splash (2004), which shared with eXasis that tiny two-cylinder Weber engine and two seats (though in parallel rather than tandem) but was otherwise entirely different. Is the Splash a car? Yes: it has four wheels and could be licensed for road use. Is it a boat? Yes, again: it floats and can move about on water under its own power. Is it a plane? Ah, here we are into a grey area of definition.

The Splash is an aeroplane in the sense that it can take off from and land on water. However, like the Spruce Goose, it does not fly very high, and you could not fly from Leeds to Wigan with it, except via the canal, and it would be far quicker to use Splash in car mode, or even to go by bus. Splash answers all the transportation questions you have ever asked, except "Why?"

Having sown confusion, let me explain. Imagine you are driving Splash. Via a suitable ramp, you approach your chosen stretch of water and drive in. You put on your sou'wester and skipper's cap and are now liable to be arrested by a different set of government officials than when you were on dry land only a few moments previously. And then you can transfer to hydrofoil mode[3].

Frank actually drove across the English Channel in Splash, which nearly turned into disaster in choppy conditions. He unsportingly declined my suggestion that he should try crossing the Atlantic.

Rinderknecht's connection with the Geneva show began roughly when I first reported from there, in the late 1970s. His first show car, in 1979, was a turbocharged petrol version of the VW Golf with a modified grille and rectangular headlights. He was just another tuner/modifier, but, only two years later, he began answering questions that nobody had asked, with the Aliporta gullwing Golf.

One or two of Rinspeed's other creations might have been suitable, or at least tolerable, for my annual trek to the Geneva Motor Show.

[1] There is surely room for further development of this technology. Try entering a one-way street from the wrong direction and you could be given electric shocks of increasing magnitude to the nether regions. If your personal hygiene were not up to the required standard, Senso could take you directly to an automatic cleaning centre, locking your seat belt until you'd been given a thorough wash and brush-up. If you were in roadrageous mode, a gloved fist could come out of the steering wheel and punch you repeatedly on the nose while an East End voice from the fascia asked, "Do you like hospital food, pal?" If you were sexually aroused ... no, let's not go there. If you died suddenly, Senso could pull into the nearest layby and incinerate itself, while playing Verdi's *Requiem* at full volume.

[2] Allegedly.

[3] A custom-designed transfer case permitted power delivery to the rear wheels, the propeller, or both. At a minimum water depth of about 51in, you, the driver/captain/pilot, could deploy Splash's hydrofoils; the rear spoiler ('Formula 1-style') rotated 180 degrees and came to rest below the Splash. To the left and right of the high sidewalls of the cockpit, two hydrofoils integrated into the outside skin rotated 90 degrees to point straight down before unfolding into their lifting V shape. The angle of attack of each hydrofoil could be adjusted individually by the driver/captain/pilot to suit various operating states. Already at low speeds, the vehicle began to lift itself out of the water. The fully suspended position could be reached at under 20mph.

Splash, with its wheels above the waves, then travelled as a hydrofoil, at an altitude of about 2ft above the water. Yes, you were technically flying, but more in the sense of forward motion than of lift. I have written this note in the past tense, correctly I think.

21 The decline of the Routes Nationales

ONE OF THE PLEASURES of driving through rural France used to be that one could find excellent yet inexpensive restaurants and cheap and cheerful hotels just about anywhere on the routes nationales. This was still generally the case until the late 1990s.

I used to enjoy the annual trip to Geneva, first from England, driving through the Jura and then, after I moved to France, from the Var, using parts of the Route Napoléon. In the latter case, I observed the drastic decline brought about by the expansion of the autoroute network.

In those days, when it was more possible to consider speed limits as advisory, the journey could be done in a little over five hours, plus a stop for lunch. I set off from my shack in the Var for Geneva just before 11am on the first Monday of March 2006, in my Ford Focus. It was one of those magical late winter days, cold but with a bright blue sky, and I experienced one of those journeys that one gets rarely: traffic was light and each time I came upon slower vehicles, it was at a point where I could overtake immediately without having to slow down.

I had timed my departure so that I would arrive at lunchtime at a roadside restaurant just north of Serres on the RN75[1]. A couple of years earlier, I had consumed a delicious osso bucco there. The place had been packed. I was a bit taken aback when I arrived this time at half past 12: no lorries or vans with the logos of EDF (Electricité de France) or France Télécom were outside, in fact no lorries at all, and there was only one car, which turned out to belong to the new proprietor. This was an unmistakably bad omen, but I knew that there were no places to eat after that for a considerable distance, and I was hungry.

I parked, went in and should have left immediately, remaining hungry. It just did not feel right. I had an exceptionally disgusting meal. The restaurant no longer had a proper chef, and it had ceased to be a *routier* stop.

Oh well, I thought, I shall have a decent dinner this evening in the Auberge in Allonziers (see Chapter 12).

However, I was alarmed to discover that this was under new ownership, which had not been communicated when I made my booking. They no longer served evening meals. After the show the next day, I had dinner in Geneva. The next morning, I went into the breakfast room of the Auberge, where I was told that the coffee machine was not working. I declined the offer of tea, paid my bill, got in the car and had breakfast in the routier restaurant a few hundred yards away on the other side of the road.

Just as the railways brought prosperity to remote places, the autoroutes have taken it away. This is what led to the sad dwindling of places to eat and of hotels to stay in on the N85 and N75, as they were once labelled, just as has happened elsewhere in France. With an almost complete end to passing trade outside the summer holiday season (and even during those few months it has dwindled), it all came to an end.

Allonziers is among the places strangled by the decline. I was not surprised to discover that the Auberge had closed for business shortly after my last visit. The routier restaurant that was nearby exists no more. The building has been flattened. The fuel station next door to it is still there, but business must be far slower now than in the old days.

Thanks to Google, I see that in 2017 the restaurant north of Serres is still in business. Perhaps it has changed hands again. And perhaps there is someone in the kitchen who can cook, but I doubt that delicious osso bucco is back on the menu. One or two other restaurants that I used to frequent have survived. One day, I may do a driving trip to see what, if anything, is left of the enjoyment of driving to Geneva from the Var, but, if I do, so I shall probably take a packed lunch. I learned a great deal during my time on *Motor* magazine, sometimes from committing crass errors, about the virtues of careful planning.

[1] As it was then. Soon after, like many Routes Nationales, it was downgraded to a series of Routes Départementales, in a cynical move by central government to transfer costs to the regions.

22 A splendid anniversary

THERE WAS A SPECIAL issue of *Motor* for the week ending 18 March 1978, to celebrate the magazine's 75th anniversary. The cover was a fine composition, with two cars that spanned the magazine's existence. In the foreground was a 1903 de Dietrich, in which Editor Roger Bell and his secretary Carol, soon to become Mrs Rex M Greenslade, were sitting, wearing Edwardian outfits[1]. Behind it was a brand-new Panther 6, the huge six-wheeled absurdity from Byfleet[2].

At the top of this front page was a stylishly superimposed pairing of logos, the early version, *The Motor*, in Art Nouveau serif typeface, with curlicue descending from the left leg of the 'M,' and the more modern red version, sans serif and sans definite article. I always preferred the *The*, though it was long before my time.

Free with that issue was a special 104-page supplement featuring 20 significant cars of those seven and a half decades and also the intermediate logo, with a long, straight left leg to the 'M'. This supplement certainly paid for itself, since 63 of the pages were advertisements, many of which were interesting. Urged on by Murray Harris[3], *Motor's* convivial 'Advertisement Controller,' the majority of the advertisers had got into the spirit of things by producing specially-created copy and artwork.

The editorial content was remarkable. One of the main components was a series of brief tests of 20 of the most significant cars of the magazine's 75 years of existence. After prolonged argument, we rounded up many of the usual suspects for our Top 20: a 1909 Rolls-Royce[4], a Model T Ford, a 1938 Citroën Light 15, a 1949 Morris Minor, a 1953 VW Beetle, a 1955 Citroën 2CV, a 1959 Mini, a 1966 Citroën DS, a 1977 Jaguar XJ12, and so on. There were others that might not now be included in such a selection, such as an NSU Ro80, which now looks like a technically interesting journey into an engineering cul-de-sac.

Among surprising omissions I would list: vintage Bentley, Bugatti, MG, Riley, Jaguar E-type, and Porsche 911; perhaps it was considered that the last two were covered by the XK and … the Beetle. This and more was admitted in a footnote to the Top 20, in which was this amusing remark: "We even considered the Edsel, as the biggest flop ever!"

At least, for the Bentley, there was a reproduction, among several Brockbank cartoons, of "CITRON PRESSÉ" in which a 'Blower' Bentley hustles a Light 15, and also an illustration by Bryan de Grineau of the Blower at Le Mans. There were plenty of mentions and photographs of Bugatti in various articles.

Also given away with this issue was a very fine poster that was stapled into the centre. And really, it was necessary to buy two copies of the magazine, because, on one side, this had illustrations of our Top 20 by Jim Dugdale and, on the other, illustrations of a selection of 24 of the greatest racing cars up to 1968. These were by the highly talented Tony Simmonds.

The creation of that poster was remarkable. As the artist explained in 2017: "You might find it hard to believe, but I painted every car on that poster in those exact positions on a large single sheet of watercolour paper, which must have been getting on to A1 size. I wouldn't even entertain doing it that way now!

"I think the timeline [from commission to delivery] was about two weeks, but it was so much harder to find the reference for those specific cars then – no Google, for example

– but I was an enthusiast and had loads of books and magazines on those kind of racing cars." Dugdale probably created his illustration by the same method.

Other artists whose work was featured in the supplement included George Lane and Bryan de Grineau. Besides Brockbank, cartoonists included Honeysett, a regular contributor at that time, and Vane, with a splendid caricature of the long-serving eccentric Sports Editor Rodney Walkerley, who used the pseudonym 'Grande Vitesse,' though he was a legendarily slow driver.

There were superb cutaways by Lawrie Watts, Theo Page, Leslie Cresswell, 'Aubois' (Dave Attwood), HJ Way, SE Porter and Brian Hatton (who was still on the staff during my time at *Motor*). Alas, this is an art form that has all but expired: it is done, if at all, on computer these days, and has lost its artistic element as far as most of us are concerned.

In addition there were numerous excellent photographs from three-quarters of a century, including several classic motor racing shots taken from glass plates in the 1930s.

A great deal of planning and hard work went into putting together the supplement, under the direction of outgoing Editor Roger Bell, who had left the magazine after nine years on the staff, the final five at the helm (which was usually more than enough for anyone), shortly before the issue went on sale.

Remarkably, almost all the photography other than the cover shot was done on one bitterly cold day in December 1977. The National Motor Museum assisted us greatly, not only by allowing us to drive some of its splendid exhibits, but also by giving us a base where we could keep warm in-between drives, and have a buffet lunch. The entire editorial team arrived at Beaulieu while the sparrows were still doing their early-morning exhalations. Our two staff photographers, Uncle Maurice and Scorch, were supplemented by a freelancer, such was the workload. During the day, as well as the museum's cars, we drove and photographed several interesting privately-owned cars which had been driven to the venue by generous and trusting owners. I drove three cars that day.

[1] In the original plan it was to be Technical Editor Rex himself with Carol in the de Dietrich, but he was taken ill and Roger had to stand in for him.

[2] The bodywork was designed in his spare time by Geoff Lawson, while working for Vauxhall, with assistance from his colleague, Wayne Cherry. Lawson later became Jaguar's Director of Styling and was one of the finest designers of his era. He died suddenly in 1999, aged just 54.

[3] Nephew of Air Marshal Sir Arthur 'Bomber' Harris.

[4] From the purist's point of view, as Roger Bell pointed out in the text, this car is not quite a Silver Ghost. However, as Daisy Ashford might say, you'd hardly notice.

23 A cold day in the New Forest

TWO OF THE CARS that I drove on that sunny but bitterly cold December day in 1977 have stayed firmly fixed in my memory[1]. The first of these was the museum's 1913 Vauxhall C-type, the model known as the 'Prince Henry.'

Two Vauxhall C-type prototypes had competed in 1910 in a gruelling 1200-mile motor sport event (in some senses the precursor of the German Grand Prix). They did not win the *Prince-Heinrich-Fahrt*[2] but performed impressively and thus what is widely regarded as the forerunner of the vintage sports car acquired the Anglicized name of a German prince who seems to have been a far more likeable character than his elder brother, Kaiser Wilhelm, not that that was difficult.

The C-type Prince Henry had a particular connection with *Motor* magazine. Its creator had been the celebrated Laurence Pomeroy (1883-1941), Vauxhall's chief engineer, whose son Laurence Pomeroy Junior was Technical Editor of *The Motor* (with the *The*) from 1937 until 1959. One of his distinguished successors as Technical Editor (and later Editor) of the magazine, Charles Bulmer, drily recalled Pomeroy Jr as follows: "... probably *The Motor*'s most famous and certainly most flamboyant Technical Editor although, in my opinion, not technically the best because his knowledge outside the engine field was limited."

'Pom' as Laurence Junior was known, acquired a 1914 Prince Henry in 1931 or 1946 (accounts vary, but the latter seems more likely), and owned it until his death in 1966. At a Bonhams auction in 2016, this car changed hands for £516,700 (including 'premium').

I climbed aboard the high and mighty four-seater tourer and slid across behind the wheel; the driver enters from the passenger side to avoid having to clamber past the gear lever and handbrake which are located outside the car, in the airstream. Because of this arrangement, I was silently swearing at myself for having forgotten to bring my gloves, which was a foolish error on that day.

Four-wheel brakes were not common on motor cars until some time after the First World War; it took a great amount of engineering work to find a way to obtain a satisfactory balance between front and rear. There is a pedal in the Prince Henry that operates a transmission brake, but I was given strict instructions not to use it except in the direst of emergencies, because it had a tendency to burn its linings if applied frequently. The external handbrake operates the tiny, and rather hopeless, rear drums. I was advised to restrict my deceleration to this, and to engine braking ... and to look far, far ahead. Fortunately, the gradients in the New Forest are rarely severe.

I was expecting sluggish performance, an unpleasant gearchange, agricultural handling and, of course, a severe lack of braking power. I was absolutely spot on concerning the last of these, but otherwise the car was a revelation.

The old Vauxhall weighed less than I had expected, about the same as a 1978 VX4/90, a large four-door saloon[3]. As far as performance was concerned, the Prince Henry was understandably slow by the standards of 60 years after its production. Nevertheless, the four-litre four-cylinder engine was more lively than I had anticipated and, once one had coaxed the big machine above 50mph, it could retain that quite easily, and the car continued to feel reassuringly stable, though it was necessary to maintain a beady eye on the road ahead in case it was necessary to shed speed, which, as explained, required forward planning. You certainly get a good view from the wheel of a Prince Henry, sitting at the roof level of most cars. And you do see some funny things in the forest ...

At one point, tanking along at 60mph (probably 15mph below the car's maximum), I was surprised to observe a cock pheasant flying across the road from right to left at about windscreen height. The oddest thing was that it was flying upside down. It took me a second or so to realize that it was being carried by a bird of prey which was evidently very close to the limits of its operational capability. I did not attempt any braking, but, happily, collision was narrowly avoided by lifting the right foot.

Although the steering was heavy at walking pace, once on the move it lightened up and above all it delivered the most marvellous 'feel,' which is the magical ingredient that the steering of all cars should deliver, though few ever have. Grip from the skinny beaded-edge tyres was better than expected, but 'tenacious' would not be the adjective of choice. The car was a joy to drive.

The nicest surprise was the gearchange. The prescribed technique in these old Vauxhalls is to get into fourth gear as early as possible, and then let the engine's substantial torque do the work for you, rather than revving hard in the lower gears as in a modern car. I had worried unnecessarily that it would be obstructive. It was not fast, but it was precise and easy to time smooth engagement, thanks in large part to the excellent clutch activation. In fact, shifting through the gears was a perfect exemplar of that elderly cliché of motoring hackery, 'rifle-bolt action.'

Apart from my frozen right hand, this had been one of the most enjoyable drives I have ever had, and the Prince Henry made me keen to have a go in its famous successor, the OE-type 30/98, which first appeared in 1922. My grandfather had owned one in the early 1920s. I had the opportunity a couple of years later to drive the Vauxhall Heritage Collection's 1926 example. It looked gorgeous, but I was disappointed in three respects: the brakes were still somewhere between feeble and non-existent, the steering required more effort and was less responsive than the Prince Henry's, while the gearchange was not nearly as nice; I think it may have been due for an overhaul.

The Prince Henry was the first car I had driven that had been designed before the First World War. My next assignment could hardly have been more different. This was my first Lamborghini, a Miura, among the privately-owned cars.

With its body designed by Marcello Gandini when he was working for Bertone, the Miura was undoubtedly one of the most beautiful cars of all time. It was also one of the least practical. The chassis and the complex drivetrain, with the V12 engine mounted transversely behind the cockpit, had been devised by three Lamborghini engineers in their spare time, without Ferruccio Lamborghini's knowledge.

It was then hastily turned into a show car and the coachwork was commissioned for that, but there was no intention to put it into production. However, it caused such a sensation, with wealthy enthusiasts placing deposits for it, that the Sant'Agata company felt obliged to go ahead, despite some engineering innovations that were not really suitable for production, such as the engine and gearbox sharing the same oil[4].

It also had a severely cramped cockpit, which is not surprising in such a compact package: the Miura is about 5in shorter and 7in narrower than Ferrari's F360, for example. For anyone over six-foot tall, getting in and out requires a degree of athleticism. The same is true of the later Countach, with the important difference that in the latter one does not feel too uncomfortable once one has inserted one's person behind the steering wheel. With some difficulty, I clambered in, and the proprietor, a pleasant chap in his 50s, sat beside me.

We set off across the forest roads, and I took great care not to push the car too hard. I kept the revs well below the limit, did not brake too hard or too late, and concentrated simply on getting a feel for what it was all about. I was driving a fairly quick car at about six-tenths of its capabilities, but suddenly I realized that the car's owner seemed to be on the edge of a 'petit mal.'

He was gritting his teeth, his arms had gone rigid, and his fingers were grasping the seat. And he had that rabbit-in-the-headlights look, just like the Removatop girl at Donington (see Chapter 39). I eased off further and we headed back to base. It turned out that the poor man had never been above 100mph before and it did not seem to agree with him. I expect he sold the car soon after that.

One other marque that, surprisingly, did not make the cut into the Top 20 was Lotus. I would have chosen a Seven rather than an Elan or the later stuff, because it encapsulated Colin Chapman's obsession with lightness.

[1] The third was a 1928 'Bullnose' Morris Cowley, which was disappointingly unmemorable. I also reported on a 1904 Lanchester owned by Alan Warner of holiday camps fame, but, on the day appointed, to drive it the weather was foul. The roads had been salted, and, alas, I never had a chance to drive the car.
[2] The winner was an engineer of Czech origin named Ferdinand Porsche, driving a far-more-powerful Austro-Daimler.
[3] Few people under the age of 50 will have heard of the VX 4/90 – and they will not have missed anything of importance. It was not among the cars in our special supplement.
[4] I know, I know, there is the Issigonís Mini and most motorcycles, but it has never seemed to me a good idea, especially with a 12-cylinder engine.

24 Where Russian poets go to die

WHEN I WAS A magazine editor, travelling to cover foreign Motor Shows with a small team (a photographer and another reporter), I picked hotels carefully. There were two main criteria: the establishment had to be convenient for getting to the show, and it had to be as cheap as possible, on the principle that we would save our money for essentials such as good food and wine.

In those days one could still find some very cheap and shoddy hotels in big cities if one knew where to look, and I became skilled at seeking them out. It took a while for those who worked with me to understand the logic of this policy, but they soon appreciated the two benefits: we ate very well and IPC's managers never questioned our expenses.

The dump in the 13th arrondissement of Paris that I favoured in the 1980s, when attending the biennial Salon de l'Automobile, was a case in point. It was memorably described by my colleague Andrew English[1] as "the sort of place where Russian poets would go to die." Several years later, I discovered that it had been the hotel of choice of the wandering (non-Russian) minor poet Jean Genet. I may even have passed him on the stairs of the Hotel Rubens at some time. My pocket was not picked, but Genet's thieving days were probably long past by then. He had become internationally famous and was not short of cash, but he never bought a house or even rented an apartment, preferring to stay in cheap hotels.

If the Hotel Rubens, in the street where they used to make splendid Delahayes[2], had not been fully booked on the evening of 15 April 1986, Genet, then aged 75, would perhaps have died there, rather than a few hundred yards away on the other side of the Boulevard de l'Hôpital, in another of my regular haunts. The old dear was in a bad way by then, with throat cancer, but he shuffled off after tripping and cracking his head on the way to the lav.

Oddly, Jack's Hotel in the rue Stéphen-Pichon has no plaque on its outside wall to commemorate this historic event. An English rendition of this might read "Jean Genet, minor poet, absurdist playwright, vagabond, petty thief, homosexual prostitute, ex-con, motor racing sponsor[3], total fruitcake, etc, checked out here (without checking out)." I was not even able to discover in which room he had snuffed it. An impressive response to my question would have been, "Ah, Monsieur, vous voulez la Suite Genet? C'est un petit peu plus chère …," but they simply did not know. The French are sometimes surprisingly poor at marketing. It is, of course, a nation of fonctionnaires.

Whenever I was not picking up the tab, on the other hand, I generally stayed in four-star establishments that would have resulted in difficult conversations with IPC's managers if I had put the bills on expenses.

[1] Later the Motoring Correspondent of *The Daily Telegraph*.
[2] Not many people born after World War II are aware that France once had a proud reputation for creating high-quality cars – Amilcar[4], Bugatti, Delage, Delahaye, Talbot-Lago, among others.
[3] As backer of the driver Jacques Maglia. Known outside motor racing circles as 'Jacky,' Maglia was the stepson of Lucien Senemand, one of Genet's numerous homosexual partners. Jacky was primarily heterosexual, but apparently his early exploits as a car thief were at least partly an attempt to attract the eccentric poet's attention.
In 1959, tiring of his then-protégé, a young Arab who had had to abandon his career as a tightrope artist after a fall, Genet transferred his attentions to Maglia and became possibly the most improbable motor racing sponsor in history. Genet followed Maglia wherever his racing took him, even living with

him for a while in Norwich, where he bought a Lotus for the young racer. While they were there, Maglia married the daughter of a local policeman. Genet signed as a witness to the Church ceremony, giving his profession as 'voleur' (thief).

Maglia had demonstrated considerable promise in his racing career, but it came to an end with a serious accident in a Formula 2 race at the spooky Solitude circuit to the west of Stuttgart in 1965. It was also the last ever race at Solitude. Abdullah the ex-tightrope walker having committed suicide, Maglia was the sole beneficiary in Genet's will.

[4] It was in one of these superb little light cars (rather than a Bugatti as is often incorrectly stated) that the loopy dancer Isadora Duncan had her third from last ride (after that it was the ambulance and then the hearse). The last thing she said to her proposed jockey for the evening, or, indeed, to anyone, was "SCAAAAAAAAAARF!"

25 Not picking up the tab

GOOD HEAVENS, I THOUGHT while watching *Hors de Prix* (2006), directed by Pierre Salvadori (not a close relation of Roy[1], I think). The English version of this French film was called *Priceless*, losing a rather good but presumably unintentional pun. It stars the dreaded *actrice* Audrey Tautou and the mildly irritating actor/comedian Gad Elmaleh, but both are excellent in their respective roles, she as a manipulative four-star hooker, he as a waiter on the make. However, it was not their performances that provoked my surprise …

The film is set mainly in swanky French resort hotels. "That's Le Grand Palais in Biarritz," I said during the first scene. That was the modest holiday home built for Napoleon III and Princess Eugénie in 1854[2]. I have stayed there as the guest of Jaguar and a couple of other car makers.

A few minutes later, I said, "Ah, that's the Carlton in Cannes" (where I have stayed at the expense of Ford, Chrysler, Maserati, BMW and perhaps some others), and a while afterwards, "… that's l'Hotel de Paris in Monaco." Few people who have seen the film can have stayed in all three of these establishments. Possibly only motoring journalists like me. Otherwise, you'd have to *pay*, which would be absolutely frightful.

Those were probably the three best big hotels I have stayed in, not just in France but anywhere. There was also a scene in a large house with terrace and garden on a rocky Côte d'Azur promontory. I had dinner there once, with Mercedes-Benz. As if the war had not ended, the company bizarrely brought a German chef. And for entertainment they also brought a famous German mime artist who was so spectacularly unfunny that he almost made me laugh.

When I spent a Saturday night in the Hotel de Paris as guest of Ferrari[3], I had a stupendously enormous first-floor room with double terrace opposite the Casino, affording a splendid view of Casino Square, all the way from the tricky entrance to the Massenet left-hander at the top of the hill to the right-hander that leads sharply downhill towards Mirabeau. Those who have neither walked nor driven the circuit will have no understanding of just how steep that descent is.

There was a huge television on the wall of the room. The Armco barriers were in place, ready for the Grand Prix. Unfortunately, the race was the following weekend.

I have also stayed in numerous excellent small hotels. Perhaps the most memorable was a 2006 Audi launch at the Cap Estel at Eze, an exquisite little place, originally the Mediterranean dacha of a wealthy 19th century Russian, when they perhaps had a better class of oligarch. The present owner is also a Russian.

The entire hotel had been recently hired for a month by a Russian whose surname may begin with 'A'; it must have cost a fortune. I was put up in 'Room 210,' apparently the most splendid of all. This turned out to be an extravagantly large suite. It had a living room measuring about 9m x 10m, in all it was about 24m long and lavishly furnished, in modern good taste. There were three flat-screen televisions; the one in the living room was the largest I have ever seen, the one in the bedroom merely quite large, while the third was above the bath. There was also a shower room, and two loos.

Eight French windows gave access to an enormous terrace almost directly over a charming little cove (though the sea looked far from inviting the morning I was there), with a view of Cap d'Ail. There was a grand piano in the main room, a table for ten people, a settee and several large armchairs, and a fully-equipped kitchen area that could be closed off by sliding doors. The only missing elements were a snooker table, and half a dozen scantily-dressed handmaidens.

At dinner, I complained to the Audi UK press relations people of the "insulting smallness of the accommodation" that I had been offered. They were puzzled, so I said that I would give them a guided tour and they would immediately understand my complaint. This was an international press launch so, successively, the press from various countries were invited in groups. In these cases, a core team of the manufacturer's people remain throughout the event.

They couldn't stop laughing during the guided tour, especially when they saw the piano. I don't know why I was given such a lavish apartment, in which on a warm evening one could easily hold a party for a couple of hundred people without it seeming crowded. Perhaps it was because I wrote for *The Daily Telegraph*, which meant something at that time, perhaps because I had become a 'doyen'[4].

Well, those were fine hotels, all with pleasant and helpful staff, which is usually a sign that the manager treats them correctly, and, as a motoring hack, on foreign 'first-drive' trips, one lived like a multi-millionaire for 24 hours or so, and the staff of the manufacturer concerned went out of their way to make sure that things ran smoothly.

One of my early foreign test drives was entirely untypical in this last respect. It was to try a new BMW, and, for some reason, we were based in Turin. At that time, the German manufacturer sold its cars in Britain via an independent company, BMW Concessionaires (GB) Ltd, whose managing director was a somewhat overweight world-class spiv by the name of Anton Hille. The normal routine was followed in the early part of our evening in the hotel in the centre of the city – press conference, dinner, adjourn to bar.

In the bar, Mr Hille held forth with his habitual arrogance. Then, just before 10.30pm, a pair of spectacularly fruity tarts arrived. To the evident dismay of his PR team, Mr Hille announced loudly, "Right, all you journalists can fuck off." Not long after that, perhaps not coincidentally, BMW acquired full control of its British subsidiary. And now, I shall recount my experience of a *very* weird hotel.

[1] Roy Salvadori (1922-2012), racing driver and team manager. The high point of his driving career was victory in the Le Mans 24 Hours race in 1959, sharing an Aston Martin DBR1 with Carroll Shelby.

[2] Almost half a century later, le Prince Bertie de Galles was recreating there with his mistress (great-aunt of Camilla, I think) when news arrived that his midget mother, Queen Victoria, had snuffed it and the he had to change his name to Edward VII, which was frightfully inconvenient.

[3] I was testing the Ferrari Superamerica, not a very good car in my opinion. Google 'Ferrari Superamerica' and 'Peter Dron' to find out why.

[4] Old git.

26 A singular experience

IN GENERAL, THE HOTEL in which one stayed on a car launch bore little correlation to the car. I recall a few nasty hotels from which I drove some nice cars, and sometimes I tested some mediocre boxes on four wheels whilst being entertained in five-star luxury.

Of course, many plutocrats' cars were matched with multi-millionaires' hotels, but the most unexpected match of car and hostelry was the Volkswagen Dune and the HI Hotel in the avenue des Fleurs in Nice, parallel to the world-famous pavement for ostentatious joggers and cyclists, the Promenade des Rosbifs.

This was in 2006, and I felt that, if I had been Doctor Who, my police box had arrived in the wrong century. I did not understand the point of either the car or the hotel. The headline in *The Daily Telegraph* on my report (of the car, not the hotel[1]) was "WHY?"

Let us get the car out of the way first. Funny name, Dune … makes one think of a ludicrous, rambling sci-fi novel, or perhaps of Lawrence of Arabia. The ideal place to test it would surely be somewhere with baking sun and lots of sand. So, we drove the VW Dune at the Alpine resort of Isola 2000, which, as the name suggests, is 2000 metres above sea level (more or less). There was a thick layer of snow during our visit …

Snow, sand, what's the difference if you have four-wheel drive? That would be a reasonable question, except that, in the Dune, as in the Polo on which it was based, power was transmitted via the front wheels only.

To complicate matters, the Dune was badged as Dune in Britain only. Elsewhere, it was called CrossPolo, which was deemed unsuitable for the UK, perhaps because it sounds to English ears like transport for equestrian transvestites in the throes of road rage.

The CrossPolo's predecessor (based on the previous Polo) was called Fun in Germany, though, strangely enough, Dune in France. Volkswagen shifted three times as many Funs as it had expected, but the Germans then decided that they did not want Fun any more. I hope this clarifies matters, even if it is not very interesting.

Here I quote from the press pack: "Designed in the style of a small SUV, the distinctive four-door with a large hatchback[2] presents itself as a practical and lifestyle-oriented all-around talent with can-do qualities." Don't we all, dear?

Well, that's enough about the Dune or CrossPolo or whatever. Let's examine the HI Hotel[3]. The name led me to expect something life-changingly ghastly, and I was not disappointed. I was taken aback, nonetheless. The entrance of this unusual inn prepared me for the monumental absurdity of what followed[4].

The ramp was fairly steep and covered in the kind of easy-clean grey gloss paint used in garages. It was raining heavily when I arrived, so the ramp became almost as slippery as sheet ice. This type of paint was also used in the bedrooms and one might say in the bathrooms, too, except that there weren't any bathrooms. My room had a glass-panelled shower in the bedroom, raised on a plinth, entered via three steps.

The throne-like lavatory was even more of a display item in the bedroom, also approached via steps (four in this case), and also glass-panelled, but only on three sides: there was no door. The floor was painted the same slithery battleship grey as used at the hotel's entrance, as was the skirting board on which was stencilled the word 'stocker,' meaning 'to store.' What and where and, indeed, why, never mind how?

Above that, a strip of pale yellow bore the words 'se reposer' (and why not?) but all-over pale cream, for example, and at least a door on the lavatory, would make that a great deal easier.

Next up was a narrow white strip, with the legend 'se hydrater,' which is, indeed, what happened to the room when I used the shower: water flooded out down the steps and onto the floor. I wondered, and not only concerning this detail, how much the hotel's insurance premium was.

Next colour up was pale green, for 's'energiser,' then, in mauve (also used on the floor around the lavatory) 'décompresser' (relax – but how could one in such surroundings?). Finally, at the top of the wall and on the ceiling, was pale blue, but not even an attractive and authentic azure blue. The command here was 'rêver.' A nightmare seemed more likely. I actually had a weird dream in which I was having a vigorous argument with Jacques Chirac, who was France's President at that time. In my dream, he was out for the evening with a tasty piece of totty who complained to me, "Now you've upset him. He was going to take me to a really smart nightclub."

Anyway, back to reality, or at least to the HI Hotel. The bed was comfortable, but its steel legs were set at an angle, threatening to break the ankles of anyone walking by. The shower and wash basin fittings were of the finest quality, but above the basin was a ludicrous jutting shelf that made things like brushing one's teeth more complicated than usual.

The fancy-looking, wall-mounted, flat-screen television did not work properly, with poor reception and, astonishingly, no terrestrial French channels. It was also awkwardly placed. Part of the handle on one of the sliding French windows fell off when I touched it. There was no minibar. The price for this, for those who were paying, was 210 euros per night, and mine was not the most expensive room. Two other members of our party had televisions that did not work at all.

I found a piece of paper on the grey-painted low wooden box that served as a bedside table. Here I was welcomed to the 'HI experience' with a cryptic explanation, possibly a blank-verse poem:

HI is a new urban hotel concept
where you can realise an singular experience
nine room's concept can be discover
as unique life space
HI was invented by matali crasset

I thought 'matali crasset' must be an anagram (I, STALE ART SCAM, perhaps), and that the whole thing was a surrealist joke by someone who had spent too much time watching Jacques Tati's films. But matali crasset, I discovered, is female (so much for the feminist theory that women bring greater practicality to design). She is a former collaborator of Philippe Starck. Who would have guessed?

She was born in 1965 in "Chalons-en-Champagne"[5]. After working in marketing, she decided she wanted to be A Designer. She does not make jokes, as far as I can see, except inasfar as overcharging punters while mocking them might indulgently be regarded as a joke (provided one is not paying). Instead, she makes *statements*, all in lower-case sans serif, of course. Is anyone ever expelled from art school for having ridiculous ideas?

I was informed that ms crasset was "that woman sitting over there" and that she was available for interview. I politely declined the kind offer. I had already formed my opinion without the need for corroborating evidence. I prefer more traditional hotels.

[1] I attempted to persuade *The Telegraph*'s Travel Editor to take a review of the HI Hotel, but this was turned down, for the obvious reason that the Travel section was nothing more than advertising bait, and did not run anything critical.

[2] This is what most people would call a five-door.

[3] In the interests of fairness, I have written this entirely in the past tense. I stayed at the HI in February 2006. The hotel may have been entirely transformed by now and may no longer resemble a Dadaist experiment. I do hope so.

[4] I presume they called it the HI Hotel rather than the Hotel HI to avoid the sort of telephone conversation that goes:

"Hi. I'm in the Hotel HI …

"Oh. Hi."

"No. Yes … I mean I'm in the Hotel HI."

"Yes. You said that. And I said Hi too. Hi again."

And so on.

[5] In those days it was called, with less pretension and greater geographical precision, Chalons-sur-Marne. I caught a train from there once (before it was renamed), when the engine of a modified BMW I had been cruising for a couple of hours at as close to its max of 150mph as possible holed a piston spectacularly, and emptied its sump via the exhaust system onto the autoroute. Smoky.

27 Crashing into dustbins

THE EXTRAVAGANCE OF MOTOR industry hospitality peaked in the 1980s. Sometimes, journalists were invited to the Arctic Circle to drive cars on ice lakes. There was always a good story with which to fill some pages, but sometimes these things were arranged specifically because senior executives had mistresses in Finland or Sweden. Yes, really.

On other occasions, the main reason behind a 'feature opportunity' was to ensure that the Press Department's budget would be maintained, or, indeed, increased, for the following year, just as armed forces in countries not at war, or not much, tend to fire off lots of ordnance and send fighter pilots on test flights in December.

Occasionally, a car manufacturer would invite journalists with wives/husbands/ partners somewhere for an entire weekend, for no particular reason. One such invitation came from BMW in 1985. For the weekend of the Monaco Grand Prix, we were to stay in the Mas d'Artigny, a luxury hotel on the forested hillside near St Paul de Vence, with a splendid view over Antibes and the Mediterranean. Apart from that weekend and several other BMW events, I stayed in the hotel over the years on numerous occasions at the expense of Renault, Rolls-Royce, Ford, Audi, Volkswagen, Subaru, Toyota, Volvo, Porsche, and perhaps other manufacturers.

I am not sure whether to use the present or past tense about the Mas d'Artigny. Following a major lawsuit against the owner, it closed its doors in January 2017. Let us be optimistic and use the present tense in the hope that there may be a future for it.

The hotel has a large main swimming pool. Numerous satellite rooms at ground level have their own smaller pools. In its heyday, lapsing into the past, it had one of the finest restaurants in France.

It is popular for car launches because it is within easy driving distance of Nice Airport, and it is right on the edge of some of the finest driving roads in the world: after a five-minute cruise, one began the fun with a blast up the Col de Vence. For a while, it had a monopoly as the sole luxury hotel with these specific advantages, but two or three others sprung up over the years, notably the Chateau Saint Martin, built beside the ruins of a fort of the Templars at the base of the Col de Vence, and the Mas de Pierre, lower down the slope towards Villeneuve-Loubet.

The Mas d'Artigny has had its moments of fame over the years. One Saturday night a few years ago, the manager was shot and robbed of the week's takings when driving home on a Saturday evening.

In 1990 I was due to go on a Porsche launch. The evening before I was due to fly to Nice, my wife phoned me from Paris, where she was working for a couple of days. She asked what was the name of the hotel I was staying in. When I told her, she laughed and said that it was a major item in French news bulletins and that I might find that there were no Porsches to drive.

A gang of villains had broken into the large locked garage. They then forced the safe off the wall, took it half a mile down the road and blew the door off it, returning with the keys to six brand-new 911 Turbos (the Type 964). They then headed towards Nice, but one of them did not manage to do half a mile, the driver dropping the Porsche into the deep ditch on the steep downhill approach to the junction with the D7, which connects La Colle-sur-Loup with St Paul. The five others were thought to have been shipped to the Middle East or Australia, after passing through Italy and the Balkans. In fact, they were found a year later, gathering dust in a warehouse near Nice. The gang had executed the heist with considerable skill, apart from the ditch incident, but had not put sufficient planning into the next stage of the operation.

Porsche's people excelled themselves, pulling half a dozen cars off the production line and rushing them from Stuttgart to the Mas d'Artigny. There was a full complement of test cars when I arrived. But back to that weekend in May 1985 ...

We flew to Nice on the Saturday morning and were transported from the airport to the Mas d'Artigny by bus. For the evening, because the restaurant had another booking that occupied most of the restaurant, we had to drive a few miles away for dinner rather than stay in the hotel. We were divided into parties of two couples and each party of four was given a Renault Espace. This turned out to be a very bad idea – though the Espace was not at fault.

My wife and I were paired with another couple. I had shared test cars with the husband on launches and we got on well. I had met his wife a couple of times and she seemed all right. I agreed to drive to the restaurant and my friend gave route instructions. I cannot recall the method by which we decided who would drive us back to the Mas d'Artigny (and therefore drink sparingly during dinner), but it turned out that it would not be me. Inwardly I rejoiced, but later I had cause to regret this. It was decided that it would be my friend's wife.

My wife and I and my journalist friend sampled without unnecessary restraint some excellent local wines that accompanied a very enjoyable dinner. I paid no attention to the wine ingestion of my friend's wife.

We set off on the return journey. It was a dark, utterly moonless night, and part of the route was a winding road through a forest. I am not sure if the driver had had too much to drink, but she was driving far too quickly for her evidently modest ability, trying to show off, I would say.

She ignored my quiet suggestion that she should slow down and then she ignored my loud command, which I delivered with added gerundive emphasis. We came to a tight left-hander. She braked much too late, locked up the front wheels and skidded straight off the road. Luckily there were no trees at the edge of the road, but there were three wheelie bins which the Espace struck and sent flying like skittles. We came to a halt.

"You stupid fucking bitch," I remarked, slowly and quietly, without using an exclamation mark. My wife said that there was no need to be rude. I replied that there was every reason to be rude and I had barely got started. The husband remained silent.

We got out and inspected the front of the Espace. Remarkably, it was undamaged. We continued on our journey, and now the husband kept telling his wife to keep the speed down, which she did, more or less.

The next morning, after a leisurely breakfast and a grovelling apology from the lady driver (under instruction from her husband, I was certain), we all boarded the Espaces, this time driven by BMW staff. We were taken to the harbour at Antibes, where we boarded a delightful old motor yacht with a teak deck. It was, I guess, not being a boaty person, about 120ft long.

We set off into the sparkling Med under a bright blue sky and our party of a dozen or so was served a delicious early lunch in the large seating area at back end of the vessel[1]. We arrived at the entrance to Monaco harbour at around 1pm, in plenty of time for the race.

A small boat came speeding out to meet us, with two uniformed men on board. The senior of them turned out to be the harbour master, an unpleasant-looking ruffian, who demanded that the captain of our little ship should give him 3000 francs (about £300).

"But that is our berth over there," said our captain, pointing to a gap in the harbour wall, by the swimming pool section just wide enough to accommodate us.

"Yes," said the piratical harbour master. "But you are here and you have to get there, n'est-ce pas?" Raymond Playfoot, BMW GB's Communications Manager, resignedly took out his wallet and handed over a wad of notes.

We berthed, and then my wife and I went to inspect our allotted spectating area.

The track was only 20 yards from our boat. However, the viewing point was somewhat hopeless – one could see only about 40 yards of the circuit as the cars flashed past from right to left.

Raymond Playfoot mentioned to me that the huge and hideous floating gin palace immediately to the east of our elegant little boat had been hired by a group of American BMW dealers, that it had a screen almost big enough for a cinema … and that we would be welcome on board.

So we watched the start on the screen, and when the cars reached Portier on the first lap, just before the tunnel, we went to our spectating area and got the full benefit of "VROOAAW" (See Chapter 85) as 18 cars blasted past on the first lap, Berger and Tambay having tangled soon after the start. This was the peak of the 1.5-litre turbo era. Those high-revving Grand Prix engines were seriously loud, especially a full pack of them. In 1985 there was a mix of straight four, V6 and V8 turbos, with one or two naturally-aspirated three-litre Cosworth V8s rumbling along towards the back of the field.

Then we returned to the BMW gin palace, and watched the rest of the race on the big screen. It is better to watch the Grand Prix on television unless you are privileged to have one of the prime viewing sites for the Grand Prix. These are mostly apartments, such as those overlooking Sainte-Devote, with a view of the harbour part of the circuit. There are also some hotel rooms, such as the one I had on the wrong weekend in the Hotel de Paris (see Chapter 25). But you would have to be very keen indeed on Grand Prix racing to pay the price of either of those options, and I do not think that many people retain that keenness these days. Certainly I do not.

If we had been there in 1985 to observe the performance of the BMW-engined cars, there was not much to report. The German company's four-cylinder turbo, which, installed in a Brabham, had powered the unspeakable Nelson Piquet to his second World Championship title in 1983, was no longer competitive. The unspeakable Piquet, who had qualified in 13th place, did not finish the race, having crashed his Brabham-BMW heavily while attempting to pass Riccardo Patrese into Sainte Devote. The most successful BMW-powered car of the weekend was the Arrows of Thierry Boutsen, sixth on the grid and ninth in the race.

On the rare occasions that I was obliged to share a room on press trips, it was always with my wife. Others were less lucky.

[1] Aft is the correct term, I believe. Or possibly poop. Or stern.

28 "Let's go back to the hotel ..."

ONE MONDAY MORNING IN July 1984, when I had been Editor of *Fast Lane* for a few months, I received a telephone call. A cheery voice announced, "Hello, this is John Morgan," which meant the square root of fuck nothing to me. He resolved the problem by mentioning that he was Jaguar's European Sales Director.

"You may recall that we met in the Gatto Nero in Turin." I did recall an enjoyable evening in the Gatto Nero – then, and perhaps still, one of Turin's finest restaurants – on the eve of the Motor Show, at Jaguar's expense.

I remembered a succession of delicious pasta dishes, accompanied by some excellent Verdicchio and Montepulciano, and that, after an hour or so, I felt that I could eat nothing more for about 24 hours. Then the main course, exquisite rack of lamb, had arrived.

Now that my memory had been jogged, I vaguely recalled this chap, who had mentioned that he had known my grandmother in Southend 'before the war' (as one used to say). He was 60ish, flabby, florid-featured and conversationally tedious. I spent most of the evening chatting to more interesting people from Jaguar; PR men, engineers, and so on.

"What can I do for you?" I asked, warily.

"Ah," he said. "I'm going to Spa next weekend with the team, and wondered if your young chap – what's his name? Tim, I think – could come along for the ride. There'll be a good story out of it, I should think." He had met Tim at a recent Jaguar event.

I visualized the opening spread with a photo from the top of Eau Rouge of the closely-packed field roaring through the dip immediately after the start, led by the TWR XJ-S team. Yes, that would be just right, especially with all expenses paid, apart from photography.

"Hang on, I'll ask Tim if he's free. 'Tim, what are you doing next weekend?'"

"Nothing much. Why?"

"Fancy going to Spa for the ETC round?"

His eyes lit up. "Yes, fantastic!"

I spoke into the telephone. "That's a definite yes. I'll put you through to Tim to discuss details."

The following Monday, Tim entered the office shortly after 10am. If you believe in auras, his would have consisted of three-foot high red and yellow flames.

"How was Spa?" asked Brian Bennett, the Deputy Editor, after several minutes during which Tim had gazed blankly at his desk. Observing this from my office, with the door open, I pretended to be engrossed in paperwork.

"Why didn't anyone warn me about that fat fairy?" Tim demanded tetchily. He gave a detailed account of his weekend, becoming increasingly angry.

They had caught the Ostend ferry, then Tim had driven while the fat man snoozed and snored after his heavily-lubricated lunch in the executive-class restaurant, having instructed Tim to wake him up when they approached Brussels. Tim did so and was given directions to their hotel.

"I was surprised that he had booked us into a double room rather than two rooms. But at least there were two single beds. I sort of assumed that he must be under some kind of budgetary restraint ..." Brian's fist was pressed hard to his lips to prevent any noise from emerging.

"And then?" I asked.

"We went out to dinner at 7.30."

"Which restaurant?"

"Er, it was, um, *Comme Chez Soi*, I think."

"Well, so much for budgetary restraint," I said. "That's probably the best restaurant in Brussels."

"During dinner we discussed the racing team and road cars and all sorts of stuff. It was fine until coffee was served ..."

"And then?"

"Suddenly, I felt this fat, clammy hand on the inside of my thigh." A deep, gargling noise rose from Brian's throat.

"Ah," said I, between gritted teeth. "And then?"

"He said, 'Let's go back to the hotel and have some fun'. I spent the rest of the bloody weekend fighting the bastard off. The worst thing was that everyone in the racing team thought I was his latest rent-boy. One mechanic asked how long I'd been on the game."

Brian[1] emitted a series of sounds, beginning with a long, tenor whine and ending in uncontrollable laughter. This had a domino effect: everyone laughed, except Tim, who ended his day's work without having done any, violently slamming the door behind him[2,3].

I believe Tim remains convinced that I intentionally set him up for this amusing weekend of humiliation. I plead not guilty in this instance, though I confess that I have played a few practical jokes over the years ...

[1] Brian subsequently went over to 'the other side of the fence' and enjoyed a successful career in motor industry PR. Brian joined the Ford Motor Company, as, several years later, did Tim Holmes, who, despite being Director of PR for Ford of Britain, was at the time of writing unable to visit Detroit, because he was born in Libya (where his father was a serving RAF officer).

[2] Tim did not get round to discussing the results of the race with us. For the record, the 1984 Spa 24 Hours, a round of the European Touring Car Championship, was won by the Jaguar XJS of team leader Tom Walkinshaw (1946-2010) sharing with Hans Heyer and Win Percy. They beat the BMW 635 CSi of Tassin/Cudini/Snobeck by three laps, two other BMWs finishing third and fourth. Walkinshaw went on to be ETC champion that year. Tom was widely regarded as a Scotch hard man, and considered himself to be as hard as nails until he met Signor Flavio Briatore.

[3] About ten years later I told this story to Nick Scheele, then the boss of Jaguar, who seemed to find it highly amusing. Mr Morgan had retired by then.

29 Jabba and the Bleeptron

THE IDEA CAME TO me while rummaging for paper clips in a desk drawer. Amongst a jumble of rubber bands, pencils, pens and stuff, I found no clips. But I did find the Bleeptron. Gleefully, I examined it. "Yes!" I shouted silently.

I intensely disliked the Deputy Editor of *Motor* at that time, who was referred to behind his back as Jabba (as in The Hutt) – and the antipathy was mutual. Whenever the Editor was away, Jabba's most toxic qualities emerged, rather as in those days a deputy bank manager[1] might get above himself when his boss was on holiday. That morning, Jabba had gone too far. I left the building, strolled around Sutton, and sat in a coffee shop to calm down. On my return, the answer presented itself, just like that.

I had received the Bleeptron for review and had tossed it into the drawer as beneath satire. I then completely forgot about it. The Bleeptron was a small device in an old-fashioned tin – the sort of tin in which John Bull bicycle tyre repair kits were sold[2]. Instead of sticky patches, glue, chalk and other stuff, it contained a tiny speaker, an adjustable vibration sensor, a printed circuit, and space for a nine-volt battery.

The purpose of the Bleeptron, introduced at a time when compulsory seat belt usage in cars was being widely discussed[3], was to remind people to attach their belts. It did this by emitting a high-pitched, loud bleep when the door was slammed. Double-sided sticky tape was provided for attachment to the door trim.

All the keys for *Motor*'s road-test and long-term test cars were kept in the top right-hand drawer of the desk of the Editor's secretary, who was in charge of distributing them each afternoon under the instructions of the Road Test Editor. The drawer was never locked. At a quarter past 12, when the secretary was in the canteen having lunch, I took the keys of Jabba's brand-new Mitsubishi and set off for the car park. I opened the driver's door of the Trooper, carefully detached a corner of the door trim, held in place by push-fit plastic widgets, and stuck the Bleeptron, its sensitivity set to maximum, as far up inside as possible, then carefully popped the trim back into the doorframe. I sat in the car and slammed the door, provoking a satisfyingly screechy bleep; it was oddly difficult to determine where it came from. I locked the car, returned the keys to the desk drawer, and joined my colleagues in the pub for lunch.

The following morning, Jabba came into the office at 9.30, which was late for him, and he was evidently in a very bad mood. From next door, in the Road Test Department's office, I heard him telephoning the local Mitsubishi dealer. He gave the Service Manager a very hard time, complaining about an appalling electronic noise from the Trooper. This noise, he explained, was a kind of high-pitched electronic whine. It was provoked by the mildest irregularity of road surface, or even by accelerating, braking or cornering on completely smooth asphalt.

Mitsubishi's man was informed that the noise was "intolerable" and brusquely instructed to collect the defective car at his earliest convenience, check out what caused this abysmal fault, stop it forthwith, and return the vehicle in a condition fit for use asap. I could understand from Jabba's end of the conversation that the car would be collected that afternoon and returned the next day. At lunchtime, I paid another visit to the rooftop car park.

I was out the next day, but apparently, as I learned the day after, the Mitsubishi people had been unable to find any fault whatever in Jabba's car that could account for the strange noises allegedly heard. Someone overhearing this conversation said that he got the distinct impression that the Service Manager thought Jabba must be "having psychological problems."

Extraordinarily, Jabba had said, the noises had now vanished. Not for long, however ... This time the Bleeptron was inserted inside the passenger door. And so on, for several weeks, until one day I was away testing and was thus unable to remove the device before another inspection by the Mitsubishi mechanics, who found it after an extended search.

I was surprised to read a mention of this prank in a long-term report in the magazine: "This appears to have been somebody's idea of a practical joke. Very funny, I don't think," wrote Jabba the Hutt. He might have added, "Everyone seems to think I am a complete prat. I cannot imagine why."

[1] At least, in those days, we had bank managers.
[2] Nobody under the age of about 50 will know what this is.
[3] Clunk click, guys 'n' gals. You can trust me – I'm a television presenter. Now then, now then.

30 Frank and the Tardis

FRANK THE YARD MAN always wore his brown leather coat and brown leather trilby, whatever the weather. Frank's command post, popularly known as 'The Tardis,' was a small glass-reinforced-plastic cabin in the yard behind Surrey House[1].

Through the window of the Tardis, in which he brewed endless cups of tea, chain-smoked Woodbines and stimulated his mind by reading *The Sun* and *The Racing Post*, Frank surveyed the entire yard, which IPC[2] shared with a department store. Frank's main job involved logging delivery lorries in and out.

He also had the task of keeping the yard clear. He would be out of his cabin in a flash if anyone parked a car there. To senior IPC directors he was obsequious; anyone else got short shrift. He particularly disliked sarcastic, long-haired young men in jeans driving flash cars, so the road test staff of *Motor* were his *bêtes noires*.

We parked in the yard only for brief visits, which always involved a tedious argument with Frank. We had our own car park, shared with IPC men in suits, above the staff restaurant, accessible via two lifts in one corner of the yard. You drove the car into the lift, slammed the heavy folding doors shut, pressed the button and the lift slowly rose 20ft to the car park. Then you parked and came down in the car lift, the entire operation taking about two minutes, but often there was a queue. Squeezing in and out of wide cars inside the narrow lifts was difficult and I had to clamber through the window on several occasions.

One busy morning, five seconds after I had slammed the doors shut and pressed the button to ascend, the bell rang. Someone kept his finger on the button the whole time I was going up, parking and returning.

The awful ringing, which resounded deafeningly inside the steel cage, stopped shortly before I opened the doors. Five cars, occupied by a couple of directors and three colleagues, were waiting in grid formation.

"OK," I shouted, "which of you clowns was ringing the fucking bell?"

One of the directors smiled and said, "It wasn't us. It was Frank."

Around the corner I found Frank, in his brown leather coat and brown leather trilby, standing outside the Tardis.

"What was that about, Frank?" I asked, provoking an incomprehensible rant that might have slotted seamlessly into a Samuel Beckett play. I kept trying to interrupt him to present my point of view, but he carried on ranting. Eventually, all patience spent, I grabbed the brim of his brown leather trilby and attempted unsuccessfully to force it down over his ears. Then I turned and entered the building.

Half an hour later, I was summoned to the Publishing Director's office. He asked what had occurred between me and Frank. I explained, expressing my disappointment regarding the trilby and the ears. He laughed and said, "The man's a complete pain, I agree, but we have to maintain good relations. Be a good chap and apologize, will you?"

I opened the door to the Tardis. I said, "I have something to say, Frank. Please remain silent." Surprisingly, he did. "My boss has asked me to say I am sorry. Right, then ..." I paused. He smiled. I continued, "I am very sorry ... that you are such a cunt."

Some months later, I landed at Gatwick after a foreign car launch, the 737 approaching the runway at an angle of 45 degrees in a vicious crosswind, the pilot deftly straightening up at the last moment. The gale had not abated when I reached Surrey House half an hour later. The wind accelerated around the building, which had been constructed in the Brutalist style without regard to vortex shedding and the Strouhal Relationship[3].

While I was opening the lift doors, an exceptionally violent gust headed directly, like a heat-seeking missile, to the Tardis, which blew over, landing on the concrete, door downward, with a loud smack.

I strolled over and peered through the window. There was Frank, trapped, gesticulating wildly. I stared at him and cupped a hand to an ear. "Speak up, Frank," I said. I could not hear what he was shouting, so I smiled and waved, then returned to my car.

[1] A 17-storey concrete-and-glass blot on the Surrey landscape, erected in the 1960s.
[2] A large publishing company of the 20th century. Surrey House was one of two hideous skyscrapers that it occupied in Sutton.
[3] It has since been demolished and replaced with an equally hideous block of flats.

31 The training scheme

WHEN ONE BECAME AN IPC[1] Editor, Men in Suits, who mostly neither knew much nor cared at all about magazines[2], decreed that one should attend 'training schemes'. Some were enjoyable and useful, such as one run by Vincent Hanna[3], preparing one for ordeal by radio or television interview.

Mostly they were pointless. A typical example was a 'Management Techniques' course, designed specifically for people who, unlike me, wanted to become Publishers and Managing Directors; most were Advertising Managers. The course involved three days of classwork and 'an adventure weekend,' the 'highlight' of which was to be a paintball contest.

In the classroom in the 'Low Rise' part of Surrey House, I recognized one or two editors. The lecturer, in crap suit and silly tie, had exaggerated face furniture and a ponytail.

"Right," he said, grinning stupidly, "this will be tremendous fun, boys and girls. First, we shall discover how we want to learn."

I put my hand up.

"I'll take questions later," he said dismissively. "First, would you, miss-in-the-front-row, be kind enough to hand out these questionnaires?" he asked of a blonde with pointy tits and pert buttocks.

I said, "It's a simple question."

"Oh, very well."

"You are here as a lecturer. If *you* don't know how we should be taught whatever it is you are planning to teach, how do you expect *us* to know?"

He attempted a glare, but looked nervous. "Just fill in the form and we'll discuss it afterwards."

The blonde handed me a stapled four-page questionnaire containing numbered statements to which one was required to respond, marking them on a scale of one to five with, from 'Very Inaccurate' to 'Very Accurate.' The statements were generalizations, for example, 'I tend to be more comfortable with the known than the unknown.'

I filled in the form, far more rapidly than anyone else, then switched to *The Telegraph* crossword.

After several minutes, the lecturer said, "Time's up, guys 'n' gals." The blonde with the tits and buttocks was instructed to collect the questionnaires. Our lecturer repeated that his objective was to find out how "the class" wanted to be taught.

I interrupted. "I have a supplementary question …"

"Please wait until I have finished my presentation. Now …"

"No," I insisted. "I do not intend to wait until the end of your presentation."

"Very well," he said testily.

"Supposing everybody ticked the answers at random, what would that tell you about the price of bananas?"

"I don't understand your problem, Mr …'

"Dron. I don't have a problem. Or I didn't until I met you."

"What do you mean *exactly*, Mr Dron?"

"Well, if you take 'Very Inaccurate' as '1' and 'Very Accurate' as '5,' I answered Question 1 with 1, Question 2 with 2, and so on until I got to Question 6, when

I reverted to 1. And so on until Question 102. One, two, three four, five; one, two, three, four, five …"

"That is very childish. I shall disregard your frivolous answers and your gratuitous rudeness … we shall move briskly on."

"That's what I'm going to do," I said, standing up. "I'm moving briskly on. I'm leaving. I'm not coming back. I will not attend your weekend seminar. I will not play silly games in the woods. I have a job to do and my weekends are sufficiently adventurous without playing paintball and bonding with advertising persons. Good day." I just managed to stop myself from adding that, if I did, I would go after him with live ammunition.

As I headed for the door, the lecturer said, "I shall make an official complaint to your Publishing Director."

"Go ahead," I said, giving him the name and extension number. "Toodle-oo." I paused and addressed the class in general, "As for you lot, you should read about the Forer Effect[4]."

I went straight to my Publisher, one of the better Suits, and explained what had happened. He laughed and said, "I do wonder about senior management sometimes."

Incidents like that made me wonder what it would like to be sacked. It's not so bad, really. It can even be a release.

[1] In the 1980s, IPC had a fleet of vans which proclaimed, 'World's Largest Publishing Company.' It had a collection of good magazines, but the managers, with a few notable exceptions (see note 2 below), were probably better suited to selling baked beans or plastic widgets.

[2] Among several exceptions to this was a jovial rogue named Graham Sheath, who once confided that, "Things are so tough in this company, you can even be stabbed in the chest." He was delighted when he visited Paris for talks on joint ventures with Hachette to find that his opposite number from the French publishing corporation was a Monsieur Condom.

[3] Vincent Hanna (1939-1997), one of the best and most original British political journalists of the 20th century, who alas died young.

[4] Look it up.

84

32 The man who shot Lord Haw-Haw

I COULD HAVE WALKED away with a wad of cash, over 40 grand. I should have done, as I told myself repeatedly, and still do from time to time. Instead, nine months after making the wrong decision, I stopped on the way home one Friday afternoon and bought a bottle of champagne. "What are we celebrating?" my wife asked. "Oh, nothing much," I said, "I've been fired."

Faced with the choice between, on the one hand, the pay-off and far less certain life of a freelance journalist, and on the other, staying on under new bosses, I had decided to remain as Editor of *Fast Lane* magazine. It was not only the financial security of regular employment that influenced my decision; I believed it would be interesting to work with this big German publishing group. Well, there is interesting and there is interesting, and this was interesting in the Chinese sense. Everybody, I suppose, must do a few stupid things in life. Certainly, despite fierce competition, this was by far the biggest single stupid mistake I have ever made.

I knew that the Huns were operating through a small British company. For reasons I could not understand, I was not permitted to meet the new owners until after the sale, so I had to take a punt, in the dark. As soon as I met Horst Pinschewer[1], the small and undistinguished boss of the small and undistinguished British publishing company, and even before I had been given my new draft contract of employment, I realized that I had voluntarily leapt into a deep, polluted well, landing neck-deep in the nitrogenous. Horst immediately struck me as a pompous blivet. But I was committed, or should have been.

Commuting to central London was a nightmare. I lived in East Grinstead (see Chapter 80). Admittedly, the commuting journey, either through heavy traffic by car or by the slow and rattly suburban railway, would have been more acceptable with a less grim destination. It was a gloomy set of offices just off the north-west side of Oxford Street, and the working atmosphere was tense. I used to see the famous loony sandwich-board man with the sign announcing that 'The End is Nigh'[2] and occasionally thought of telling him that he did not know the half of it.

I was rarely able to have direct contact with the Germans who had bought the magazine. Communication was a problem and face-to-face meetings were rare. During one of these, I pointed out the impossibility of carrying out a recent directive. "Ah," said the chap breezily, "ven vee Stuttgarters make a suggestion, it can sometimes sound like an order." You can say that again, I said drily, thinking of adding that my German Shepherd Dog did not seem to think I was being serious unless I shouted at him.

Sometimes, the orders or requests bordered on the bizarre. I was asked to arrange some debenture tickets for the Wimbledon tennis championships.

I hated the Oxford Street area, though it provided interesting diversions from time to time. One morning, within a couple of blocks of the office, I was sitting at a red traffic light, and there was a chap pacing about on the pavement, smoking, checking his watch nervously. I thought, "I know that man." Well, I didn't know him. It was Tom Stoppard. He did not seem to have Fortune on his cap. There was some scaffolding outside a building nearby and a workman spoke to the distinguished playwright, who then handed his cigarette to the man for a light, took it back and continued pacing about, puffing nervously. It was rather as if the Prince, waiting impatiently for his carriage, had an encounter with Dogbery or Verges, rather than Rosenkrantz or Guildenstern.

Having been fired, after I had cleared my desk, I needed to go back to the office one more time to remove some personal files and some larger stuff, in particular a rather nice bookcase with glass doors that IPC had let me keep. I was in the process of tying this up on the back of the Mazda pickup that I had borrowed, when a Jaguar XJ12 pulled up. The uniformed chauffeur stepped out and opened the back door for his passenger. It was Jeremy Beadle[3].

Mr Beadle looked directly at me and walked towards me. I thought, "Right, this has all been an elaborate wind-up." He carried on walking, straight past me, and he did not look back. I drove off in the Mazda and did not look back either[4]. It is vital to focus attention on the unfolding event horizon.

[1] Or Geoffrey Perry, as he preferred to be known. At the end of the war, as part of a group under the leadership of another noted post-war British magazine publisher named Captain Ján Ludvík Hyman Binyamin Hoch (later known as Robert Maxwell), Lieutenant Pinschewer shot William Joyce, otherwise known as Lord Haw-Haw, in the buttocks, for no particular reason. Joyce, admittedly a ghastly fellow, was nursed back to full health, tried and then shot again, this time not in the buttocks, having been convicted as a traitor even though he was not a British citizen. That's British justice for you.

[2] Stanley Green (1915-1993), no relation of Whispering Gavin Green (see Chapter 35, Note 1), as far as I know, was convinced that an excess of protein was the root of mankind's problems. So it was obviously not that that killed him. *Ashes to ashes, and dust to dust, if the women don't get you, the liquor must.* And if not that, it will be protein. Or something else.

[3] Jeremy James Anthony Gibson-Beadle MBE (1948-2008) TV prankster, with the famous catchphrase, "I say, *cavee*, you fellows! *Gibson-Beadle's About*, don't you know!"

[4] The attempt by the large Stuttgart publisher, motorpresse, to establish itself in the British market came to be nicknamed 'Operation Sealion 2' (though not by the Germans themselves). Having bought *Fast Lane* from IPC in 1990, they then closed it and launched a new monthly, *Complete Car*. This folded in 1997 after 18 months of publication. Operation Sealion 2 therefore lasted considerably longer than Operation Sealion 1, but the result was essentially the same, though happily without the death and destruction.

33 Just a second, or two

I HAD BEEN WARNED that Chris Schirle, TVR's Competition Manager/chief engineer, could be ferocious. Our first encounter, at Oulton Park in 1986, confirmed this.

He nodded silently when I introduced myself. Regular driver Steve Cole did a couple of warm-up laps. Another chap was due to drive the yellow 420 SEAC before me. This other driver spun on his out lap. Schirle called him in immediately and tersely invited him to disappear.

Then it was my turn. Chris gave me a pep talk, accompanied by unblinking, steely blue eyes. He told me that nobody in the team had wanted me to drive the car; he had agreed only because TVR's PR man had made the arrangement. The tirade continued, with warnings and threats.

As I began climbing into the winged racer, I asked, "Tell me ... what's a good time around here in this?"

He gave another fierce stare, then replied gruffly, while a grinning mechanic helped tighten the harness, "If you get round in under 1 minute 34, I'll make sure you get a fucking Grand Prix drive."

I promptly stalled. Next time I got it right and exited the pits. I had visited Oulton several times but never driven there. I had no previous experience of driving on slicks.

My first flying lap was signalled as '1-40,' encouraging as I had been cruising, learning the dips, bumps and swooping curves of Cheshire's mini-Nürburgring. Gradually, I whittled this down to 1min 32.5sec. From then on Chris and I got on very well. He invited me to join the team for the weekend's race, a four-hour relay.

The team consisted of three TVRs. I was engaged as fourth driver, sharing the SEAC with Cole. Steve did the first and final stints. After one of our team cars conked out, I ended up driving for an hour and five minutes. I had never previously completed more than 15 consecutive laps of a circuit.

I played squash at least once a week at that time and was fairly fit, even though I was a smoker, but I soon found that previously unknown muscles were aching. Also, I had pushed the seat rearwards one notch and my back seemed to have come into contact with a cross-member, which was mildly uncomfortable. Maintaining full concentration was the toughest thing, though, particularly because of the performance variation of the cars. After a difficult patch halfway through my session, I found a rhythm.

The SEAC was the third-quickest car on track at any time. There was a team of beautiful, super-rapid Chevrons. They appeared as if from nowhere, flashed past and vanished into the distance. There was a 911 gang whose cars just had the edge over the TVR on the straights, but we easily outperformed all but one of them overall. There were about 30 teams altogether, with all sorts of cars – Caterhams, BMWs, Minis, Fiestas, a Lotus Elan ... The slowest team was the most bizarre: a Lotus Cortina, an Austin A35, a Morris Minor and a Ford Mustang.

With all this traffic I never had a clear lap. Nevertheless, almost all my laps were around 1min 35sec (we were running on harder-compound tyres than on the previous day). One lap lasted over 1min 37sec, when I spent too much time looking in the rear-view mirror at the quick 911 bearing down on me.

He was gaining along the pits straight, but, as I descended towards Cascades, he had dropped back, probably having had a moment in Old Hall. Then suddenly he was catching me again. I missed my braking point for the banked Island bend, scrabbling around the outside, but just avoiding the necessity to run away and join the Foreign Legion.

The breakdown of one of the team's cars dropped us to 19th place overall, but, at the finish, we were up to fifth on the road and sixth on handicap. Mr Schirle was smiling after the race and complimented me on my consistency.

Yes, but I was consistently doing 1m 35sec while Cole was consistently just below 1min 34sec. As anyone who has ever raced will attest, it's that last second or two that's the toughest part.

Some years later, in qualifying for a Tuscan Challenge round at Castle Combe, I had the opportunity to follow Steve for several laps. I hoped that there would be one bend where I was getting it wrong. Then I might rectify that, by changing my braking point or the line.

Alas, it was not like that: we were both braking at the same points and our lines seemed identical. Yet I was losing a tiny bit at every bend. I ended up sixth (out of about 24) in qualifying, finishing eighth. Steve was on the front row and he won the race. You ask yourself: how does he do that? Alas, there is no obvious answer.

34 Going to the wall

SURFING THE INTERNET IN search of some TVR Tuscan Challenge[1] information, I chanced upon a German article mentioning me by name. As I have no German, life being too short, I tried a Google translation. Here it is:

> But then a rough existence remained directed the model on the tracks. In the frame of the Tuscan Challenge from 1989, he drifted over the Curbs of fire Hatch, Oulton and Mallory park or Snetterton, at the steering wheel hard and determined men such as the serious Gerry Marshall[2] who confessed always candid, let he be in this world only because of the beer. "We are," about Tuscan pilot went to confession Peter Dron in the lead foot organ almost Lane, "just as bescheuert[3] such as the people of TVR and should be locked in actually in rubber cell. Consider: 400 HP for 800 kg!" Hardcore freaks resourceful only a couple slipped somehow by the stiches of the law and acquired a street allowance for its Tuscan.

There I was on the grid at Silverstone on 30 July, 1989, along with 23 other *bescheuert* blokes in identical TVR Tuscans, all powered by modified Rover V8s[4] knocking out, as our Hun commentator suggests, around 400bhp.

For once, I made a perfect start. It was difficult to get a Tuscan cleanly off the line: all that power, combined with light weight (the majority bearing on the front axle), and not especially grippy tyres, necessitated delicate coordination of clutch and throttle to be in the narrow margin between excessive and insufficient wheelspin.

That afternoon, I found that margin. I started from tenth position, in the middle of the fourth row, after a damp qualifying session. The track was dry for the race.

By the time I had snicked into second gear I had passed the cars in the row ahead. Immediately after changing into fourth, which meant just over 100mph, I was up with the four professional racers who were fiercely battling for the championship.

We were approaching the braking zone for Copse Corner. I reckoned I could hang onto fifth place through there and perhaps be at the head of the rest of the field. I might even manage to stay close enough to the quick men for a few laps to learn something.

Then it all went seriously wrong. Something rapidly entered my peripheral vision from the left, followed by a loud bang. One chap had decided that he might make up places by putting his left wheels onto the grass verge. This was unwise, considering the attributes of these cars mentioned earlier. He rejoined the action at an angle of 45 degrees and collided heavily with my left door.

During incidents like this, a race track suddenly seems very narrow. I had hit the brake and clutch pedals and turned the wheel into the slide, but the car was gyrating wildly. I knew that I was heading for the Armco on the outside of the track, and I was fairly sure that it was going to hurt.

I must have spun five or six times. Each time I was facing back towards the start/finish line, I could see Tuscans bouncing off each other and off the pit wall and the outside barrier. I hit the Armco backwards, luckily at a relatively shallow angle, still travelling at about 70mph, bounced away, half-spun around and struck it hard again with the front left.

A photograph of this stage of the incident shows my car riding up the wall, the right side several inches off the ground, the large glassfibre bonnet detached and flying several feet above, a track marshal in orange overalls ducking for cover, and mayhem behind me.

I considered doing the Gilles Villeneuve thing of sticking it in first gear and gunning it, but as all four wheels were pointing in different directions there was no point. I undid my harness and climbed out, with a sore neck.

In the following week's *Autosport*, the magazine's reporter diligently described what he thought he had seen. As an afterthought, he added, "Peter Dron was also involved, but only peripherally." That was a relief. Once again, I had got away with relatively little damage.

Accidents happen in motor racing, and this one did not really bother me too much after my anger had subsided, because I knew it was not my fault. However, I was beginning to understand that, having started late and shown some modest promise, I was not really making satisfactory progress as a racing driver. I was *nearly* quick enough, but not quite, and it was difficult for me to analyse precisely why.

I felt that I was doing everything almost perfectly and I was close to the pace of the professionals, but it was just that last bit, to do with finesse rather than bravery, that was lacking. I knew it was all in that zone between applying the brakes and hitting the apex of the turn – that's where it all happens; everything else is just drag racing.

Unless you are one in a million, blessed with exceptional talent, you cannot expect to jump into a racing car and beat the professionals straight away. The quick men in the Tuscans had been racing every weekend of the season for ten or 20 years, or even longer.

But you can get there if you are persistent. The first Tuscan test session was held on a bitterly cold day at Oulton Park in April 1989. It was difficult to get the tyres up to temperature, and the Tuscan's slicks were not very grippy anyway. I was puzzled at first that on the long straight towards Knicker Brook (this was before the chicane was installed), the revs rose every time I crossed the ridge about two thirds of the way along. I think there may have been some ice there; whatever it was, the revs were rising because the driven rear wheels were spinning slightly … at about 150mph in fifth gear.

The least experienced driver there was a chap called Martin Crass. He had never raced and had hardly ever been on a racing circuit. He had a huge accident going up the hill into the fast and tricky Druids Bend. His car was badly damaged and he was briefly hospitalized with concussion. With some help from TVR Chairman Peter Wheeler, his car was repaired and six weeks later at Castle Combe he began a long racing career. At first he was at the back of the grid, hopelessly off the pace. But he worked at it, and I think he ended up taking part in more TVR races than anyone else … and he won a few of them.

Perhaps I could have been a serious contender, but you have to be obsessed to do that. I decided that, although I enjoyed it, I was not the obsessive type and, in any case, I was too busy with other projects to find out if I could cut away that final second or two.

[1] A well-supported one-make series introduced in 1989. Unfortunately, the brilliant TVR Chairman, the late Peter Wheeler, made a couple of crucial errors, which is all that it takes. See Note 4.

[2] 'Larger than life' is the way Gerry (1941-2005) was habitually described. Among other abilities, he could balance himself on his bald head on the top of a bar and carry on drinking his beer.

[3] 'Bescheuert' means bonkers, apparently, which is about right, though one would expect the Germans to have a longer compound word for that.

[4] Later versions of the Tuscan and TVR's road cars used the Blackpool company's own engine. Most observers would agree that that was Peter Wheeler's biggest mistake. I think he agreed, too, because he sold the company to a young Russian mug with loads of cash. TVR went bust, but, at the time of writing, is under dynamic new ownership with ambitious plans.

35 The subtle art of seduction

WHILE WAITING TO GO out in my Tuscan race at Oulton Park one Sunday in 1990, I watched a fiercely fought and painfully noisy Honda CRX race. Whispering Gavin[1] was the leader in the early stages, with a group of five closely following, more or less bumper to bumper, and then the rest strung out behind them.

He seemed to have it in the bag at half-distance, but then I could hear that his exhaust was no longer making the full screaming noise[2]. Instead, it was now popping and banging. He gradually dropped to the back of the leading group, his car not whispering but making uncouth farty noises. He whispered afterwards that he had run a bit wide and put the two outside wheels over a kerb, which had flattened the exhaust and reduced power output by a significant percentage.

Behind this leading pack of experienced, highly-skilled, semi-pro drivers, battles of similar intensity raged. On the final lap into the final, tricky Lodge Corner, consisting of a sharp right turn into a steep dip followed immediately by a steep rise into a more gentle left-hander, contact was made by two of these cars, one of which crossed the finishing line on its roof.

No injury resulted from this, but the chap who ended the race inverted angrily blamed the young woman driver with whom he had been disputing tenth or 11th place.

Later, after my race, I was walking through the paddock and there she was, with a group of people gathered around her. I noticed a journalist friend among them and went over to have a chat. It was quite evident that she was not cut out for this kind of thing. Far too nice and far too ready to admit that she had made a mistake …

"I'm never going to make it as a racing driver," she said between sobs. Boo-hoo, blub-blub, and so on and so forth. She was the sister of a chap who was one of those many drivers touted as the next superstar, but somehow it did not work out for him. Apparently, he was not too bothered, provided he could go surfing. But his sister was fiercely ambitious and severely self-critical.

She desperately wanted to succeed on track but was beginning to realize that, although competent, she did not have the spark of talent. Her brother, perhaps, had the talent but not the ambition.

Neville, the famous racing commentator (well, famous in the small world of national motor racing), was there. He was now in full relaxation mode at the end of a very hard afternoon's work, and wished to offer some solace to the unhappy damsel in her moment of gloom and disappointment.

"Never mind, dear," he said cheerily. "I bet you're a terrific fuck."

This effort at consolation did not seem to comfort her in the slightest. Her sobbing became even more intense; indeed, convulsive. However, the same style of chat-up line had possibly worked well for Neville in the dawn of his career, back in the 1950s at Goodwood, when I expect he was a dapper young fellow, probably wearing the same clothes: cavalry twills, brown/beige sports jacket with leather elbow patches, and the sort of shirt and tie that you can spill pints of beer and gravy on without it showing too much.

[1] Australian-born Gavin Green, quietly-spoken long-time contributor to and former Editor of *CAR* magazine. Excellent journalist, imaginative editor, talented amateur racing driver, failed Publishing Director. Well, one has to be crap at something.

[2] The sound of a full field of CRX racers was physically painful, yet they always passed the regulation

sound tests without difficulty, whereas the rumbling V8s in TVR Tuscans barely scraped through. The problem of these tests is that they are based on decibel levels rather than pitch, and pitch is the bitch that hurts the eardrums.

36 Crashing a motor caravan

I ARRIVED AT LLANDOW motor racing circuit in Glamorgan early on a Friday afternoon in August 1973, changed into racing overalls, climbed into the vehicle, strapped myself into the full harness and put on my helmet and gloves.

The vehicle was a Bedford CF motor caravan, its engine and suspension modified by renowned Vauxhall tuner Bill Blydenstein[1]. The wheels and tyres had also been changed: more about that later.

I had been roped into taking part in a 24-hour run in this motorized bedroom which also had a 'kitchenette,' but no en-suite shit-and-shower facilities. The target average speed was 60mph. I did a warm-up lap, finding out where the bends were. There were not many: a tight, wiggly section at one end, and two right-handers with a short connecting straight at the other[2]. Then I did two flying laps. At the end of the second of these, a mechanic held out a board showing the time for the first one – around 60 seconds.

The circuit was almost exactly a mile long, and I knew that the other drivers had not got within two or three seconds of my time. I backed off, did some rapid mental calculations, and decided I would park the van and drive back to London.

Before that, I was going to explain that I could not maintain that pace for long, that the other drivers had been slower, and that there was not the remotest chance, even without fuel stops, that an average of 60mph over 24 hours was attainable. I was going to add that it would be quicker and safer, as well as less effort, if one chose a stretch of the M1 or M6[3].

I was relieved to get out of this nonsense, because the vehicle felt rather unstable. I wound down the driver's window[4] and cruised back to the pits. I turned into the first of the two right-handers at the far end of the circuit from the pits at a lower speed (below 60mph) than on my hot laps, and then disaster struck.

Without warning, the vehicle suddenly listed to port. I thought for a moment that it might settle back but instead it flicked into three or four violent barrel rolls, ending on the infield. At one point, the doorframe and roof clamped my full-face helmet and tried to yank it off my head; at another I got a face full of Welsh dirt through the window.

Eventually, the tumble-drier motion stopped. I found myself suspended, upside down, still strapped in. Everything was silent, except for the ominous ticking of the petrol pump. I could smell petrol. This was five days after the unfortunate Roger Williamson had been burnt to a crisp at Zandvoort[5].

With some difficulty, I found the ignition key and switched it off. Then I tried to find a way of getting out. The driver's door was blocked by close proximity with Planet Earth; it would have to be Plan B. I looked upwards and to the left for the passenger door; it seemed distorted. I decided to give it a try and, if that did not work, I would crawl towards the back door. I was about to unbuckle my harness, when I heard voices and people running towards me.

I waited until they lifted the Bedford so that I was almost the right way up, unbuckled the harness, and fell out into warm summer air, I think through the driver's door. People sometimes say funny things when they are in shock. Apparently, I said, "I must wash my hands."

I was sitting in the sunshine, smoking a cigarette, in considerable pain[6], waiting for my friend and colleague, Andy, to sort out a few things and then take me to Cardiff Infirmary, when the owner of the motor caravan company came over.

"Are you all right?" he asked.

"I'll survive," I said, or something to that effect.

"Bloody irresponsible, aren't you?" he said, rhetorically. Andy was on the point of slugging him, but decided that getting me to Outpatients was the priority.

I later discovered that, without asking Blydenstein's advice, this twerp who traded in motor caravans had insisted on a different size of wheel from those recommended by Dunlop (because they looked nicer in photos). The tyres moved laterally on the rims, enough for the flange of the loaded left front wheel to dig into the tarmac; a photographer noticed the gouge marks[7]. I should have sued the bastard[8].

And now for someone else's accident. They are always less serious.

[1] A highly-respected engineer who intelligently scoffed at power outputs and 0-60mph figures, pointing out that torque and 20-100mph figures were far more important in the real world.

[2] After lying fallow for some years, the circuit has been revived in recent times (though constantly under the threat of disappearing under a housing estate), and it now contains a couple of chicanes, so is even less suitable for 24-hour record attempts.

[3] At that time, Millbrook circuit, which would have been ideal for that type of exercise, was not available for use by outsiders, but perhaps if someone had asked Bill Blydenstein or someone from Dunlop to intercede, it might have been possible.

[4] We did that kind of stuff manually in those days, chucky.

[5] His accident was also caused, it seems, by tyre failure. He was apparently uninjured, but was trapped in his overturned March 731, and died of asphyxia, despite the heroic efforts of fellow driver David Purley to rescue him.

[6] I had crushed two vertebrae together, and for several weeks suffered the worst pain I have ever experienced. I was lucky to find a brilliant osteopath. When the young racing driver Pascal Wehrlein dropped out of a couple of Grands Prix early in 2017, television commentator and former Number 2 driver David Coulthard displayed his ignorance of such injuries by making some critical remarks.

[7] Legend has it that the motor caravan had been fully equipped and that numerous pieces of cutlery were discovered, lying around on the track. I have no idea if this is true.

[8] I mean the motor caravan merchant, not the photographer.

37 Immediate and accurate correction

MY FIRST VISIT TO MIRA[1] in October 1976 was dramatic. With Gordon (*Motor*'s Road Test Editor) and two other testers, I spent a bitterly cold, damp morning, timing four cars around the 'high-speed circuit' (a 2.8-mile triangular track with steeply banked bends) attaching and removing test equipment, and so on.

None of this was out of the ordinary, especially the weather. The long, hot summer of that year already seemed a distant memory. The testing routine soon became dull, with numerous moments of irritation and frustration, and a few of terror, but on a tester's first day it all seems new and exciting. Those occasional moments of terror generally occurred on the triangular 'high-speed' circuit if you entered its banked curves at more than 125mph, or at the ends of the acceleration straights, or if you got out of shape on the aptly-named 'Number 2' circuit, used mostly for brake-fade tests. Its bends were helpfully marked out by oil drums filled with sand; these days, they have girly plastic posts.

At midday, Gordon, who was in charge, said, "Right, time for lunch." Gordon had recently had an argument with the publican of the splendidly-named Oddfellow's Arms, overlooking MIRA, so we headed off in convoy in two cars to a more distant hostelry, on roads made treacherously slippery by melting snow and a liberal coating of cow shit. Gordon was leading, in a Toyota Corolla Liftback; I was driving the second car, a Honda Civic.

Gordon was a highly skilled driver, but was, perhaps, rather too keen to prove it that day to the new boy. Despite maximum attack on the slithery lanes, he had no chance of getting away from the Civic in the unimaginably crude Toyota. Eventually, he was so sideways in one right-hander that I said, "Shit, he's lost it!" Uncle Maurice the photographer said optimistically from the passenger seat, "No. He'll hold it." He did not hold it. The Corolla fell off the road with a soft thud into the snow-filled ditch on the left.

We stopped and ran over. Gordon was banging his fists on the steering wheel. Mike, his passenger, was gaily sobbing with laughter. Both were unharmed and the Toyota seemed unscathed, though stuck. We dropped our furious leader at a garage, and the rest of us headed off for a convivial lunch.

An hour later, we found Gordon and an uncouth grease monkey with Widley Braggins sideburns who was driving a Transit pickup which had a small crane on the back. The Transit had a slipping clutch and was merely dragging the car backwards and forwards in the ditch.

We all jumped into the ditch and pushed. Immediately, the Liftback popped out like a cork, now with all the panels on the left side severely crumpled. The suspension seemed undamaged, so we took it back to MIRA and did the acceleration runs. Our times beat the manufacturer's claims. This may have been a result of the makeshift aerodynamic modifications reducing the frontal area; more likely, it was due to the Road Test Editor's pent-up fury.

Motor's road test of this car, published in December 1976, advised, "On slippery surfaces, [the Corolla's] Japanese-manufactured Dunlops lacked grip and a combination of rear-end steer (due to poor location of the live axle) and indifferent traction could cause the tail to step out of line, calling for immediate and accurate correction ..." Yes, indeed. QED.

Of course, while an apology had to be delivered to Toyota, there was no reference to the ditch incident in the road test. That's the way it is with magazines. Unfortunate 'out takes' are never featured. For example, I have a copy of *Autocar* from 5 May 1999, which contains an eight-page comparison test between a Ferrari 360 Modena and a Porsche 911 Carrera 4. There is no mention in the text (or a photograph of the incident) that both cars were seriously damaged when the Porsche crashed into the rear of the Ferrari.

MIRA was first used by *The Motor* and *The Autocar* (both magazines retained the definite article in those days) in the 1950s (the bleak place had been a relief bomber aerodrome during the war). A famous road-testing incident occurred in the early days. A proto-nerd tester named Stuart, on his second visit for *The Autocar*, while showing his colleague Ronald 'Steady' Barker (See Chapter 7) around the facilities, failed to distinguish between the shallow water-splash trough (for cars) and the deeper trough designed for lorries[2] and made an incorrect choice.

Apparently, the Singer Gazelle convertible remained afloat for an impressively long time, enabling the testers to scramble onto dry land. Then, with a gurgle, it sank out of sight in the murky water. The tank was drained, and the filthy Singer towed to the Members' Garage, where the sump was emptied and refilled with fresh oil and the electrics dried out. Remarkably, it restarted on the first turn.

Our hero Stuart then drove home in the soggy Singer with the heater turned up to max in an attempt to dry the interior out. This made the windows mist up, so he opened them. There followed a series of popping noises, as the kapok stuffing in the hood lining expanded and burst its seams, floating away along the A5 like gossamer on the breeze. Forty years on, Steady, who viewed this while sitting in a comfortably dry car behind the Gazelle, would still start crying with laughter when retelling this tale.

[1] The Motor Industry Research Association's test track, near Nuneaton.
[2] These troughs were used for cooling off during brake tests.

38 Testing, testing

METHODS OF MEASURING THE performance of cars have developed rapidly over the years. *The Motor* had begun checking and reporting on the maximum speed, acceleration and braking of cars in the 1920s, against strong opposition of the industry, but it was not until the 1970s that measuring equipment began to be more technically advanced than a set of stopwatches.

When Lawrence Pomeroy Jr[1] was Technical Editor of *The Motor* in the 1950s, according to legend, he submitted a bill for an expensive pair of high-quality saucepans which he said that he had acquired to be used for standing quarter-mile acceleration runs on a B-road somewhere, timed as usual with stopwatches. By some means, he had supposedly calculated the distance between the two shiny saucepans.

"Where," asked the Editor, examining the claim form dubiously, "are these saucepans?"

"Well, that's the funny thing," replied Pomeroy. "When we had finished our test runs, some bugger had pinched them."

The long-suffering Editor of the magazine was accustomed to Pomeroy's eccentricities. According to the late Bunny Tubbs, a staff man on *The Motor*:

"One day when the war was just over and one could move about a bit, Pom came in to find a fuming ginger-haired Editor. 'There you are, Pomeroy,' cried the Editor. 'You weren't in Thursday or Friday, you didn't turn up on Monday and you weren't here yesterday. What do you think you are paid for, I'd like to know?' Pom drew himself up on his stiff leg, screwed his monocle into his eye and surveyed his angry boss. 'It is a fact which cannot be too widely appreciated,' he drawled, 'that Pomeroy works on Wednesdays.' "

From the mid-1950s, *The Motor* and *The Autocar* were able to use the Motor Industry Test Association's facilities (see previous chapter). This brought big improvements in testing methods and consistency, for several reasons. All cars from then on were accelerated on the same surface and all, except those that were too fast, were maxed around the triangular high-speed circuit with its banked bends. The measured ¼-mile posts on the horizontal straights and the circuits were useful.

Vauxhall's testers were required to perform quite slow gearchanges when doing acceleration runs. As a result, we generally beat their 0-60mph figures by more than a second. On the other hand, their maximum speeds were always about two-to-three per cent better than ours. This was because they tested at Millbrook, which, until about 1980, was not made available to outsiders.

When I joined *Motor* in 1976, by which time it had dropped the definite article, more sophisticated methods of testing had begun to creep in. We had a fifth wheel which was clamped to the rear bumper of test cars for acceleration runs.

Initially, this had been connected to a simple speedometer, at first analogue and then digital. The tester in the passenger seat would click stopwatches as different speeds were reached – usually 30, 40, 50, 60, 70mph.

By the time of my arrival, however, the stopwatches were not used any more for acceleration runs. The cable was no longer plugged into a speedo but into a complex electromechanical box of tricks. I shall come back to that. On the other hand, for many years, stopwatches were still used for maximum speed runs.

After integrated plastic nerf panels were introduced, hiding the bumper, attaching the fifth wheel became more of a challenge. We had to detach the panels – and then put them back on, which was often far more difficult. The toughest that I recall was a Jaguar XJS.

We even had a dummy bumper fabricated, to which the fifth wheel could be easily clamped. We attached the dummy bumper to the ugly stuff behind the plastic panel by fair means or foul. Sometimes this involved drilling. I do not think the car makers ever found us out.

There were several manufacturers of these fifth wheels. Shortly before I joined the magazine, one of these had detached itself from a car being driven by Road Test Editor Gordon Bruce and flown over the barrier at the far end of the horizontal straights. There was a substantial drop to dense undergrowth below. Gordon was despatched by Technical Editor Curtis to retrieve it, but he could not find it. Perhaps it is still there.

The replacement for that wheel was from Peiseler, a German company specializing in precision equipment of various types. Dr Peiseler, the founder of the company, was still in charge in those days. He was a friendly, bespectacled chap, who always wore a white coat. He pretended to speak no English and had a woman translator who always wore a leather coat, and who looked like a prison guard. Her command of English seemed somewhat basic. Peiseler's headquarters were at that time near Munich, in a village called Dachau. Oddly, Dr Peiseler always seemed to understand what I was asking, and even laughed at my jokes, but his translator always seemed to be struggling.

A cable ran from the Peiseler wheel, tank-taped to the bodywork on the way to stop it from flapping about, to a large, very heavy electro-mechanical box of tricks, also from Peiseler, which we put on the floor on the front passenger side of the car. This was powered off the test car's battery, and it produced a printed read-out on a roll of graphite paper.

Then Peiseler made our job much easier in two ways: the wheel could now be attached to cars by suction clamps, as mentioned in the previous chapter, and the recorder became fully electronic, smaller and far lighter.

However, for maximum speed runs at MIRA – and later at Millbrook – we still used old-fashioned stopwatches. And they were truly old-fashioned – Heuer mechanical analogue stopwatches. But they were accurate and it was not difficult, using the windscreen A-pillar, to click at exactly the right moment.

These five stopwatches were set into the top of a splendid stopwatch board, below which there was a sprung clip for holding the A4-sized printed test sheets. This board had been constructed by Maurice Rowe, who had a high level of woodworking skill and an inventive mind, as well as being an ace photographer.

The tester in the passenger seat would click the first watch to start at one of the quarter-mile posts and then after slicking to stop that watch at the same post after a lap, would click the start the next one at the next quarter-mile post. And so on.

In the 1990s, new technology allowed testers to conduct tests of all aspects of performance without any external attachments. Devices such as the VBOX, using GPS (Global Positioning System) allowed absolute accuracy, but at a very high purchase price.

All the testers I ever knew far preferred thrashing around test tracks or racing circuits to the laborious business of recording performance figures.

---

[1] 'Pom' was Technical Editor of *The Motor* from 1936 until 1958. He was the son of LH Pomeroy (1883-1941), the distinguished Vauxhall engineer, responsible for the 'Prince Henry' and the 30/98.

39 Have you done this kind of thing often?

A USEFUL AND ENJOYABLE annual event was the SMMT (Society of Motor Manufacturers and Traders) Test Day, which took place in late spring. The first few that I attended were at Silverstone. Then it was moved to Donington Park, and, after that, to the Millbrook test facility in Bedfordshire.

Nearly all indigenous manufacturers and importers attended, bringing along all or most of their model ranges. Occasionally, there would be an interesting new car that nobody had driven previously, and this caused a mad rush to get on the list to try it. But mostly, it was an excellent opportunity for provincial journalists to sample all sorts of cars that they might otherwise not have a crack at, while, for people like me, it had other advantages.

In the late 1970s and throughout the 1980s, I probably drove 100 different cars per year, but there were always a few interesting machines that I had missed, and the SMMT gave the opportunity to fill in the gaps, and to reassess cars that one had driven in different circumstances: for example, if it had rained incessantly during the loan period. There were options of driving cars on the circuit or on surrounding roads. Also, of course, it was just a lot of fun hacking around a race track in different cars for several hours.

There were surprisingly few accidents over the years; none involving serious injury. Probably the most spectacular crash was achieved by Leonard Setright (see Chapter 7), who managed to cartwheel a Jaguar XJ12 into a ball of scrap at Silverstone. The bend at which this occurred, the old Club Corner, I think, was evidently insufficiently fast for his sublime talent. I understand that he then harangued the Jaguar engineers, explaining that they had got their spring and damper setting wrong.

One fine May day in the 1980s, I arrived early at Donington armed with a list of cars that I wished to drive. After signing in, however, I was briefly distracted. I noticed a rather remarkable blonde girl, wearing a bikini top, tight pink hotpants and tall red stilettos, beside a car with a large sign announcing that this was the place for demonstrations of the Removatop sunroof. Along with many others that day, I discovered an interest in after-market sunroofs of which I had hitherto been unaware. I got her to do her routine, took a deep breath, and then went off to work my way through my list.

A couple of hours later, I was about to get into a BMW 3-Series when the blonde came over. She said it was her break, and wondered if I'd be prepared to drive her, because she had never previously been to a race circuit and was curious to know what it was like. I told her to hop in.

We set off from the paddock into the pit lane, and then I was waved through onto the track. We squealed through the first right-hander, Redgates, in third gear. From there it is 'flat' in most cars, including that BMW, all the way down to 'The Old Hairpin,' which is not really a hairpin in the usually-accepted sense, but a right-hand bend of slightly more than 90 degrees. Yes, the Craner Curves are flat, but this is surprising to those who have not been there before, because it is pretty well blind. First there is a wide-radius right and then a tighter left where the descent becomes suddenly steeper.

As we came through the second part of this, which is nearly-but-not-quite like falling off a cliff, a squeaky voice from my left stuttered, "H-h-have you d-d-done this kind of thing often?"

As I braked hard for the Old Hairpin, I looked across to my left and realized that my passenger had become very tense. The blood had drained from her face, her arms had gone rigid, she was gripping the seat at each side, and she had that rabbit-in–the-headlights expression.

I gave her my practised leer and remarked, "I bet you ask all the boys that." She calmed down after that, and even seemed to enjoy the experience after a couple of laps.

The splendidly eccentric Lord Strathcarron[1] used to take Perry, his beloved parrot, to the SMMT Test Day. Perry's cage would be wedged into the passenger footwell or, if David had a passenger, strapped onto the rear seat.

Sometimes, particularly powerful cars were available for passenger rides only, piloted by professional racers. On one such occasion, the driver was Beppe Gabbiani who asked, while I was strapping myself into the harness, "OK. You wanna that I go fast or fucking fast?" I replied that he might as well make it fucking fast. And he did.

I was disappointed when the SMMT transferred its Test Day from Donington to Millbrook, even though it was more convenient for me to drive to. Within the test facility there is an excellent test circuit which used to be called the Outer Handling Track because there was once an Inner Handling Track.

They were both quite short, with lap times of well under 45 seconds. They were like typical English country lanes, and were useful for testing braking and handling: the outer with some fast corners, the inner much tighter. The inner was transformed into a boring stop-start thing for checking fuel consumption in something approximating to the real world, and there were too many drivers attending the Test Day for it to be practical to use the outer handling track.

Instead, the Hill Route was used. I never liked that much: it had some quite good bends on it, and, in places, was a bit like an Alpine road, but one or two of the bends were unlike anything I have encountered on real roads. I recall entering one of them that was tight and with an absurdly sharp brow, and all I could see over the bonnet of the Aston Martin that I was driving was the sky, for several seconds.

One of the good bends was a medium-speed downhill right-hander. On my first run on a Test Day, I came into this as I had done on many occasions in private testing, braked, changed down into third, turned in sharply and gave it some throttle. A marshal jumped out, angrily waving at me to slow down.

He did the same thing on the next lap, and on the one after that. This time, I was waved down at the top of the following hill by a chap who turned out to be the Chief Marshal. I opened the window and nearly said, "Aren't you Steve Parrish[2]?" I am sure that I identified him correctly.

He told me that his marshal at the bottom of the hill had complained that I was going into the bend too fast. I said, "Well, you can tell the anal-retentive little twat that if he jumps out again I may not take the trouble to miss him." Steve Parrish, if it was Steve Parrish, laughed, but then started to explain the job he had been given. I interrupted him and said, "Look, no hard feelings, but if it's going to be like that, I'll stick to the road route," which is what I did from then on.

[1] David William Anthony Blyth Macpherson, 2nd Baron Strathcarron (1924-2006).
[2] Former professional motorcycle racer and truck racer. British Superbike Champion 1981. He once owned a car with the registration PEN 15.

40 Look – no hands!

THE SPEED AROUND MILLBROOK'S bowl – a circular track with five lanes, the uppermost of which has a circumference of 2.03 miles – rarely bothered car testers, provided that speed was not much above 160mph. It was fear that the heavily-loaded front right tyre might explode that concerned us. The general rule was to raise the tyre pressures by a few psi, do a warming-up lap, two flying laps, a slowing-down lap and then get the hell out of there.

My fastest Millbrook lap was just above 165mph, which I achieved in three or four cars. I remember someone else in the 1980s doing a lap at over 175 in something more grunty and feeling impressed but not remotely envious, just thinking about that front right tyre. Once a colleague and I, having maxed an Aston Martin, found that a patch of rubber three inches across had half-detached itself from the sidewall, unusually from the right rear. I informed the Avon Tyre company about this. The Avon Tyre company expressed no surprise.

Tyre loadings in a quick car at maximum speed around a banked circuit are *far* higher than anything likely to be encountered in fast road driving, even if there were no speed limits, and far higher, consistently, than might be generated by driving on a racing circuit.

A banked track has something called a 'neutral-steer speed,' colloquially and aptly known as the 'hands-off speed,' at which the driver can take his hands off the steering wheel and the car will maintain its trajectory without adjustment. It's spooky the first time, but not half as spooky as going around a banked track at maximum speed in a quick car the first time. I used to enjoy subjecting new recruits to that introduction.

Sitting at an angle of more than 21 degrees to the vertical at over 160mph, it feels as if your internal organs are being pulled skywards by some invisible force (as indeed they are, in a sense[1]). Being rather tall, I tended to duck my head to get the fullest view of the event horizon to which one was heading as if a curved zip were being undone at something over 230 feet per second. It was vital to see as far ahead as possible because at 160-plus you would very rapidly catch up with a car toodling along at only 100mph[2]. Also, I always thought that the limit of vision on the banked curve would be just about where one would end up if something went badly wrong *HERE*. Aaaaaaargh!

I had previously verified the neutral-steer speed (86mph) at MIRA, and I did the same one day at Millbrook, where it was 100mph in Lane 5. I folded my arms and did about half a lap (carefully watching the rear-view mirror) before becoming officially bored and deciding it was lunchtime. A couple of distinguished motoring hacks of my acquaintance went further than this. No names, no pack drill; let's call them 'Steven' and 'Colin.'

They had maxed a Rolls-Royce, and were cruising back to the exit from the Bowl, when the conversation turned to the hands-off speed and Colin said to Steven, let's check that. Steven said, that's a good idea and set the cruise control at 103mph, a genuine hundred. The car maintained its course, neither climbing higher nor descending.

After half a lap of this, the novelty was wearing off and Steven said to Colin, "You know, we could sit in the back of this barge and it would drive itself around like this on automatic pilot for a couple of hours until it ran out of petrol or got stuffed up the arse by some inattentive shitbag in a supercar."

After a moment's reflection, Colin, marginally the less responsible and undoubtedly the more imaginative of the two, replied, "I bet it could … let's try it. All the other testers have gone to lunch."

So they removed the head restraints and clambered towards the rear seats, first Colin and then Steven, and sat in the back[3]. The car continued serenely on its path. But electronic systems can be mysteriously temperamental. Even on expensive cars, they can suddenly switch themselves off, for no apparent reason. Two-thirds of the way around the lap, that was what occurred. The cruise control system abruptly downed tools, the throttle faded away and the Roller, losing speed, began moving steadily leftwards in a stately downward trajectory.

"Shit! Grab the wheel!" shouted Steven, the more responsible of the two. Colin hurled down the newspaper that he had been casually reading and leaned forward. He managed to steer the car on a more or less straight course by observing the dotted lane lines, but could not see where it was heading. Meanwhile, Steven scrambled as fast as he could into the front passenger seat, took over the wheel and moved across into the driver's seat. They never tried that experiment again. Explaining the circumstances of this to Rolls-Royce Motors in the event of an accident would have required some creative thinking, but they had previous experience of that.

[1] In fact, it is more complex than that. Your stomach, kidneys, liver, spleen and all the other bits wish to go straight ahead, resisting the centripetal force. ('Centrifugal force,' like phlogiston, does not exist.)
[2] Most testers at Millbrook were alert and would drop down the banking as soon as they saw a faster car, headlights ablaze, catching them, but occasionally it was necessary to abort the high-speed run. We always notified Control by short-wave radio when this happened and Control then delivered a preliminary dressing-down to the miscreant and an invitation to visit Control's office, which provided some entertaining listening.
[3] Not being very safety-conscious, they neglected to fasten their safety belts, which was probably a fortunate decision.

41 Brake fade

ONE OF THE MOST enjoyable and instructive parts of working for *Motor* was the two-day, four-car group test to Wales, which had been introduced several years earlier by the Editor who hired me, Roger Bell.

These exercises always operated to the same format, though they were always memorable in different ways. The first day began when three writers and a photographer assembled for breakfast, usually at the Toddington service station on the M1.

From there, we would head west on a variety of challenging A and B roads. Roughly every hour, we would stop at the roadside, scribble some notes, and swap cars. There was no better way to assess competing cars. Usually on the first day, we would get some photos in the bag, if it was not raining too much. It was vital to do this on a fine day, because, if the Sun was shining, that was usually an indication that it would tip down the following day. Also, there was the possibility that somebody might crash one of the cars, though that hardly ever happened.

This was long before the days of mobile telephones. We did not drive in a tight convoy. Each driver went at his own chosen speed and we arranged ourselves carefully in descending order of speediness. But it was essential to avoid losing touch with each other. We had a system that was foolproof, or nearly.

Whoever was in charge of the test, the quickest driver but not necessarily the one in charge of writing the test[1] set off first and he was responsible for the following driver, who was responsible for the driver behind him, and so on. The rule was that if you came to a Stop sign or if you were turning off onto a side road, you stopped and waited. Likewise, it was the team leader's decision when to stop for a car change.

The sole occasion when this went wrong, in my experience, was when the first three of us had pulled into a layby and waited for the fourth car. This was driven by a new recruit. He came past us, not noticing the three cars, or the three of us jumping up and down and waving our arms. Gordon the Road Test Editor took off after him, but got stuck behind a lorry and returned to the layby with his aura in flames.

Eventually, after about half an hour or so, the young chap reached a T junction and, not seeing a car parked at the roadside waiting for him, vaguely remembered the instructions that he had been given. He telephoned the office and a secretary gave him the terse message that Gordon had sent from a phone box. He returned to the layby to receive an almighty bollocking. He was almost fired on the spot. It turned out that he was a hi-fi maniac and had been adjusting the woofers or tweeters of the car's stereo system, and had not been paying much attention to anything else.

After that, whenever I was the leader on a group test, which was on all those I took part in after Greenslade had left the magazine, I gave severe instructions to the other drivers to leave the radio/cassette player off. For one thing, part of the assessment process was listening to engine and transmission noise and road roar. "You are not here," I would point out, "to assess the radio/cassette player or the speakers," adding gerundive emphasis.

Our route passed through a fine swathe of old England – we passed through Buckingham, Aynho, Deddington, Chipping Norton, Stow-on-the-Wold, Tewkesbury, Ledbury and Ludlow. The most challenging section was shortly after this, the winding descent from Clun towards Newton, in Powys, which is very much like an Alpine pass, with a mixture of tight- and medium-speed bends, shedding a lot of altitude en route to the valley.

This was as tough a test of brakes as could be found anywhere in Britain. On one occasion, we were comparing four two-litre coupés with sporty pretentions: a Ford Capri, a Toyota Celica, a Vauxhall Cavalier, and a Volkswagen Scirocco.

On the outward journey, I was in the Capri following team leader Rex Greenslade in the Cavalier, and I was managing to stay within a few lengths of him. The other two were some miles behind us. The idea of these exercises was to compare the cars rather than to have a road race. Nevertheless, there was always a competitive element to it.

About halfway down the hill, probably at the point that one passes from England into Wales, the Ford's rather feeble brakes gave up the struggle, succumbing to severe fade. The pedal went straight to the floor and I had a long, scary moment, pumping hard to restore some pressure and hurling the car sideways into a left-hander to scrub off some speed.

My heartbeat gradually returning to normal, I then cruised gently down the rest of the hill to the junction with the A489. There I found Greenslade in ostentatious pose. He was leaning against the Vauxhall's front wing and pretending to read *The Daily Telegraph*. I parked behind him and switched off the ignition, leaving the car in first gear rather than applying the handbrake.

I got out of the car. Rex looked at me and asked sarcastically, "What kept you, old chap?"

I was beginning to explain what had happened when we noticed a nasty odour. Then we saw smoke wisping out from the Capri's front wheel arch. And it is true that there is no smoke without fire. We could see a flame an inch high above the pads. Greenslade rolled up his newspaper and gave the wheel a smart smack. Surprisingly, this put the fire out. But a few seconds later the flame popped up again, like a pilot light.

Greenslade's firefighting method was clearly flawed, so I leapt into the car and drove up the main road to the east for five minutes. I returned to the T junction, stopped, got out … and the pads instantly lit up again, so I repeated the procedure. This time it worked. Our two colleagues having caught up, we continued on our way towards our overnight halt, a splendid hotel with a very good restaurant on the edge of Lake Vyrnwy.

On the return journey the next morning, once again I was following Greenslade closely, but along a very different stretch of road, near Tewkesbury. It was a long series of curves with such clear visibility that they could be taken more or less in a straight line. At one point we flashed past a Rover SD1 with four men in it. Rex and I were flat out in top gear, at about 115mph. I noticed some signwriting on the driver's door of the Rover: 'BRITISH LEYLAND SCHOOL OF HIGH-PERFORMANCE MOTORING.'

I did the trip to Wales about once a month for several years, and on every occasion it rained either on the outward journey or on the return, sometimes both. The only accident I recall was when photographer Maurice Rowe went off through a hedge in the Welsh borders, avoiding a tractor that had pulled out of a field directly in front of him.

[1] *Motor*'s tests were all collective efforts. Each was written by one person, incorporating the notes of all the other testers. There were often long arguments before the final text was sent off to the printers. Greenslade and I occasionally ended up raising our voices. Then we would adjourn to the pub.

42 Insurance claims

FROM TIME TO TIME, the insurance industry cunningly promotes itself by issuing a collection of strange and often barely credible claims submitted by customers hoping for compensation after a mishap. One of my favourites is, 'Vehicle damaged on safari park outing by rhinoceros named George.' It's the detail that counts.

Filling in insurance claim forms was an inevitability when one worked on a motoring magazine. For example, on *Motor*, we had more than a hundred cars in for test every year, as well as our own long-term test cars. I should think the magazine's staff exceeded 300,000 miles annually, to which I generally contributed more than 40,000. There was bound to be the odd biff and bump.

The two weirdest claims I can recall both involved Jaguars, and both could be described as passive accidents, in that the person behind the wheel did not cause them. Indeed, in each instance, the vehicle was stationary when the damage occurred.

Before handing back test cars to delivery drivers, we always topped up the fuel tanks and, unless it was raining, we put the cars through the automatic car wash in Throwley Way, Sutton, down the hill from our offices in Surrey House.

On one occasion three of us were performing the vehicular ablutions. The first car had gone through the machine. The second car was a Jaguar XJS coupé, and I was sitting a few feet behind it, waiting my turn in the third car.

The horizontal top wheel of the car wash spun noisily over the Jaguar's long bonnet, but then it hesitated and stopped. I could see why. The dangly fronds of the top wheel, whatever they are called, had become tangled in that handsome aluminium grille that runs across the XJS, just forward of the base of the windscreen. This component serves as a ventilation intake and the windscreen wiper spindles and washers are also located in it. I was curious to see what would happen next. I did not have to wait long to find out.

The immense torque of the autowash's top roller predictably won the day. The aluminium grille was wrenched out of the Jaguar. The roller resumed its rotation and headed in a southerly direction towards the boot. It was still clinging tenaciously to the heavy aluminium grille, which it thumped violently on the roof and then the bootlid, before hurling it rearwards, causing some damage that would require the services of one of Brown's Lanes panel beaters. The grille missed the roof of the car I was sitting in by a few inches, and crashed loudly into the wall behind me. Since that day, I have never used an automatic car wash, even for cars that I did not own.

Several years later, a few miles away in Croydon on a very blustery day, I was sitting in a Jaguar XJ6 in a queue of traffic, waiting for the lights to change, when suddenly the sky fell in on my head, as in the tragic tale of Chicken Licken. Well, of course it did not, really, but it sounded as if it had. Something solid had hit the roof of the Jag with an extremely loud bang directly above my head.

I stepped out to investigate. There was an indentation, approximately eight inches long and half an inch wide and deep, directly above the driver's seat. I was wondering what might have caused the damage when I spotted some pieces of broken roof tile lying in the gutter. Two and two made four. If I had been sitting in a convertible, I would have been unable to complete the sum.

The next morning, I telephoned Jaguar's press office and explained what had happened. The press officer told me not to worry, and said that she would send me an insurance form. I described the incident exactly as above. I even enclosed a drawing of a Jaguar XJ6, a large Victorian house, and a falling roof tile.

About a week later, the woman in Jaguar's press department rang me. "We've received your insurance form, Peter," she said. "And that's fine, but, um ..."

"But what?" I asked.

"Well," she said, "we'd like to know what *really* happened. We're running a book on it." She was not joking, and she sounded disappointed when I failed to offer an alternative explanation. Sometimes it is difficult to persuade people to believe the plain, unvarnished truth.

43 By Bentley around Europe

AFTER THE WALL STREET crash wiped away much of the fortune of the remarkable Woolf Barnato[1] (who had previously kept Bentley afloat), Rolls-Royce had, through crafty sleight of hand (to put it euphemistically), snatched the ailing company from within the (probably more sympathetic) grasp of Napier: Bentley cars were nothing but shameless examples of 'badge engineering' for 50 years. The Mulsanne Turbo was the first step towards recreating Bentley's separate identity[2].

I had vaguely suggested to Pluspenis[3] that we should do something with the Mulsanne Turbo other than an ordinary road test. A while later, he invited me to lunch and introduced me to Gadzooks[4], a prematurely bald Anglo-Italian journalist who had proposed driving a Mulsanne Turbo to all ten capitals of what was then called the European Economic Community[5]. During an excellent lunch, forgetting to ask why, I unwisely said that I was up for that.

One Sunday morning at crack of dawn I found myself at the Rolls-Royce/Bentley showroom in Conduit Street in the company of Gadzooks, R-R service engineer Dave, and John from Avon Tyres, who stepped in at the last moment to replace a journalist, whom I never met, who had been severely injured in a motorcycle accident. We set off towards Holyhead with minimal luggage crammed into a boot also containing four spare petrol cans, an extra spare wheel, a trolley jack, sundry spares, and a sealed tachograph. It takes some skill to fill the boot of a Bentley, but we managed it.

We had a full set of maps and highly-detailed route instructions from a chap at the RAC, who had meticulously calculated distances and possible average speeds, making particular note of timings of the four return ferry crossings that would be necessary[6].

I cannot remember why, but we stopped after only 5.6 miles to fill up with fuel, appropriately in Cricklewood, very near where Bentleys were manufactured in the 1920s when the company was independent.

The plan was to go first to Dublin, then to Amsterdam, Copenhagen, Rome, Athens, Paris, Luxembourg, Bonn (Germany's capital until the Wall came down), Brussels and then back to London. We took it in turns to drive, map-read, and attempt to catch a nap.

Everything went well until shortly after midday on Day Three. We were ahead of schedule, Gadzooks at the wheel, flat out on the autostrada north of Bologna. He suddenly slowed and pulled onto the hard shoulder. I thought that we were being pulled up by the Carabinieri rozzers, but, when I looked round, I saw only a cloud of smoke. The power steering pump had overheated, a pipe fractured, and all the fluid disappeared into the famously clean air of Emilia Romagna.

We cruised into Bologna, Gadzooks reporting that the steering had become very heavy minus assistance. We arrived at the premises of the local R-R agent, who also expertly resurrected rotting old Ferraris and Maseratis. It would have been a fun place to visit in other circumstances. The Bentley was raised on a hoist. Dave and John spent a long time fiddling about, achieving little apart from burning their hands and wrists.

Time flew by. We had a ferry to catch, 487 road miles to the south. Eventually we decided to press on. I was assigned the task of going for it. I thought there was little chance of reaching Brindisi in time to catch the ferry to Igoumenitsu in Greece, but I tried hard. The average speed for the journey was just over 90mph, though the rain was belting down, and the unassisted steering was unimaginably heavy. The sun came out in Apulia. We arrived in Brindisi just in time to see our ferry 'steaming' out of the harbour.

The 24-hour wait for the next one ruined our schedule, but at least allowed us a night in a hotel, which was a dump, but which seemed like luxury after all that time on the road.

Another Rolls-Royce engineer, with a box of spare parts, was flown out to Athens, and he and Dave spent ages, to no avail, attempting to put the system back in working order. In the end, we drove over 3900 miles without power assistance. Nevertheless, we completed our mission, and arrived back in Conduit Street after 6243.8 road miles at an average speed of 40.1mph. (The running average was approximately 70mph ...)

Looking on the bright side, we did some useful development work for Rolls-Royce/ Bentley. After relatively simple under-bonnet modifications, production versions of the turbocharged Bentleys did not fry the power steering. The company's test drivers had perhaps not driven the car flat out in high ambient temperatures for sufficient distances to encounter this problem. It's only when you drive like a German that you find out things like that[7].

I slept for about 12 hours when I got home. At least none of us had fallen asleep at the wheel.

[1] Besides being Bentley's major shareholder, Woolf Barnato (1895-1948) was its leading racing driver (the most highly regarded by 'WO'), winning the Le Mans 24 Hours race three times in a row, 1928-1930. He was unrelated to Leonard Woolf and, unlike Toto Wolff, the Mercedes-Benz executive, was not named after Dorothy's little dog in *The Wizard of Oz*.

[2] However, there was no expectation at that time that the two marques would become as separate as they are today ... and especially not that one part of the manufacturer whose engines powered Spitfires, Hurricanes, Mosquitos, Lancasters, etc, would be owned by the company whose engines powered Messerschmitts and Heinkels, while the other (which had produced the Sopwith Camel's rotary engines in the First World War) would belong to a rival German company, whose engines were used in Fock-Wulfs and Stukas.

[3] Ian Adcock, a journalist who for a while posed as a motor industry press relations man, often supplied me with cigars after I gave up smoking definitively (other people's cigarettes and cigars don't count). All motor industry PR people have nicknames. For example, Ken Cannell of Ford was 'Fur,' Wayne Bruce, who worked for SEAT, Volkswagen and Nissan before joining McLaren, is 'Manbat.' N Barrington 'Barry' Needham of Alfa Romeo was 'that arsehole.'

[4] Richard Gadeselli, who went on to be a big wheel within the Fiat machine. He is now Dottore Ingegneri Cavaliere Gadeselli. Doff your caps, and keep behind the barriers when he passes, riff-raff.

[5] Anyone considering such an exercise would be well advised to wait until the EU has shrunk back to more manageable size.

[6] Holyhead-Dun Laoghaire, Dover-Calais, Puttgarden-Rodbyhavn, Brindisi-Igoumenitsu. Brindisi, supposedly in 'the heel' of Italy, is in fact where the tube will be attached if an enema is required.

[7] Also, an excellent chassis engineer joined the company from Ford, and the springs and dampers were considerably stiffened. The Turbo R, which succeeded the Mulsanne Turbo, had a far stiffer shell and was a nice car. You can pick them up quite cheaply now. But then you have to pay for the running costs.

44 Asleep at the wheel

UNTIL DECEMBER 1980 I was rather cockily confident that *other people* fell asleep at the wheel, but not *me*. I was 31 years old, fit and healthy, despite smoking a packet of Gauloises per day.

On a Saturday, I flew to Nice Airport and spent that night at the Mas d'Artigny hotel, near Saint Paul de Vence. The next morning, I set off back to Blighty. The drive to Calais, about 750 miles, was quite demanding, especially in the early stages on the Route Napoleon. The sun shone brightly, but the temperature was low in the Alps and there were snow-covered sections and icy patches.

I would have liked to stop for the night in Paris, but I had deadlines to meet for *Motor* magazine: test the car on Monday, process the figures on Tuesday, complete the copy by Wednesday.

I arrived home in Sussex late on Sunday night, and set off at 6am on Monday to drive the 150 miles to MIRA (near Nuneaton), where colleagues and I did the figures on three cars: maximum speeds, acceleration, brake-fade tests, and all manner of other stuff that I always suspected was of interest only to schoolboys of the trainspotting tendency. We were so busy that day, we did not have time for lunch at The Oddfellows Arms.

Also, we had been delayed because one of the Fuego's headlamps, held in place by a cheapjack spring/slot system, typical of rubbish Renaults of that era, had popped out and destroyed itself, so I had to hang around and wait for a man from Renault to deliver a replacement. I was told later that every Fuego on that press launch lost at least one headlamp. However, worse was to follow …

By mid-afternoon, only the most tedious test remained on the Fuego: steady speed fuel consumption. This involved fitting a fiddly device between fuel pump and carburettor[1] and doing a three-mile lap of the high-speed track at every 10mph increment from 30mph to 100mph. This procedure always seemed to take forever.

The banked curves of the anti-clockwise 'high-speed' circuit were lined in that era with two steel hawsers linked by vertical wooden posts, spaced at 8ft intervals. At 80mph, which felt like walking pace, I fell asleep at the wheel. Instead of entering a banked turn, the Fuego struck the first wooden post amidships. It was either the impact, or the terrified scream of my passenger that woke me. I clearly recall the sensation of having been 'beamed down' into someone else's accident.

I was still attempting to steer, pointlessly of course, after the steel hawsers had ripped out the linkage, as well as the exhaust system and whatever else it could remove from the underside of the car within the time available. The Renault finally came to rest at the top of the banking. I got out gingerly, as there was a 30ft drop on my side. My co-pilot Howard Walker got out gingerly, too, and we both slid down the steep banking onto the infield.

I had knocked down 36 of those vertical wooden posts, which was apparently a MIRA record at the time, though it did not stand for long. A couple of Rolls-Royce testers were lapping in close convoy at over 120mph a few weeks later when the lead car shed part of its exhaust system, which disabled the steering of the second car.

I felt surprisingly calm as we were transported back to the Control Tower, which was much as it had been when the place was a relief bomber airfield during the war. I telephoned the office to inform the Technical Editor, Rex Greenslade that we urgently needed another Fuego for photographs. While I was explaining why, Rex cackled with laughter. It was only then that I realized I was in shock: I could not stop the hand holding the receiver from shaking.

I have been ultra-careful about drowsiness ever since, but whenever I was going for it, there was no likelihood of dozing off.

[1] We were all delighted when the advent of fuel injection with high-pressure fuel systems rendered our steady-speed consumption tests impossible.

45 Dee-dah, dee-dah

I HAD LIFTED MY foot slightly from the throttle the previous occasion I had approached this tricky downhill S-bend in the Mazda, but, thinking about it afterwards, I was sure it could be taken flat. So here I was, in experimental mood, on a traffic-free A23, with the sun recently set on a balmy July evening in 1980, flat out, full throttle. I was about to put my theory to the test. With the benefit of a long run-up, the speedometer was indicating 138mph.

In fact, I was probably doing at least 10mph less than that. Following the advice and assistance of Dunlop, I had recently had the wheels and tyres changed on the RX-7[1]. The replacement wheels were of slightly larger diameter than standard and, although the new tyres were lower in profile, the overall result was an increased radius. This might have mildly raised the maximum speed, especially downhill, but not by a significant margin.

Without any suspension modifications, this change of equipment gave better precision, much improved transient behaviour, and enhanced grip, especially on wet roads. However, I had not bothered to have the speedo recalibrated, so what had previously been a small exaggeration of velocity became gross. Even so, I was undoubtedly tonking along at something over 120mph in a 70 limit, and, even in those days, one could get into serious trouble with The Law for that kind of thing.

I turned gently into the first left-hand curve, and then eased the wheel to the right, making use of the entire two-lane width of the dual carriageway. The indicated speed did not drop, any mild scrub-off being compensated for by the steep downhill gradient.

I was just thinking how serenely easy it all was, with no need to lift off or to make steering corrections, when I noticed the jam sandwich in the feed lane from Handcross on the left. No sooner had I noticed it than I also noticed that the team had turned on the blue flashing light on the roof. They were in pursuit mode, and I was the hare. The experimental science part of the episode, though successful, had ended abruptly.

I had a head start. After the esses, the A23 ran dead straight for a mile before my turn-off onto the B2115 towards Cuckfield, where I lived at the time. Straight, but not level: there were two steep hills with a deep dip between them. At the bottom of the dip there was a farm track to the left and I happened to know that the farm belonged to a Mrs Palmer, who was the mother of racing driver Dr Jonathan Palmer[2].

I was Jonathan's personal fitness coach at that time. Once a week we would play squash. I would stand on the T at the centre of the court, and he would run around all over the place getting red-faced and rather cross. Grand Prix drivers hate losing, whatever they are doing. He then became even crosser ... while he was drinking one of those repulsive isotonic substances, I would put away a pint of Harvey's and smoke a Gauloise.

I had a few moments between the S-bend and the farm track to make some rapid calculations. If I took my usual turn-off or continued southwards, I was worried that I might get caught in traffic, or that my pursuers could radio ahead and trap me. So that left Option Three.

As I descended from the first hilltop, I slammed on the brakes and, in the dip, I swung the car violently to the left, switched off the lights and accelerated hard up the farm track. A few seconds later, in the mirror I observed the police Rover, blue light flashing away, blasting past, its siren blaring. I expect they went all the way to Brighton. Dee-dah, dee-dah, where did that bastard go? Those were the days.

You cannot do that any more for several reasons, one of them being that the road layout has been ripped up and is totally altered. Perhaps I set the all-time record for speed through that S-bend. Besides, these days, the odds are stacked against the hare and in favour of the hunting dogs.

Mrs Palmer was surprised to see me. I told her casually that I was on the run from the police. She said, "Oh dear. Well, you'd better have a cup of tea, young man."

If I had taken on James Hunt at squash, the result would have been the other way round: he would have been standing on the T, and I would have been chasing vainly after the ball. At least after the game we would both have drunk beer and smoked cigarettes.

[1] Mazda's claimed top speed for the car was 200km/h (124.3mph). *Motor's* test, conducted at the MIRA test track, gave a maximum of 117.4mph, the lower figure resulting partly from the banked circuit and perhaps partly from an engine that was not fully run in. The RX-7, introduced in 1978, was part of Mazda's decades-long struggle to overcome the combustion inefficiency of the elegant Wankel rotary engine: a valiant but doomed project.

[2] Palmer, born 1956, took part in 88 Grands Prix between 1983 and 1989, his best result a fourth place. He enjoyed more success in sportscar racing and later in 'touring cars,' before becoming a big wheel in British motor sport as Chief Executive of the company that owns Brands Hatch, Oulton Park, Snetterton, Cadwell Park, and so on.

46 What should I talk about?

IN EARLY 1993, WHILE walking upstairs in the Royal Automobile Club in Pall Mall, I crossed the path of James Hunt. He was heading for the dungeons to play squash.

He said cheerily, "Hello, Peter, what are you doing here?" I told him that I was on my way to a committee meeting of the Guild of Motoring Writers. He said, "Oh, isn't that full of old farts?" I replied that he must have been misinformed, because I was its Chairman.

I had recently, to my surprise and dismay, assumed this honorary post[1], which turned out to be harder work, and to entail far more hassle, than I had anticipated. The worst bit was having to deliver a speech at the annual dinner in December.

I dislike giving speeches, but, on several occasions over the years, I have been obliged to do so. The speech at the Guild dinner was the greatest ordeal, in front of over 200 people – journalists, motor industry press officers, racing drivers and engineers, and so on.

I decided that my speech should be impromptu, so I began preparing it six months in advance, updating it as things came to mind. During this period, to the shock and sorrow, especially, of all who knew him well, James Hunt died suddenly, aged just 45. I cannot recall whether it was because of this or purely coincidental that the Guest of Honour at that year's 'black tie' Guild dinner was Alexander, Lord Hesketh.

Guests for the top table with me were mostly selected by the Committee[2]. That year, apart from Lord Hesketh and Chairman Me, they included the Guild's Driver of the Year Damon Hill[3] and his wife, plus Peter Wheeler, proprietor of TVR. The Guild Chairman was allowed two personal guests, and I chose Raymond Baxter, the famous ex-broadcaster, because I correctly thought he would be amusing company, and my friend, Andrew English (a former colleague on *Fast Lane* magazine, later to become Motoring Correspondent of *The Daily Telegraph*).

Lord Hesketh arrived a little late, just as we were sitting down. He was full of apologies: for being late, and for having a fever (sweat was pouring from his brow), and he also apologized because he was going to have to rush off for a vital vote in 'The House' (he was at that time Government Chief Whip in the House of Lords) at about 9pm. He added that I should not worry, because his chauffeur was waiting outside and would get him back rapidly. But of course, I did worry.

As announced, Hesketh left just before nine o'clock. A few minutes before I was due to make my speech, I went outside the dining room and had a shot of malt from my hip flask, which helped. It all went better than I had feared. I had a sympathetic audience, and they laughed politely at my off-the-cuff jokes.

I had just resumed my seat when Alexander Hesketh returned, still sweating profusely. He mopped his brow and sat down to my left. He apologized again and asked, "What do you think I should talk about?"

I thought, oh shit, this is going to be a total disaster. I said, er, well, you could talk about being boss of one of the last of the privateer Grand Prix teams, what it was like working with James, maybe about your time as a motorbike manufacturer …

He scribbled a few notes and then he was summoned to the dais. Without once removing those scribbled notes from his pocket, he spoke for about ten minutes. He was fluent, funny, informative, moving … in short, brilliant. Some bastards just do that kind of stuff naturally.

[1] Among the members of the Guild I had and still have many friends. However, I resigned my membership in 2009. I received an e-mail asking if I meant that I wished to be transferred to the 'Retired' list and replied, thank you, no, I wish to resign.

[2] This was going to be a spectacular name-dropping paragraph, but I have forgotten a couple of people who were there. It's still quite impressive, though.

[3] Damon had won three Grands Prix that year, his first season with Williams-Renault, finishing third in the Championship. He is perhaps the most underrated World Champion of all.

47 Mr Plod takes a dip

I HAD KNOWN JAMES HUNT since 1968, when he raced in Formula Ford against my brother. He was one of the most extraordinary people I have ever met. He had the combination of exceptional ability[1] and fierce ambition that is essential for success in motor racing. As is well known, he also knew how to have fun.

James would not fit into the Formula 1 scene these days and was on the edge of being anachronistic even in the 1970s. He was more like a 1950s racer, and one could easily imagine him in the company of Mike Hawthorn and Peter Collins.

I attended a party with James in Harrow-on-the-Hill during the long hot summer of 1976[2]. This, of course, was James' championship year, as featured in the fantasy film *Rush*, and he was already a superstar. It was a few weeks before Lauda's dramatic near-death experience at the Nürburgring.

I cannot remember who the host was, but it was a most convivial evening, held on a large terrace at one end of a vast swimming pool. Delicious snacks kept appearing from somewhere. Musical entertainment was provided mainly by the genial Guyanese calypso singer Cy Grant and by some excellent rhythm and/or blues records, when he was taking a break.

The volume was not excessively, rave-like loud. Nevertheless, at about 1am, two policemen arrived, saying that there had been a complaint about the noise. This, of course, was Ploddese for, 'We were passing, heard some music and thought we'd blag a free drink.' Within a couple of minutes, they were socialising, soon realizing that there were some interesting people at the party.

One of the coppers was at the poolside with James and me. He started recounting his thrilling career chasing speeding motorists. Only one, it seemed had got away. This had occurred a couple of years earlier, when he was stationed in Surrey, on the other side of London.

"We were parked on the bypass around midnight and this white Mustang came past, doing well over the ton, heading towards Sutton. So we gave pursuit in the Rover, with the blue light flashing and the siren going. The target turned left towards Epsom …"

"Ah, at Burgh Heath," said James.

"Oh, you know the area, do you, Mr Hunt?"

"Yes, quite well."

"After a couple of hundred yards there's a right-hander. The bloke in the Mustang took it flat, didn't lift. So I followed in the SD1 …" The officer paused, his eyes glazing over at the memory.

"What happened then?" asked James, with a twinkle in his eyes.

"We went off the road, through a hedge and finished up in a field."

Before this tale could be pursued further, there was a sudden movement and the police officer was pushed into the swimming pool. He disappeared beneath the surface. His peaked hat floated, upside down, then took in water and sank. The policeman reappeared, looking rather cross.

It turned out that the other policeman had been chatting to James' girlfriend of the evening and had dared her to push his colleague into the pool. The drenched policeman, having emerged from the pool, picked up James' girlfriend and threw her, fully dressed, into the pool. There then followed a swimming session, both cops having stripped down to their Y-fronts. The host kindly provided some towels. One policeman had a dry uniform to get back into. The other, of course, did not.

How all that panned out back at Dock Green[3], we never discovered. The cop with the wet uniform had some explaining to do, but he was more worried about a soggy incident book, from which it would be difficult, perhaps impossible, to extract the details of various motorists that they had nicked earlier in their shift.

As the two guardians of The Law were heading back towards their patrol car and their version of normal life, James said quietly, "I wish I hadn't sold that Mustang."

[1] Some motor sport hacks (most of whom could not drive a nail into a block of wood even if supplied with an illustration and detailed instructions) have suggested that he was only moderately talented and merely struck lucky by getting possibly the best car on the grid for 1976. But Niki Lauda and other contemporary drivers rated him very highly, which is more credible testimony.

[2] At that time, most climatological experts were predicting the imminent approach of a new Ice Age.

[3] More interesting might be what happened when the drenched policeman arrived home, where his wife or girlfriend might have asked, "Here, how did you get all wet like that?" and he would reply that he had heroically rescued someone who had fallen into Regent's Canal.

48 Bernard

BERNARD CAHIER WAS A jovial old rogue. He was an excellent photographer and one of France's leading motor sport journalists. He helped John Frankenheimer make the film *Grand Prix* and even appeared in it, playing himself, with not much more exaggeration than he gave to the role in real life.

Bernard was 81 when he snuffed it in 2008. He came from an interesting family. In some ways he might have been regarded as 'well connected.' In others, perhaps, not so much.

Bernard's father was a general in the French army, and his sister married Robert Mitterrand, elder brother of the sinister François. Thus Bernard was the uncle of the amusing, arty Frédéric (who became French Minister for the Arts).

His own uncle, Eugène Deloncle – I once suggested to Bernard that he should write a memoir entitled 'Mon oncle Deloncle' – was a co-founder in the 1930s of La Cagoule, an extreme-right organization, and a committed Pétainist during the war. Deloncle and his son were assassinated by the Gestapo in 1944, apparently because of connections with the Abwehr, so it was not only the French who fought amongst their own side. Bernard himself held entirely different views, though I am sure he was never on 'The Left.' He joined the Resistance, aged only about 17, well before D-Day, and was then a soldier under the estimable General Leclerc.

Here is a story from the internet ... Bernard was posted to Cameroon after the war, and there he became friendly with a rancher who kept a pet leopard. One evening they were having pre-dinner drinks on the terrace, when the leopard approached them, snarling and clawing aggressively. "Mais qu'est-ce qui te prend?" shouted the rancher, who stood up and smacked the leopard across the face with his hat. The leopard trotted off. They then went inside for dinner and were astounded to see the leopard fast asleep on its bed. So the leopard on the terrace had been *a* leopard, not *the* leopard.

Well, those are the facts as recounted by someone on the internet. However, when Cahier told me the story, he said *guépard* rather than *léopard*, which makes more sense, because leopards are notoriously unpredictable and violent, and they have retractable claws, whereas cheetahs are more easily domesticated and have claws like those of dogs. The internet version sounds like a story that has 'improved' with the retelling. Similarly, most English readers mistakenly believe that Lampedusa wrote a novel entitled *The Leopard*.

In about 1965, I was walking along the King's Road near Oakley Street and a tall, eminently bonkable blonde bird, presumably a model, and probably being filmed by someone I had not spotted, walked towards me with a cheetah, complete with diamond-studded collar, on a lead. "Nice pussy," I should have said. But I had a curious aversion to blondes at that time and feigned sophisticated indifference, stopping to check the time on my cheap wristwatch. Anyway, enough of pussy cats ...

I recall one press trip, to Majorca, in the early 1990s. It was for the BMW M3, and I was doing it for *Fast Lane* as a freelance. Another journalist, who shall remain nameless, was trying to keep up with me. He went off the road, fortunately without personal injury, but the car was wrecked. Actually, it was rather difficult not to lose it on those roads, which were not only bumpy and twisty but polished, breaking up, dusty, and, in places, liberally coated with diesel fuel. I had a couple of rather tricky moments, and Brian Laban, with whom I was sharing, had a *huge* moment, keeping us on the road thanks only to his great skill ...and a rather large helping of luck. But I ramble, as is my wont ...

For some reason, the trip began with our British group, a batch of Germans, and one or two frogs, including Cahier, assembling in Switzerland, before flying on, early the next morning, to Majorca. The first stop was a Holiday Inn close to Basle airport. On leaving the terminal with the other Anglos, I spotted Cahier putting his luggage into the boot of a taxi.

I went over to say hello. He greeted me warmly. I said I presumed he was doing this M3 exercise. He said yes, so I said why don't you join us on our bus? But he was in a hurry to get to the hotel because he needed to get some work done. I got on the bus, we arrived at the crap hotel in about five minutes, I showered, changed, had a couple of drinks in the bar, then there was a technical presentation, and then dinner. I looked around, but there was no sign of Bernard. I assumed he must have been in his room working.

The main course arrived, and then Bernard came in, eyes blazing, evidently in an unusually bad mood. It turned out that his hopeless taxi driver had assumed that he had meant the Holiday Inn in the centre of the city, had had difficulty finding that, and then got totally lost, in Spades. "We travelled so far, he had to reset the meter at one point!" Bernard had been in the cab for something like three hours. He soon calmed down and became his usual jovial self, and we smoked cigars together after dinner.

The last time I met Bernard was in 2005, on a press launch based in a hotel at Gassin, next to Saint Tropez. The hotel was a bit pretentious, but the food was good, and from the restaurant there was a superb view of the bay. He was having lunch when I arrived. He looked a very old man by then, and I think the stress of his wife's illness had taken years off his life expectancy. She was still struggling along at that point, and they were even planning a trip to the USA (she was American). This sounded mad to me, but perhaps she wanted to stay there and die.

There was an odd coincidence later. I knew that Cahier's house was somewhere on the winding ascent between Grimaud and La Garde Freinet, but had never discovered exactly where; he invited us once, but we were unable to go and I regret that.

That road was part of the prescribed route. I drove up to La Garde Freinet, then came back down the hill, and pulled off at a track at the side of the road to make some notes. As I was about to leave, I looked up and saw the sign, Mas de Miremer. That was it, la maison de Bernard. I could not see the house from the road, but there was a No Entry sign and another reading 'Maison Piégée,' which was not an invitation to the casual visitor to drop in.

49 No way out, José

ATTITUDES TO SPEEDING IN Italy had long been lenient, to the point that they seemed no more than advisory. A newly appointed Transport Minister changed this abruptly in the late 1980s. There was some resistance for a while. A group of wealthy Lamborghini and Ferrari owners paid some larrikins to destroy all the speed cameras on the autostrada between Bologna and Milan.

After that, the speed cameras were set in reinforced concrete and gradually the new, intolerant policy was imposed. The Carabinieri no longer turned a blind eye. It took a while for those outside Italy to become aware of this. José Rosinski discovered the transformation in an expensive way.

Rosinski[1] was French, despite the Spanish first name and the Polish surname. After reaching a high level in journalism, he had a reasonably successful motor racing career, during which he won a French national sports car championship. He competed in single-seater formulae, up to Formula 2, and six times at Le Mans.

Then he became one of France's leading motoring journalists and was a Grand Prix commentator for TF1, the French television channel. He was a stylish writer, and an amusing character with slightly ornate facial furniture, a trim moustache later joined by a beard. When I first met him in the mid-1980s, he lived in an ornate 17th century apartment in an expensive part of Paris.

He always had the latest technology. Some time in the early 1990s, he boasted to me about his brand-new, enormously expensive radar detector. It was not legal in France, but he said that *in extremis* he would throw it out of the window. He said it gave him "absolute security."

His confidence turned out to be misplaced, though to his surprise the problem occurred not in France but in Italy, where he had been testing some mega-fast Porsche in the company of a photographer.

Alerted by a warning bleep, he had time to shed enough speed before they could register a seriously high number. Nevertheless, the blue-and-white Alfa 75 pulled out of the layby where it had been lurking, blue roof lights flashing, siren blaring. José hastily grabbed the radar detector from the top of the dash and stuffed it into a jacket pocket. He decided not to throw it out of the window. It had cost him the equivalent of a couple of thousand pounds, and anyway, he was in Italy, so there would be no big problem, he thought.

Understandably, the Carabinieri did not recognize Rosinski's face or name from his French television appearances (which might have given him a slim chance in France, though that is unlikely). They were aggressive and unpleasant, and they demanded to know where the radar detector was.

José unblinkingly said that he did not have one. The police said they knew he did, and that it would be better for him if he produced it. A prolonged argument followed. José remained calm, but the police became angry, shouting and waving their arms. He and they knew that they had no right to search him or his car, and he did not believe that they would bother to call in Customs and Excise, who can do whatever they want, whenever, wherever. Again, his optimism was misplaced.

Rosinski and the snapper were told to sit in their car (the cops had removed the keys). The cops contacted their bosses. Rosinski was ordered into the police car and a cop drove the test car with the photographer beside him. They travelled in convoy, at well over the speed limit, to the nearest equivalent of Dock Green or Five-0, where they were made to sit on a bench, each handcuffed to a radiator.

Rosinski thought for a while and then told the desk officer that he needed to go to the lavatory. He was detached from the radiator. The policeman pointed casually to a door. José opened it, closed it, pushed the bolt across, silently unscrewed the button surround on the cistern, lifted the lid, dropped in the detector, silently refitted the lid, had a piss in case he might need one later, pressed the flush button, washed and dried his hands, and opened the door to return to the reception room. But there were three grinning Carabinieri outside the door. They were not queuing to have a slash.

One of them unscrewed and lifted the lid of the cistern, pulled out the detector, laughed and asked, "Che cosa è questo?" Rosinski said he had no idea whatever and that it was nothing to do with him. The Carabinieri all stopped smiling.

The customs men arrived and gave Rosinski the third degree. One of them, a motor racing fan, recognized him from his TV commentaries. He said that he was in deep enough trouble already; if he did not confess, the penalties would be far more severe. So he confessed and paid the fine, and of course also lost his radar detector, even supposing it was still in working order after its submersion.

There was no escape for me in Germany, either.

---

[1] José Rosinski (1936-2011), RIP.

50 No escape, but in credit

GERMAN AUTOBAHNS HAVE NO speed limits, right? Wrong, actually. If you don't believe it, try treating those signs with numbers on them as advisory and see what happens, but make sure you have plenty of cash for the on-the-spot fine (and it could be worse than that, if you are substantially in velocitous tort).

In the old days, it was true. With a fast car, you could get from one side of the relatively-lightly-trafficked old West Germany to the other in a remarkably short time. Lane discipline (a concept that never caught on in Britain) was the finest in the world. Speed-limited sections, often without obvious justification, began creeping onto the autobahns during the 1980s, a process that, er, accelerated after The Wall came down[1]. The autobahns became far more crowded, and road manners deteriorated.

One day in the late 1980s, I was near the Rhine, testing a Hartge[2] BMW, a 3-series saloon with the 'big-six' engine crammed under its bonnet. White-faced photographer strapped into passenger seat, I joined the Luxembourg-Saarbrucken autobahn at Merzig and gunned it.

Immediately, I noticed something in the mirrors, in the far distance, obviously travelling fast. The rate at which it gained on us diminished as we accelerated towards maximum. By the time we were doing 130mph, I had identified it as a 5-series, at 140, I could see it was an M5 and, as we struggled over 150, I noted the Luxembourg registration.

Our top speeds seemed similar. We were in convoy, flat out, for about ten minutes, with almost no other traffic. We passed one vehicle (which alas turned out to be an unmarked police car) as we entered an interestingly bendy section with '150' signs, at a steady 155. However, the signs were in km/h and we were doing 155mph, more than 60mph above the limit.

Soon after, the traffic increased as we skirted Saarlouis, still on an autobahn, but running through a built-up area. I eased off and the M5 drew alongside. Its occupants, a man and a woman in their 40s, with their teenage daughter in the back, grinned and waved, and we grinned and waved back.

Suddenly, half a dozen green-painted police vehicles surrounded us. They included a VW van with an illuminated sign saying 'FOLLOW ME' (in English). A fat policeman unnecessarily leaned out of the front passenger window waving a big red lolly.

We and the M5 were escorted to a slip road, where we were invited to stop. We accepted the invitation and armed police stood around us ready for action, looking as if they hoped we would try to do a runner. The elegantly-dressed Luxembourgeois family, still grinning, stepped out of their car. We all shook hands, which seemed to bewilder der Fuzz[3].

As previously mentioned, my command of German is negligible. I don't think I could ever master those long, ugly compounds: *Europäische Wirtschaftgemeinschaft*, for example. So the M5 driver acted as translator as well as fellow-defendant. First came a request for identity papers. Second, we received a short lecture on the purpose of German speed limits and how irresponsible we had been to ignore them.

Finally, we were told to pay 200DM[4] (about £70). That seemed very reasonable compared with French fines of that era, but I had only about £30 on me in various currencies. The photographer had no cash whatever; like royalty, they never do. But I could see a bank nearby and was discussing the possibility of withdrawing cash from it with a plastic card.

The Luxembourg businessman, overhearing this, said, "Look, that's too complicated." He handed me 200DM and his business card and said I could repay him by post. I thanked him, paid the policeman, said goodbye to everyone cheerfully, and we were on our way again.

I had not understood at the time that the 200DM was a sort of deposit and that a court hearing would subsequently examine my crime *in absentia*. A while later, I received an envelope containing a pink slip of paper, full of those compound words in German officialese, with some figures printed at the end.

A German friend confirmed that my reading of it was correct: the court had fined me and charged costs, the total amounting to 196DM. I considered taking this paper with me to Germany and handing it to police as a credit note the next time I was stopped for speeding. On balance I decided that might be unwise.

When The Wall came down it was not good news for everyone.

[1] German Reunification joke:
"Ach zo, Fritz. Vot must you do after you T-bone a Trabant mit your S-class at 250 kilometres per hour?"
"I do not know, Hans."
"You must flick your headlamp vosher svitch."
[2] The Hartge brothers – car dealers and engine tuners. Herbert, the eldest and most flamboyant of them, stuck with BMW, while the others switched to Mercedes-Benz. Herbert had no patience with fancily over-equipped cars, disapproving of anything, such as cup-holders or a remote control to open the boot, that did not directly improve performance and efficiency. "Non-stop nonsense!" he would say.
[3] Or should that be '*die* Fuzz'? Life is too short for it to be worthwhile to learn German.
[4] A currency, replaced for a few years by the euro, which had not yet returned to circulation at the time of writing.

51 Achtung! Take cover!

WHEN THE BERLIN 'WALL' was up, most Germans, whether they lived to the East or the West of it, wanted it to come down. But its presence suited Volkswagen very well, giving it an advantage not shared by any other manufacturer. Its test track at Ehra-Lessien, ten miles north of the Wolfsburg factory, is very close to where the border was, and, for that reason, the area was designated a 'no fly zone.'

The accidental benefit of this to VW was that NATO's edict prevented light aircraft owned by rival manufacturers from flying over the site to photograph secret prototypes. Large car makers invest substantial sums in espionage, using various methods. They spend nearly as much on counter-espionage, and anything that limits or distorts the flow of information to competitors is highly valued. For many years, The Wall gave VW an edge.

In that area of Lower Saxony, and, indeed, for most of its length, 'The Wall' consisted of an electrified fence, a minefield, and a series of sinister observation towers from which heavily armed sentries scrutinized life beyond their Communist Dream World through Zeiss Ikon binoculars (perhaps the only world-class product of the old East Germany).

Ehra is set in a vast area of attractive woodland and includes numerous test tracks, the most impressive of which is a 13-mile high-speed circuit with straights over five miles long, one rather longer than the other thanks to the kidney shape that was chosen to use up less woodland, linked by high banked corners. If you stand at one end of the straights you cannot see the other, even on a clear day, because of the curvature of the Earth[1].

I lapped the track flat out in 1979 in the first-generation Porsche 911 Turbo[2].

In those days, there was no available circuit for such speeds in Britain, Vauxhall not yet having opened Millbrook to outsiders. So we drove the British-registered car all the way across Belgium and Germany to Ehra, where VW had agreed to allow us 30 minutes of track use.

The result of my flying lap was a two-way average speed of 160mph, which was considered fast for a road car in those days[3]. To be precise, it was 160.1mph. I always hated it when a standard-setting car ended up with a figure like that: it looked as if one had decided on 160mph and then bunged in an extra tenth to make it seem more realistic. In fact, the speed was recorded by Volkswagen's electronic timing system. We were handed a small piece of paper like a Setright bus ticket[4] to prove it.

I remember how surprisingly easy it was to go through the banked corners without lifting the throttle and how weird it was that I could take my hands off the steering wheel along the straights and the wheel would constantly shift gently a few degrees either side of straight ahead, first one way then the other, although the car tracked perfectly, not straying off dead centre. Porsche had yet to sort out the aerodynamics – there was evidently some lift at the front, to put it mildly. More recently, first McLaren, and then Bugatti and one or two others, have made that Porsche speed seem pathetically slow. The F1 set a speed of 240mph in 1998, which would have been enough to claim the Land Speed Record until 5 February 1931.

When Andy Wallace did his record run in the McLaren, he wisely kept the speed through the banked curves down to about 130mph. He had evidently studied the place carefully, as he explained in Andrew English's test of the Bugatti Chiron in *The Daily Telegraph* in April 2017:

"The big problem with Erha-Lessien is getting back on that dog leg with sufficient speed …
Then you'd be running against the way the Tarmac has been pressed and moulded down.
That might heat the tyres too much."

As soon as the Cold War thawed in 1990, Ehra was no more protected from aerial surveillance than any other test track, and, shortly after German reunification, spy planes from Ford, General Motors and others were frequent fliers over the test centre. VW countered these intrusions by building roofed dugouts and installing a military-specification radar system. When anything suspicious appeared on the screen in the control tower, test drivers would be alerted by radio and ordered to head for the dugouts until the all-clear was given.

VW did not go to the extreme of installing anti-aircraft batteries, but the temptation to do so must have been strong. Only a few years later, all that light aeroplane palaver was completely outdated by satellite imaging. How could that be countered? Covering the whole test area with a roof would be expensive. Objections might be raised if satellites were knocked out by guided missiles. I have another idea …

[1] However, the Flat Earth Society still exists and would doubtless suggest that this is a devious plot by Volkswagen, the purpose of which is unclear to us gullible Flat Earth deniers.

[2] Porsche's model number for it is 930.

[3] It was the road car with the highest maximum speed and best acceleration of its day. I was in a pub in 1980 when a friend's younger brother, not knowing who I was, started talking about the 911 Turbo. He said that it did 0-60mph in 5.1 seconds. I asked where he had read that. He replied, "*Motor* magazine." I said that in that case it was 5.3 seconds. He kept insisting, until I said, "Listen, boy. I did the figures."

[4] See Chapter 7.

52 Purple haze

IF THE TEST CARS running around Ehra-Lessien or another test track become invisible from above, and only the site's service vehicles can be seen in satellite imagery, then the motor industry will probably have taken a great new leap forward in plasma technology.

It may seem surprising that something of this sort has not been used in Formula 1 motor racing. However, if the cars of one of the cheap teams usually found at the back of the grid suddenly started to emit a spooky purple-blue glow and lapped the entire field, its great leap forward would be banned immediately by the FIA – and not only because timing it might prove impossible, or because it would be confusing for spectators and other drivers.

It took a surprisingly long time for aerodynamics to play a crucial role in motor racing. The 1928 Opel rocket car had negative-incidence wings to stop it taking off at 120mph and various pre-war racers were 'streamlined.' But it was not until the late 1960s that serious scientific research into downforce made aerodynamics a vital design and tuning element. Cars sprouted unsightly and sometimes dangerously fragile devices to eliminate lift without creating excessive drag. Gradually these devices have become more efficient and more complex – but no less ugly, thus disproving the old saying, 'If a car looks right, it *is* right.'

A decade later, Lotus introduced the 'wing car.' Side skirts and venturi bodywork (both subsequently banned) exploited 'ground effects.' The Brabham-Alfa 'fan-car' was not actually banned after Niki Lauda almost literally blew the opposition away and swept to victory in the 1978 Swedish Grand Prix, but would have been, if Brabham (then owned by BC Ecclestone) had decided to continue with it. Colin Chapman's Last Big Idea, the twin-chassis Lotus 88 (1981) was designed to optimize downforce while reducing driving effort. It was banned long before being fully developed.

If the regulations had not been made more restrictive, the performance capability of Formula 1 cars would by now probably be near the threshold of what the human body can stand[1], as is the case with fighter aircraft, which will soon be consigned to museums, replaced entirely by unmanned killing machines operated by technicians in remote bases.

Aerodynamicists continue to try to gain a tiny advantage without breaching the ever-tightening regulations. It is several years since evacuation of exhaust gases from the engine was considered to be the primary function of the exhaust system. But F1's last really major technological advance in 'airflow management' was even longer ago.

Some of the best aerodynamicists used to migrate from the aerospace industry to motor racing, to obtain excitement and payslips with lots of noughts on the end. Nevertheless while the 'defence' industry's aerodynamicists may not draw the million-dollar salaries enjoyed by some of their grand prix counterparts, they have huge budgets, thanks to taxpayers. Also, they do not have to compromise their designs to comply with regulations. As a result, military technology is always several steps ahead of the wacky world of Formula 1.

Do not ask me to explain plasma technology in detail: I'm too busy. It is used in Formula 1, but only as a means to stiffen structures. In experimental use on jet fighters in the 1990s, an ionised force field, up to two inches in depth, was created around the aeroplane, causing the strange *Far out, man* halo effect[2]. Allegedly, this dramatically reduces drag while rendering whatever it surrounds invisible to radar. Some scientists claim that it rewrites the laws of physics. Wow – plasmatronic!

I asked Gordon Murray,[3] for his opinion. He inquired sarcastically, "What have you been smoking?" At the time, in 2001, I replied, "A Montecristo"[4]. I might have added that, on the other hand, I was neither exceeding the speed of sound, nor, as far as I was aware, invisible to radar.

In 2006, *The Sunday Times* reported that, after a four-year investigation, British intelligence chiefs had concluded that the majority of sightings of UFOs could be explained by unusual atmospheric effects, and that when people *think* they see flying saucers, what they are actually observing are glowing clouds of "an ionised gas known as 'plasma.'" The MoD scientists' report, released under the Freedom of Information Act[5], speculated that such plasmas may play tricks on the mind, creating unusually vivid impressions in witnesses, adding that "local electromagnetic fields have been medically proven to cause responses in the temporal lobes of the brain." Well, they would say that …

[1] See Chapter 67.
[2] We can be sure that, if they could do that then, they are doing weirder stuff now of which we know nothing.
[3] Engineer of Grand Prix cars that won World Championships, creator of the Brabham-Alfa fan car mentioned above, engineer of the McLaren F1 road car, would-be car manufacturer, fan of The Kinks. Has been known to wear red plastic sandals.
[4] Sadly, I have since given up that pleasurable vice.
[5] George Orwell would have some fun with that charade.

53 Scoop!

'SCOOP' PHOTOGRAPHY BECAME A widespread practice in motoring magazines from the 1960s onwards. Hans Lehmann, who began in a small way by photographing Volkswagen prototypes near Wolfsburg, was the most famous of the spy photographers, though ironically he always shunned personal publicity.

A lot of early testing of prototypes is carried out in laboratories and on test tracks, and there are privacy laws that theoretically provide protection against photography in such circumstances. However, a great deal of development work has to be conducted in the real world. In particular, it is necessary to put a lot of miles on vehicles in extreme conditions.

Lehmann and others found out where the manufacturers went to do this work, and they followed them around the world to their testing areas in far-flung places, such as American, Australian or African deserts in summer and the ice lakes of Finland or Alaska in winter.

A network of informers, some of them working for car manufacturers, others for airlines and hotels, was built up over the years. And the motor industry developed, from the early years of mass production, its own network of espionage and systems of counter-espionage and misinformation. I used to know two men who worked for Ford: they attended all the international Motor Shows, posing as journalists. One of them gathered information and spread rumours, while the other took detail photos of interesting components of various new cars.

While I was Editor of *Fast Lane*, one of my informants was Italian. As he had a job in the industry, it was essential for him to have a pseudonym, which is how the byline 'Adriano Talpa'[1] came about. At a Motor Show one day, Lamborghini's suave PR man Daniele Audetto (see Chapter 57) asked me, "Peter, who is this Adriano Talpa?" It turned out that he was annoyed that the information provided was uncomfortably accurate, which was gratifying.

Although spy photography in the motor industry was mostly German-driven in its early days, before becoming a worldwide phenomenon, the very first photographic scoop, as far as I can tell, occurred in France.

André Lefèbvre (1894-1964), the renowned Chief Engineer of Citroën from 1933 onwards, was responsible for the Traction Avant, the 2CV, the DS and the H van, among others. He had a large holiday home named La Terrissole at Figanières in the Var, and was in the habit of bringing prototypes there in covered lorries. He and his engineers and mechanics would prepare and modify them in a barn on the property, and then drive them on surrounding roads.

These were ideal for all sorts of assessments, both objective and subjective. A minute away, on the Draguignan-Grasse Road, there is a perfectly horizontal straight more than one kilometre long, which would have been useful for acceleration runs, and there are plenty of winding roads for testing ride, handling, roadholding and braking.

All went well until 1952, when an early prototype of the DS, at that stage without its body panels, was being tested close to La Terrissole. Photographers from the weekly magazine *l'Auto-Journal* were lying in wait and they snapped it.

The photographs appeared in the magazine. This was three years before the car went into production. Citroën's senior management was furious and threatened to sue for a large sum in compensation, on the grounds of 'industrial espionage.' This anger was compounded when, three weeks before the DS was launched at the 1955 *Salon de l'Automobile* in Paris, *l'Auto-Journal* published full technical details of the car, plus a reasonably accurate rendering of Flamminio Bertoni's splendid body design. This was clearly based on inside information.

Relations between Citroën and *l'Auto-Journal* remained frosty for several years. There were complex political elements to this, particularly because the magazine's founders and owners were Robert Hersant and Jean-Marie Balestre (later the manipulative President of the Fédération Internationale du Sport Automobile, Formula 1's governing body), both of whom had been prominent collaborators during the German Occupation of France[2].

[1] Talpa is Italian for mole.

[2] Although Hersant was imprisoned for only one month, in 1945, he was sentenced to ten years of 'national indignity'[3] in 1947, though that was dropped under a general amnesty in 1952. Balestre was a uniformed member of the NSKK (Nationalsozialistische Kraftfahrkorps), a French motorized Nazi transport unit, though he later claimed that he had been a double agent working for the Resistance. All those who might have exposed this as a blatant lie were deceased.

[3] A weird French legal construction thought up by General de Gaulle in 1944. Those convicted under it had various civil and political rights removed for a specified period of time. All of them agreed that this temporary inconvenience was greatly preferable to being shot, hanged or guillotined.

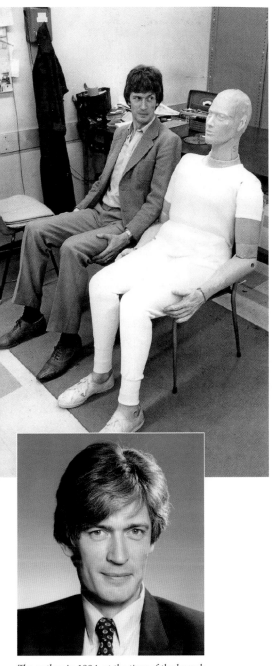

The author (left) c1980 when Features Editor of Motor magazine. This was for an article about car ergonomics, showing that many cars at that time were uncomfortable for drivers who were significantly below or above average height. (See Introduction.)

The author in 1984, at the time of the launch of Fast Lane. (See Introduction.)

Paddington Bear, the early years. (See Chapter 1.) (Illustration Don Grant)

"I didn't get where I am today through false modesty." Eberhard von Kuenheim, the BMW bigwig, delivers his frank assessment of his stupendous brilliance in his entry in the Senior Executives section of the Guild of Motoring Writers' Year Book. (See Chapter 2.)

KUENHEIM Eberhard von. Chairman of the Supervisory Board, BMW AG, Petuelring 130, 8000 Munich 40, Germany. 010 49 89 38951. *Born:* 1928. *Education:* Studied engineering, Stuttgart. *Career:* 1959 Technical Manager of automated machine tool company. 1969 Joined Quandt Group as assistant to Harald Quandt. 1970 Chairman of BMW AG's Managing Board; stood down – after 23 years' of conspicuous success – in May 1993 to take up present appointment.

Eberhard von Kuenheim

Eberhard von Kuenheim (right) in 1983, acknowledging Paul Rosche for the success of BMW's Formula 1 engine, with which Nelson Piquet won the World Championship that year, the first time a turbocharged engine had won. Rosche (1934-2016), one of the great automotive engineers of the 20th century, played a major role in BMW's success. When I interviewed von Kuenheim in 1977, he was wearing a smarter suit. (See Chapter 2.) (Photo BMW AG)

The headquarters of the Rollerball Corporation … also of BMW. The lower, mushroom-shaped building in the foreground is the BMW Museum, well worth a visit if you are in Munich. (See Chapter 3.)
(Photo BMW AG)

BL's logo – the whirling plughole of destiny. (See Chapter 4.)

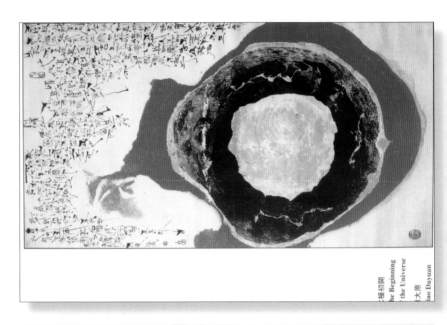

A message from China – Jean-Martin Folz visits the furthest outpost of the PSA empire.
(See Chapter 5.)

Two eccentric elderly gentlemen (both since deceased) in fierce discussion at Prescott: on the left Lord Fitzroy Raglan, on the right Ronald 'Steady' Barker. (See Chapters 7 and 37.) (Photo Paul Buckett)

Leonard Setright getting ready to let one off. (See Chapter 7.) (Photo CAR magazine)

Above and right: The Lingotto factory, one of the industrial Wonders of the World, in its early days (above) in 1928, and (right) in 2000, after its conversion into an exhibition/conference centre, with concert halls, a theatre, a hotel, and shopping arcades. Construction began in 1916, and the factory began operation seven years later. (See Chapter 16.) (Photos Centro Storico Fiat, Turin, Italy)

A memento from the splendid Palace Hotel, Bussaco. (See Chapters 17 and 18.)

A sign on the Route Napoleon (see Chapter 12) that amused me. Careful inspection is required to understand why. The sign remained in place for ten years. I should like to have taken it as a souvenir.

The special edition of Motor magazine, commemorating its 75th anniversary in 1978. (See Chapter 23.)

A gathering of former staff members of Motor, including three of its Editors, to commemorate what would have been its centenary. The author was unable to attend.

In this street (Rue du Banquier, in the 13th arrondissement of Paris) they once made splendid Delahayes. The showroom was on the left, opposite the two No Entry signs. On the right, the Hotel Rubens. (See Chapter 24.)

Cruising through Monaco in the Ferrari Superamerica. (See Chapter 25.)

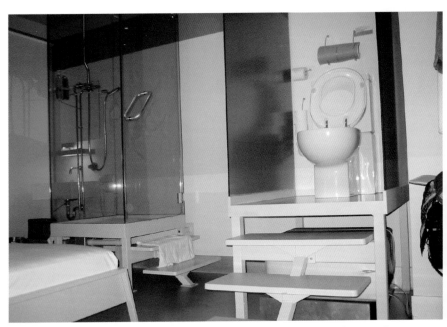

The 'HI Hotel experience' included a throne without a door. (See Chapter 26.)

On the way to sixth on the grid at Castle Combe. Not bad, but not quite good enough. (See Chapter 33.)
(Photo John Colley)

And I had made such a good start ... (See Chapter 34.)

A bad day in Bologna... Who would have guessed, when this photo was taken in 1984, that the manufacturers of the two vehicles in the foreground would one day be part of the same group? On the left, looking worried, is Cavaliere Gadeselli. (See Chapter 43.)

Bernard Cahier, in his office in 2000. (See Chapter 48.) (Photo Paul-Henri Cahier)

The southern end of Volkswagen's 12-mile (20km) high-speed test track at Ehra-Lessien in Lower Saxony. (See Chapter 51.) (Photo Volkswagen AG)

Soon after this was taken, I gave the photographer some pertinent advice on health and safety. (See Chapter 60.) (Photo Simon Childs)

Testing a Corvette at the Paul Ricard circuit. (See Chapter 87.) (Photo Peter Robain)

The Lister works in Leatherhead, with four Storms outside. (See Chapter 71.)

Michel Vaillant puts his superior penetration to good use in Paris. (See Chapter 85.)

What is the name of this car? "Don't tell him, Pike!" (See Chapter 91.)

Woollarding with my M3W. (See Chapter 94.)

My 4/4, up in the Alps. (See Chapter 95.)

54 No survivors, it is claimed

IT IS POSSIBLE THAT a few genuine examples of cars that supposedly no longer exist are dotted about here and there throughout the world, either intentionally hidden, or abandoned, forgotten and left to fade away. It is highly unlikely, however, that any examples of the Citroën 22CV survive, but dreamers always live in hope.

The 22CV was a proposed top-end version of the 'Traction Avant.' This nickname was used from the beginning by the double-chevron company itself, as promotion of what was a rare feature in cars of the period: front-wheel-drive. Other innovative elements of the car were unitary construction and fully independent suspension. It was introduced in 1934, with four-cylinder engines, later joined by a 2.9-litre straight six. But the 22CV V8 version never went on sale.

If you see a Traction Avant with some unusual detailing that differs significantly from those used in television series based on the exploits of Georges Simenon's Commissaire Maigret, you may have spotted one of the unicorns of the motor industry. Here is what to look for: a bonnet noticeably longer than standard, split front bumpers, faired-in headlamps, and, above all, the number '8' in the centre of the altered radiator grille. But of course, if you see something like this, you are almost certainly looking at a fake.

If you see such a car in Holland, then I'd put the percentage likelihood of this being so at 99.999, recurring relentlessly towards infinity, like the figure 8 turned on its side. There is one there ... and it is a fake, even though it has a V8 engine (of Ford origin).

Citroën did make at least a dozen prototypes of the 22CV, perhaps as many as 20, and they were extensively tested on public roads, which resulted in two fatal accidents.

There was a serious intention to put the 22CV into production as the top model in Citroën's adventurous new model range. The 3822cc V8 engine was based on two 11CV blocks (rather as the Cosworth DFV was derived from a pair of Cortina engines). Glossy brochures were printed and distributed, in which the 22CV was claimed to be capable of 140km/h and 16 litres/100km (87mph, 17.6mpg).

A test driver demonstrating a prototype 22CV to a potential customer near the Citroën factory in south-west Paris[1] lost control, crashed into a bridge and both men were killed. There was another accident in which a second test driver died. The local mayor, attempting to fart higher than the belt of his trousers, demanded that Citroën should stop testing cars on public roads. Naturally, the company agreed to this demand, but continued regardless, on the logical basis that proof was impossible.

In the development stage, Citroën intended to supply the 22CV with an automatic transmission with torque converter, but this was not ready in time, and it was decided to start instead with the four-cylinder model's standard three-speed manual. Three examples of the 22CV (a four-door saloon, a nine-seater limousine, and a convertible) were displayed at the Paris Motor Show in October 1934. The glossy brochures mentioned that other versions would be available: coupés with a choice of three or five seats, and what Citroën termed a 'faux-cabriolet.' This was a closed coupé with a dickey seat.

The engine caused numerous development problems. It did not deliver the planned power output, and it overheated, had an excessive thirst for oil, and a tendency to crack cylinder heads.

Because of these problems, to complete the development and testing of the suspension, brakes and aerodynamics, Citroën was obliged to acquire and install a Ford 'Flathead' V8, as used in the Model B. So the Dutch enthusiast who created his 22CV replica was not really off beam.

While all this was going on, Citroën found itself in dire financial straits, partly because of the development costs of the Traction Avant as a whole, which was rushed into production with insufficient testing and consequently encountered severe reliability problems in its early years. In particular, early examples frequently suffered cardan-shaft failures. This was naturally an even greater problem for the more powerful V8 version.

The 22CV was responsible for only a minor portion of the company's financial crisis, though it was perhaps the final straw. Citroën was forced to file for bankruptcy, and was taken over by the Michelin group. André Citroën, founder of the company and one of the motor industry's greatest innovators, was invited somewhat brusquely to clear his desk, leaving only his name behind. He was already terminally ill. He was perhaps deficient as a business manager, but he was a visionary in many respects.

The 22CV, although the engine was almost production-ready, was immediately cancelled by the new management. Citroën has never put on the market a car with an engine of more than six cylinders, though it publicly displayed a V8 proposed for installation in the DS in the 1960s.

What happened to the prototypes of the 22CV is not entirely clear. Some accounts suggest that they were all dismantled, though according to one inventive yarn, a single 22CV survived the war in a basement of the factory at the Quai de Javel but was then broken up in the 1950s. It seems more probable that they were all converted into standard 11CV models.

Citroën's head of car testing in 1934, a Monsieur Prud'homme, later insisted that he had been instructed to do precisely that, and that all parts specific to the 22 – engines, plus body and trim components – were destroyed.

Some years ago, I am informed by one who knows, numerous prototype models were gathering dust in a hangar at the Citroën test track facilities at La Ferté-Vidame, 60 miles to the west of Paris. They apparently remained secret because some had performance data superior to that achieved by later research vehicles. One was a car called the Coccinelle[2] that had a flat-twin engine, light alloy construction, three rows of seats, and a drag coefficient lower than that of a much later, publicly-declared concept model, the Eco 2000. Again, whether a 22CV was among these abandoned projects is not known.

There are plenty of scale models available of the 22CV. These, plus the nicely-crafted Dutch replica which has appeared in a few amusing spoof videos, are probably the closest that anyone will get to seeing the axed model. Nevertheless, there have been numerous reports of 22CV sightings from various parts of the world, including one in Vietnam in the 1950s, which is plausible since that was once a French colony. Occasionally, rumours circulate of a surviving 22CV, but the trail always goes cold. Intriguingly, an apparently genuine headlamp surround was found in a scrapyard in Lyon in the 1960s.

There are several missing parts to the story. Some reports suggest that the fatal accidents occurred because the V8's engine exceeded the capabilities of the chassis, to the extent that it was uncontrollable even for highly skilled drivers, though in retirement one test driver vehemently denied that this was so, insisting that the 22CV's handling had been outstandingly good. Perhaps he was the alpha tester.

I did rather hope that André Lefèbvre, Citroën's Chief Engineer, might have kept an example of the 22CV hidden in an outbuilding of La Terrissole, his holiday home near to where I live in the Var (see previous chapter). Unhappily, this seems not to have been the case. Perhaps his surviving family removed it when they sold the property and moved away some years ago. Citroën's destiny might perhaps have been different if the 22CV had gone ahead.

[1] See Chapter 68.
[2] Ladybird, though, in France, the VW Beetle is called Coccinelle rather than Coléoptère.

55 ECotY? Phooey!

ARTICLES I HAVE WRITTEN concerning 'ECotY' (the European Car of the Year award) have caused me mild embarrassment over the years, because several good friends were on the jury. But I stand by my judgement, which is that the entire concept is a nonsense.

I explained why I had reached this conclusion in a column in *CAR* magazine in December 1994, in a slot they had at the time, which they called 'Stab in the back.'

I went through the list of winners since the contest had first been held in 1964. *That* was won by the Rover 2000 – and I doubt that many people would complain about that. I suggested that others that could easily be justified included the Peugeot 405 (1985), Audi 100 (1983), Fiat Uno (1984), Renault Clio (1991) and the Ford Mondeo (1994). I suggested that "perhaps" the Fiat Tipo (1989) might be put on the credit side, which in retrospect was probably unduly generous. Another for which I felt an argument might be constructed was the "interesting but flawed" Citroën CX (1975). However, the XM of 1990 stretched the point.

Then I moved onto the negative side, with a list of cars that surely did not deserve the title. "What can one say," I asked, "about Chrysler winning the title *twice*, in 1976 with the Alpine and in 1979 with the Horizon? Many of you will have had no experience of those models; lucky you.

"And I believe it was of a version of the Renault 9 (winner in 1982) that Raymond Levy, when he became chairman of Renault, remarked, 'I am surprised that more buyers of this car do not commit suicide.'"

I mentioned that Porsche won in 1978 with the 928. This was a car that I very much liked, especially in its later 'S' versions. However, I felt obliged to point out that it was "neither epoch-making nor mould-breaking" and that it also led directly to the sacking of the company's chief executive.

However, I felt that the key argument against ECotY was not so much what had won it but what had not. BMW, for example, had never managed better than second place, and the outstanding 'E36' 3-series of 1992, the first to use the Z-axle rear suspension, did not even make it onto the podium. Mercedes-Benz had won once, but not with the first W124 with five-link rear suspension (that came third). The Volkswagen Golf did eventually win, but most people felt that this was 17 years too late. Others to have received no recognition at all included the Porsche 911 and the Alfasud, arguably the best handling front-driven volume production car of all time.

Next, I discussed how the award system was organized. At that time there were 59 jurists from 18 countries. I defended their overall integrity: "While there have been allegations of what might be termed undue interference by manufacturers, there is no evidence that it has ever been widespread. And I assured readers that the British members of the jury were beyond reproach, "and they didn't pay me to say so."

Part of the problem, I explained, is that the judges are required to make illogical comparisons. In a complicated two-stage voting system that had been introduced that year (under which only five cars went through to the 'final'), the jury had to select from, among others: Alf Romeo 145, Audi A8, Fiat Coupé, Vauxhall Tigra, Renault Laguna, Peugeot/Citroën/FIAT/Lancia MP0 and the latest Range Rover.

It would not be much more absurd, I suggested, to ask the question, "Which is best: the Bell Jet Ranger helicopter, Concorde or the Space Shuttle?"

The award's greatest flaw, I argued, lay deep within its international structure: "German jurors vote for the car that will be most significant in their own market and the Italians and French do likewise. The British once enjoyed a reputation for unusual impartiality, which almost certainly arose because no British car, until recently, was worth voting for. The nationalist bias is not so much chauvinism as an intelligent recognition of reality, but it makes a nonsense of a pan-European award."

Inevitably, I concluded, the ECotY winner "is frequently a compromise that satisfies nobody. Rather like the Maastricht Treaty, this apparent 'European unity' is a sham."

A few days after the issue of *CAR* went on sale, I received a letter from Ray Hutton, one of the British jurors. It read as follows:

Dear Peter,
CAR Magazine, December, page 178.

To use the immortal words of one of my American colleagues:
FUCK YOU!

With otherwise good wishes,
Ray

A couple of weeks later we shared a car on a launch and had a laugh about it. As far as I can see, nothing significant has changed since then. But that's enough about cars for the moment. Call me a cab ...

56 You're a cab

IN HIS EXCELLENT BOOK, *In Search of London* (published in 1952), HV Morton wrote, "The men who drive the taxi-cabs of London are naturally a race apart." Nearly half a century later, in January 2001, around 8500 so-called black cabs, produced by London Taxis International, were recalled because of "a potentially serious steering fault." I unkindly suggested at the time that this confirmed the popular view of taxis, that their most dangerous feature was the nut behind the wheel. *Boom! Boom!*[1]

That kind of pleasantry would probably not go down at all well in those mysterious green huts dotted around London where taximen congregate, when not giving us the benefit of their immense knowledge and their interesting opinions concerning Life, the Universe and Everything; this usually begins with a remark about someone or something, or occasionally an idea, and then it wanders off into the middle distance after the enticing preamble, "Not many people know this, but ..."

And then, unless we speak in anything but Estuarine or Kensington, we are treated to a guided tour of London, with footnotes, without being subjected to the dull concept of being taken directly to our chosen destination.

However, you may be shocked to learn that, while we love them dearly, cabbies do not reciprocate. The definitive work on the drivers of London taxis had just been published at the time of that massive recall.

In *Taxi!*[2] by Simon Garner and Giles Stokoe (published by Frances Lincoln), one cab driver is quoted as follows: "I hate journalists. There are three types of people who make money out of other people's misery: undertakers, journalists and solicitors." And do not imagine that you are the cabby's bosom pal if you are a stockbroker, a rat catcher or a talented amateur footballer, with or without hopes of being 'spotted' ... Another cabman puts it more globally: "We're the only profession that's truly united: we all hate the public."

I always wondered if the regulation limiting the sliding glass partition's width to 4.5in was designed to protect them, or us ...

As for those green huts, 61 were built between 1875 and 1914, funded by benefactors including the Earl of Shaftesbury, of Avenue fame, Edward VII and the Earl of Aberdeen. In 2001, 13 remained. Nine of those had, at that time, been recently restored by the London Cabman's Shelter Fund,[3] for whom messrs Jagger and Richard wrote the memorable ditty, *Gimme Shelter*.

Contrary to popular belief, cabmen, when scoffing subsidized nosh in these establishments, are not obliged to have one trouser leg rolled up to the knee. Nor are the huts of infinite internal dimensions, like Dr Who's Tardis[4].

Nor are the rooms fitted out like the staterooms in the Titanic and, apparently, it is relatively rare for cabmen to dine on larks' tongues washed down with Château Margaux. Tea remains the favoured beverage and it may only be a malicious rumour that some of the urns have not been flushed out since Victorian times.

However, I can confirm that Trappist rules operate in the huts: the cabbies remain silent, except when ordering extra tea and bacon butties. Transcendental meditation prepares them for their demanding role as entertainers and founts of knowledge[5].

"I 'ad that Bertrand Russell in the back of the cab once. So I goes, 'Well, yer lordship, what's it all abaht then, eh?' Blimey, I wish I hadn't asked."

Oddly enough, as the saying goes, one of those historic green huts is located in Russell Square, in Bloomsbury, which is named after the Earls and Dukes of Bedford, the family of the famous rogering philosopher who was no relation at all to Lord Russell of Liverpool, whose literary works could have been said to be pornographic but which of course were not.

Lord Russell and Bertrand Russell sent a joint letter to *The Times* in 1959, which had nothing to do with cuckoos in springtime. Rather, they wished to make it clear to the population at large that they were different people. But, by gad sir, did that clear up the confusion? I should say not!

If any of my readers is a cab driver, no offence intended, squire. And if you have taken offence, kindly hand it back. Or, as Groucho Marx said in *Duck Soup*, "If you can't leave in a taxi, you can leave in a huff. And if you can't leave in a huff, you can leave in a minute and a huff."

I have a suspicion that taxi drivers, like motoring journalists and, indeed, all professional drivers, as well as professional aeroplane pilots, are heading towards the category labelled 'Jobs of Yesteryear.' I sincerely hope I am wrong, but I doubt it. Professional car photographers are also in that category and few can still make a decent living.

[1] I can never recall whether that was the catchphrase of Basil Brush or of Boris Johnson. But what is the difference, anyway?

[2] The definitive work on cabmen (of London, not Huntingdonshire).

[3] A branch of the Transport and General Workers' Union.

[4] My own house is called Sidrat, because from the outside it appears to be considerably larger than it is inside.

[5] And of course, national treasures.

57 Countach!

AT 9AM ON TUESDAY, 10 June 1986, ace photographer Richard Newton and I arrived at the reception hut at the gates of the Lamborghini factory in Sant'Agata Bolognese[1]. I presented my business card and asked to see the Press Relations Director, Daniele Audetto[2].

A few minutes later, Audetto arrived and said, "Ah Peter, nice to see you! What you doing here today? We expect you next week ..." I opened my briefcase and showed him a sheaf of faxes mentioning that day's date, and 9am, with his name on them. There followed an hour or so of typically Italian panic and then everything was organized, more or less as had been agreed in those faxes.

On the first day, it was the maximum speed test. After losing a short argument, I agreed that I would do this from the passenger seat, with a test driver behind the wheel, "for insurance reasons."

I was introduced to the test driver, "Piero," a young chap with curly fair hair. We turned left out of the factory onto the Via Modena and set off towards the autoroute. The terrain around Sant'Agata is mostly about as flat as the plains of Lincolnshire and similarly has deep drainage ditches at each side of the roads to encourage careful driving.

There was a twisty section through which "Piero" gave the 5000 quattrovalvole some serious stick. He obviously knew what he was doing. Then we arrived at a village, and he slowed down to the speed limit and allowed the mad bull to burble along in second gear.

I noticed that, even though Countaches (and previously Miuras and other crazy creations) had passed through there on test runs for several years, the locals still looked, smiled and waved. I suppose this was partly local pride, but also because the car, especially with its sound effects, even at low speeds, is just such a spectacular thing to see and hear. 'Countach' is derived from a local dialectic word meaning something along the lines of, 'Fuck me! Look at that!'

I then asked "Piero" probably the most stupid question that he had heard that year: had he done any motor racing? He gave me a glance and replied, "Well, I won a Formula 3000 race last Sunday."[3] "Ah," I said in some embarrassment. I thought for a moment and said, "You must be Pierluigi Martini." As indeed he was. We both laughed and got on well from then on. What happened that day became controversial, as I shall explain in the next chapter.

I spent Wednesday in the company of Valentino Balboni, Lamborghini's famed test driver. Unlike Sandro Munari[4], Balboni was not specifically a development tester, though he had considerable ability in that area also. His primary task was to ensure that cars designed for production performed as they should, and he certainly made sure of that. He was a precise, consistent and very fast driver.

Valentino and I took turns in hacking the Countach around a variety of roads, not including autostradas, so we did not get anywhere near to the previous day's speeds – only up to about 170mph, I think.

I had brought from England *Fast Lane*'s Peiseler fifth wheel. This was attached to cars by three suction clamps of the type used by people who shift large panes of glass.

Conducting standing-start acceleration tests is an acquired skill, especially when you have an engine supposedly developing 455bhp (the real output was apparently rather more than that[5]). Trying to extrude that through the big rear tyres (345/45 VR 15 on 12J rims) requires knowledge and, although I had considerable experience of getting cars off the line, I knew that Valentino had The Knowledge of this car, so I sat in the passenger seat, operating Peiseler's electronic box of tricks while admiring Balboni's skill. He knew exactly how many revs to use and how to engage the clutch for the best effect.

We did several runs in each direction, reaching about 145mph, and the 0-140mph times did not vary by more than about a tenth of a second. Even against a Countach with Launch Control, which did not exist at the time, I doubt that Valentino would have lost by more than a few thousands of a second.

On the Thursday morning, Richard and I were taken on a tour of the factory, which was fascinatingly artisanal at that time, rather like Aston Martin, and did a couple of interviews. And then it was a farewell lunch in a splendid restaurant nearby, with various people, including Ubaldo Sgarzi[6], an ingenious fellow without whom Lamborghini would probably not exist today. The lunch was accompanied by excellent Lambrusco (with champagne-type corks and muselets, not all like the rubbish you can find in British supermarkets). I asked Sgarzi where I could buy some Lambrusco like that. He mumbled something unclear so I did not press the point.

As we were leaving the restaurant, he said, "Here is your wine." There were two cases. I asked him how much I owed him, but he refused payment. So there we have it. I was bribed. The Lambrusco travelled with me to England, exceeding 140mph a few times, and was much appreciated during the hot summer evenings of that year.

[1] In those days it was just a car factory, manufacturing extraordinary cars. Today it is a sort of lifestyle experience, complete with a museum.

[2] Audetto had been an artist and a journalist. He then became involved in motor sport as rally co-driver to several drivers, among them Luca di Montezemolo, and one of the sport's finest, Sandro Munari[4]. Audetto broke his legs in an accident and moved into motor sport management, first for the Lancia rally team, and then for Ferrari in Formula 1. Without his intervention, calling on the services of a first-class burns specialist in Ludwigshafen, Niki Lauda would almost certainly not have survived his accident at the Nürburgring in 1976. He spent several years with Lamborghini before, and during, the period of Chrysler ownership, when the company was an engine supplier for offshore powerboat racing and Formula 1, the former far more successful than the latter. After that he worked with various other companies involved in motor sport, including superbike racing.

[3] This was at Imola. At the next round, at Mugello, he set pole position and fastest lap on his way to victory. He had one further win that season, but finished third in the Championship, behind Ivan Capelli and Emmanuele Pirro. He took part in 124 Grands Prix, He finished in fourth place twice, and scored points on many occasions, despite driving for low-ranked teams (Toleman, Minardi, etc). With Joachim Winkelhock and Yannick Dalmas, he won the Le Mans 24 Hours race in 1999, driving a BMW V12 LMR.

[4] Munari won seven international rallies, all in the Lancia Stratos, and he would have been World Champion at least twice, but there was not a World Championship for drivers until the end of his career. With Arturo Merzario, he also won the 1972 Targa Florio in a Ferrari 312 PB. He later worked for Lamborghini as a development engineer/tester and also did PR work for the company.

[5] See next chapter.

[6] Sgarzi (1932-2015) was one of Ferruccio Lamborghini's earliest recruits. He was the company's international sales manager from 1964 until he retired in 1994, though after that he worked for Horacio Pagani, who had earlier been a Lamborghini apprentice. The intelligence and creative thinking of Sgarzi kept Lamborghini afloat through various crises and under different ownerships.

58 Top speed controversy

WHEN MAXING THE LOTUS Carlton (see next chapter), I used a relatively-new Peiseler innovation: this was a clamp, rather resembling a disc brake, that could be fitted to any normal wheel with three to five studs. However, this had not been invented at the time of my visit to Sant'Agata in 1986.

As mentioned, I had brought with me from Britain our Peiseler kit and we used that for the acceleration runs, in which we got close to 150mph. This was on public, but deserted public roads. It was a bit like doing acceleration runs on the Fosse Way on a quiet Sunday.

However, even if Lamborghini had allowed it (which is highly improbable), I decided that it would be unwise, for legal as well as safety reasons, to use a fifth wheel for the maximum speed runs, in which I anticipated we would exceed 180mph, mingling with the general public on the autostrada, as indeed we did. So let no one call me an irresponsible hooligan.

Travelling on a motorway at more than 180mph (190km/h) is quite different from doing 120mph in, say, a Golf GTI, not because it is actually difficult in itself on dry, straight sections, but simply because you are covering one mile every 20 seconds and 264ft every second.

Lying on a hospital bed after his huge accident at Daytona in 1975, Barry Sheene was asked by a dim BBC reporter "What's the first thing that goes through your mind at the moment of impact?" Despite having broken numerous bones including his left thigh, Bazza replied, "Your arse, if you're going fast enough."

Using digital stopwatches, I recorded the times between kilometre posts. In one direction, the time was 11.46sec, which gives a speed of 195.2mph (314.1km/h. The needle of the analogue speedometer was showing 320km/h (a digit or so below 200mph). A few minutes later in the opposite direction, the time between the posts was 12.1sec – 184.9mph/297km/h. This gave a mean speed of 190.1mph (305.8km/h).

This was faster than any previously recorded max for the Countach. Some doubt was later cast upon these figures and the method used to measure them, though never directly to me. I can only state that I conducted the tests with diligence and honesty. I later considered all possible areas in which inaccuracy could have crept in.

I had accumulated considerable experience of timing cars with stopwatches and I reckon I was as accurate as anyone. Let us suppose, however, for the sake of argument, that I consistently under-timed the car through the kilometre posts by 0.2sec. That gives an average speed through the two directions of 186.8mph (300.5km/h).

Let us further suppose that the kilometre posts in question were one per cent (that's 11 yards/10 metres) closer together than they should have been. That still gives a top speed of 185mph/298km/h.

Harry Metcalfe, founder of *EVO* magazine and owner of a Countach quattrovalvole among various other interesting machines, drove to Sant'Agata in investigative reporter mode. He wrote afterwards:

"When I did the Countach group test with Valentino [Balboni] for *Octane* magazine (January 2011), I quizzed both Valentino and Peter Dron about the Countach used in this famous *Fast Lane* feature and whether the car was specially prepared.

"Valentino told me it was a regular Countach owned by Pierluigi Martini (apparently, Lamborghini used to do special 'deals' on Countaches to well-known race drivers around this time). It had covered 6000-10,000km, so was well run in.

"The only mod was to the airbox: Lamborghini discovered you could get a few extra horsepower at high revs by lifting the airbox lid covering the top of the carburettor trumpets. To achieve this, Valentino used to add several extra cork gaskets to lift the lid further while still allowing the engine to breathe cool air ducted from outside, and while still allowing the standard engine cover to open and close.

"Together with the lack of wing on the car (which dramatically reduces drag) and higher tyre pressures (for minimum rolling resistance) the car achieved the big speed recorded in this article.

"Valentino also confirmed that standard Quattrovalvole engines were known to produce more than the stated 455bhp at the time but Lamborghini decided not to declare this at launch because they were convinced Ferrari would increase the (395bhp) peak power in the Testarossa to match the Countach and the fact that the Countach V12 was actually producing nearer 475bhp (Valentino's figure, not mine) would allow Lamborghini to up the Countach's quoted power for zero cost and jump ahead of Ferrari again! There was never any need to increase the quoted power of the Countach because Ferrari never got close to 455bhp with the Testarossa, so this extra bhp advantage was never declared."

My abiding memory of that day in Emilia Romagna will always be the moment when the rev needle was at the top end of the scale, and those two little dots in the far distance became two little Fiats in the right lane of the two-lane carriageway. Even from a long way off, I was certain that Fiat A was going to pass Fiat B.

I was thinking that, if I were in the driving seat, I'd pass them on the hard shoulder. When we were about a hundred yards/metres behind Fiat A, its driver turned to his right to speak to his wife or mistress, simultaneously steering to pass Fiat B, without first having checked his left-side door mirror. He would have seen nothing in it, anyway, because we were already on the hard shoulder, travelling something like 110mph faster.

59 Maxing the Lotus Carlton

MY FIRST DRIVE IN the Lotus Carlton was in Bedfordshire, partly on public roads and partly on various circuits within the Millbrook testing complex. When we were instructed not to exceed 140mph around 'The Bowl' I thought, at first, that this was a simple insurance requirement, but it turned out to be more complex than that.

The Vauxhall Lotus Carlton/Opel Lotus Omega was a seriously enhanced version of GM's large saloon of the period. Lotus' extensive engine modifications, with twin turbochargers, took the power output up to 377bhp.

Lotus' engineers were able to draw from GM's worldwide parts bin in creating this super-saloon. The six-speed ZF gearbox from the Chevrolet Corvette ZR-1 was used. The limited-slip differential came from the Australian V8 Holden Commodore, and the Servotronic (worm-and-roller) steering originated in the Senator (from which the self-levelling suspension was also derived). The development engineers wanted rack-and-pinion steering, but the car's build costs were already a cause for concern[1].

Brakes and suspension were seriously up-rated, and specially-developed Goodyear Eagle tyres were fitted. The interior was swathed in ruched leather in an unsuccessful attempt to conceal the car's high-end repmobile origins.

Without that speed limitation, I would have gone for it and got as close to the claimed maximum of 176mph as possible, though I would not have done so without some apprehension. I was always worried that the high lateral forces generated in such tests could lead to catastrophic tyre failure, as I have already mentioned[2].

In any case, the car would probably have struggled to get within 10mph of the claimed max, due to tyre scrub. After a bit of probing and nudging, I discovered the real reason for the speed-restriction – on the banking, the self-levelling rear suspension would apparently get confused above 140mph and jack itself up as if the car were heavily laden, with probably unpleasant consequences.

Therefore, when we had a Lotus Carlton for a full test, a short while later, we did the acceleration tests at Millbrook, but then headed to Germany for the max. In earlier years (see Chapter 38), British testers had used the famous Jabbeke Straight for high-speed runs, but, by this time, Belgium had speed limits, and they were strictly enforced. I made enquires about doing this at Volkswagen's Ehra-Lessien track (see Chapter 51), but it was fully booked for weeks ahead. So it would have to be the public highway …

After some study and consultation, I selected the A92 autobahn as our test track. This runs north-east from Munich to Deggendorf, and it is completely level and straight for 25 miles. This was a couple of years after 'the Wall' had come down, but traffic on that road at the time remained relatively light.

Gathering the minimum of basic equipment – overnight bag, electronically-monitored hub-mounted speed measuring equipment, photographer Mike Valente and his gear – I set off early one Monday to catch the 9am Dover-Calais ferry. The plan was to get the figures, take photos and be back in Blighty by Wednesday afternoon. It was a good plan …

Once we were in the Fatherland, I ran at fairly high speeds, when traffic permitted, and soon discovered that there was a violent vibration between 145 and 150mph, after which it smoothed out. The vibration was so severe that the gear lever became a blur. I decided to keep below 140 before we did the max runs.

It was foggy in Munich on Tuesday morning, but it cleared fairly soon and conditions were ideal, with virtually no wind. I attached Dr Peiseler's speed-measuring kit. We were ready for action. It is fairly straightforward on a clear, straight road to accelerate such a car up to 150mph, but after that you are struggling. The car had quite a good Cd (aerodynamic efficiency) factor but it was still a large frontal area to push through the air. Also, the power is levelling off at that speed so it takes a lot of effort to extract the last few mph.

Above 150mph, you have to be super-alert. You see specks in the far distance and very soon afterwards they materialize as three-dimensional wheeled objects. Often you get the illusion that the specks are moving towards you, which in a very real sense they are. That's relativity, as Professor Einstein would have said. You have to be prepared to abort the mission before your options finally run out.

After considerable frustration, we achieved a mean of runs in opposite directions of precisely 170mph. This was achieved in fifth, as it could not pull the revs in the absurdly high sixth (geared for a theoretical 276mph!). Analysis of the digital readout showed that the speed was flickering a few tenths of 1mph over the timed kilometre, never below 169.7 and never above 170.4mph. The speedometer was indicating close to 180. I am sure that the car had peaked and was not going to go any faster, but I wanted to do a run or two more in each direction, just to be certain[3].

But it was not to be. I had just shed 100mph or so for a speck which became two blobs which then metamorphosed into a dirty trailer-truck from Hungary passing a dirtier trailer-truck from Rumania.

I started to depress the clutch to change down a couple of ratios but there was a noise like a washing machine minus its balance weight jumping around on the kitchen floor during the spin-dry cycle. I took my foot off the clutch and we struggled back into Munich, about 70 miles away, in fifth gear, accompanied for some distance by a low-flying police helicopter.

I was seriously worried about what to do next but then we had a miraculous stroke of luck. As we arrived at the north-eastern edge of Munich, there was a very large Opel sign below the road in the distance to the right, which I correctly assumed to be a dealership. I swung the car onto a convenient autobahn exit. I stopped by the roadside, switched the engine off, brutally banged the gear lever into first, depressed the clutch pedal, turned the ignition key and, after a kangaroo-hop start, tootled to the Opel dealer.

They had never heard of the Lotus Carlton there, but they did know of the Opel Lotus Omega, though they had never seen one. I used their phone, got through to the Vauxhall Press Office in Luton and explained what had happened.

Some hours later, a low-loader arrived and the stricken car was transferred to Häusler, Munich's biggest and swankiest Opel dealership. With their considerable experience of the Corvette, which had a very similar twin-mass clutch as well as the same gearbox, they soon found that a bolt had dropped out from somewhere. By Thursday morning, they had put it all back together again before the replacement clutch that had been flown out had arrived. I was impressed. We drove back to Calais, taking care not to exceed 135mph.

I met the Vauxhall delivery driver who came to collect the car from our offices in Cheam. "I hear you had a spot of bother with the transmission," he said, smiling. "You are not the only one!"

[1] The Lotus Carlton/Omega was launched just at the moment when the economy dipped into recession. GM had a target of 1100 cars in total but only about 950 were built, one third of them with Vauxhall badges.
[2] Tyres were getting much better then. In earlier years, some cars could achieve speeds that somewhat exceeded the capabilities of the tyres with which they were fitted. But even so …
[3] For years, I was convinced that 'the 176mph Lotus Carlton' was typical Lotus dream-world bullshit. However, Chris Harris, the *Top Gear* chap, ex-*Autocar* tester and serious racer, did get a Lotus Carlton to do the claimed speed. His test car may have had a few extra miles on it or it may have been down to variations in output, probably a bit of both.

60 A bit more sideways

ON A SUNNY SUMMER'S day in 1986, I rolled up in a Ferrari Testarossa at the gates of Tangmere Aerodrome in Sussex. I had been past the entrance on the south side of the A27 between Chichester and Arundel many times, but had never been in.

I knew that it had been an important Spitfire base during the Battle of Britain and that it had been decommissioned a few years previously, but was more familiar with its satellite base, RAF Westhampnett, better known as Goodwood, only a couple of miles to the west. And I was not aware of the fascinating detail of Tangmere's wartime history.

Douglas Bader was a Wing Commander there in 1941, and, with its proximity to the Channel, it is not surprising that Tangmere was frequently used by SOE for the transit of agents between England and France. Among the many who passed through there in this capacity were 'Williams' (William Grover-Williams), who had been the winner of the first Monaco Grand Prix in 1929, and his friend Robert Benoist, one of the greatest French racing drivers of the 1920s and 1930s. Both were captured by the Germans and met sticky ends towards the end of the war, Benoist being executed at Buchenwald in September 1944, and Williams a few months later at Sachsenhausen[1].

So here I was to do some action shots with the Ferrari. It is always more relaxing to do that, especially with a quick car, at a test track rather than on the public highway. After burbling through the gates of the aerodrome, I met Simon Childs, a photographer with whom I had never previously worked.

Car photographers, by and large, are a weird bunch. Most of them are always complaining. It's too dark, or it's too sunny; they grumble about being cold, wet, or sunburnt in the course of their work (I used to drop the window from time to time and ask what the problem was); Above all, they usually insist upon working through lunchtime.

I discovered that none of that, except the irritating work-instead-of-lunch habit, applied to Simon. He did not complain. He just got on with the job. But one thing he shared with the majority of the car photographers I have met was an astonishing disregard of safety precautions. Their favourite exhortation is, "Can you get it a bit more sideways, please?" The first response to that is usually, "Well yes, but don't stand *there*, or I might kill you." Since this was our first job together, I should have discussed this beforehand, but I forgot. Anyway, one starts off working relationships in a spirit of cooperation: one does not expect people to be *completely* mad.

We went to a corner at the far end of the perimeter track, where Simon and his sidekick Mike Johnson began setting up their cameras. Simon said I should take the Testarossa back along the track, and then come through this left-hand bend, "as fast as you like."

So I did that. I approached the corner (which was blind because of the height of the corn on the infield), passed Mike (who was stationed at the entry of the curve) at something like 80mph, turned in, easing off the throttle slightly to break the grip of the wide rear tyres. The heavy lump of the 4.9-litre flat-12 moved several degrees to the south. I came back on the power, passing the apex in a mildly smoky tail-out slide, still doing more than 60 I should think. It was at this point that I found my suicidal snapper colleague lying prone in the road, *exactly* where the car would go if slide degenerated into spin.

158

"That was great," he said, after I missed him by inches. "Can you do it again?" I gave him a few terse words of advice about personal safety, and how much nicer it would be for him if he were to survive into pensionable age (he was about 25 at that time, while I was an elderly man of 35), and then we continued with the action photography, this time with a greater margin for error. However, it is the photo from that first run that is framed on my wall and a fabulous picture it is.

Some 18 months previously, I was invited to the official unveiling of the Testarossa at the Lido in Paris. This was one of the most bizarre events I have ever attended.

[1] See Chapter 76. It was suggested some years ago that 'Williams' survived the war and lived in Normandy under an assumed name with his French wife (Yvonne, née Aubicq or possibly Aupicq), a former mistress of the outstanding portrait painter Sir William Orpen, for whom Williams had been chauffeur. Robert Ryan in his definitively ludicrous novel *Early One Morning*, based with heroic looseness on the Williams/Benoist story, actually claimed that he had definite proof of this, but did not present any, on the very reasonable grounds that no such proof exists.

61 Some enchanted evening

I NEVER DID WORK out why Ferrari chose to launch the Testarossa in The Lido, a Paris nightclub where exceedingly tall 'exotic' dancers from Swansea or Prague prance around, wearing not much more than feathers, high heels and exaggerated makeup, for the titillation of gullible tourists and provincials. I suppose somebody thought there was too much competition from other launches at the 1984 Paris Salon de l'Automobile.

There was plenty of tit, but not much elation, I thought. Before the paying punters arrived, Ferrari did its presentation, unwisely showing four design projects that had been evaluated before the one with the straked intakes was chosen. Most observers preferred one of the less flashy rejects.

Then the show began. A five-piece band was cranked onstage, including a singer who may have been a retired bouncer, and a conductor resembling a used-car salesman. They played aural wallpaper in the style of Edmundo Ros[1]. The conductor behaved as if he were leading the greatest band since Benny Goodman at Carnegie Hall. Grinning relentlessly, he periodically shouted "Yeah!" or "Hey!" The singer's face muscles remained immobile while he murdered songs such as *Stormy Weather*. Barely opening his mouth, he preferred warbling through his nostrils.

Most of the clientèle consisted of foreign tourists, but this was also Big Night Out for citizens of *La France Profonde*, ladies from Lille or Roubaix bulging out in all directions from mauve or bright green polyester dresses, one gentlemen wearing a flat cap, another sporting shoes with brown plastic uppers and inch-thick crepe soles.

The band faded out and customers returned to their tables. The dance floor was swept, a still-wrapped johnny that had fallen from someone's pocket disappearing into a crack between it and the main section of flooring, not the crack for which it was intended. The stage, perhaps 50ft square, rose three feet upwards. In the centre, a smaller platform could be lowered into the depths, its place taken by either a Jacuzzi-type pool or an ice rink. I have to admit that the mechanism that allowed all the stage changes was impressive, probably dating from the 1930s.

Several set pieces ostensibly illustrated Life On Earth (minus David Attenborough), a series of excuses for the 'Nude Dancers,' who were not really nude, to kick long legs high and wiggle tits and bums, while the rest of the troupe, even less nude, wiggled as suggestively as they could manage in the background. Dancing boys with false eyelashes minced in and out of this acreage of female flesh.

The girls had bare breasts and buttocks, but their g-strings remained in place. Showgirls had not yet adopted the prenatal shave fashion, but any little tufts of pubic hair that had attempted to sneak towards the navel from the tiny protective triangle had been strimmed[2].

Cabaret turns appeared between set pieces, including a brilliant juggler, two so-so tumblers and a smarty-pants 'illusionist.' The most bizarre act consisted of a middle-aged, short, fat, menacingly ugly woman, a dim-looking muscular young man and a fruity blonde.

The ugly bag rushed upstage, pounding her chest, yelling "Mama! Mama! Mama!" The thick boy balanced his head on Mama's head and she walked up and down a ladder. The girl balanced on the boy's head and he walked up and down the ladder. Then the girl jumped to the floor, ran towards front stage, yelling in a scarily coarse gipsy voice, "*Olé, olé, olé.*"

Two elderly Indian elephants were led on for a sketch about Africa. At least they did not have false ears. They were taken away, the central platform sank, up popped the Jacuzzi. Two characters wearing Dalek-style helmets down to their waists disappeared into the bubbling water, holding flaming torches.

The rear curtain opened, revealing a huge wall with a 10ft-high image of a human face. A torrent of water crashed down. Two 'white hunters,' one male and one female, were grabbed by 'tribesmen' (all but two of them honkies in dark body-stockings, rather in the style of *The Black & White Minstrel Show*).

The tribesmen separated their captives. Perhaps to the male white hunter's disappointment, it was the female who was obliged to perform simulated rumpypumpy. A rival chief took umbrage and the two of them, one really black, the other bestockinged, waggled spears. The white lady, trussed to a swinging gibbet, was about to be dropped in the Jacuzzi, disappointingly containing no crocodiles, when the white bloke rescued her.

Then came the *pièce de résistance*, the Hindenburg. Clever machinery and lighting alternately showed wealthy German passengers enjoying their flight in the luxurious saloon, and the captain and his crew below, worrying about thunderstorms. A dancing boy played the reporter at Lakehurst Naval Air Station, rambling on about "the magnificent Hindenburg," while an object eight feet long, resembling a shrivelled marrow, swung shakily along a wire, trailing sparks[3].

The gondola appeared, and there was a loud explosion and flames. Two passengers, who had taken the precaution of wearing flameproof suits, rolled onstage on fire. It was all potentially dangerous, but there were no casualties.

[1] A Trinidadian band leader who enjoyed a lot of success with easy-listening music in a Latin-American style.

[2] This antiseptic evening of entertainment (which cost paying punters 300 francs per head, quite a lot in 1984) was quite unlike the brutally uncompromising entertainment to be enjoyed in that era in live 'fuck shows' just a few Metro stops away.

[3] Exactly as in *Flash Gordon Conquers The Universe*, directed by Ford Ingalsbe Beebe and starring Buster Crabbe, from whom the unfortunate MI6 frogman Lionel Crabb acquired his nickname.

62 The nine-million-euro dream

THESE DAYS, MY MOTHER would be imprisoned for the activities indulged in by her offspring in the garden of Rookwood, our house in Oxhey. We climbed 30ft up trees, but that would have been ignored by the magistrates as relatively trivial ...

When I was 11 and my brother 13, during school holidays we competed in time trials with a 1934 Austin Seven, as soon as Mummy had set off for the shops in her A35. My brother had ingeniously acquired the Seven somehow for about 15 quid, including delivery on a low loader. My mother probably thought it would keep us occupied. My father had perhaps not noticed that we had become probably the only three-car family within a radius of many miles.

The start/finish line of the course was at the open gates onto Green Lane, a quiet but public road[1]. The surface changed from gravel drive to dirt track to lawn, then dirt and gravel again, with a hairpin around an apple tree and an S-bend through the woods. To get a good time (under 40 seconds), it was necessary to cross the finish line with all four wheels locked, then try to stop without sliding into the public highway.

My mother's defence lawyer would point out, correctly, that she did not know that we did this, because we always waited until she had gone out shopping. Would the judge and jury accept that as a mitigating factor? Would our acquisition of cadence-braking skills have been taken into account?

My dream ever since has been to own a property with its own private racing circuit. Le Grand Sambuc[2] would suit me perfectly. Set in 1500 acres of woodland, dominated by a 2300ft crag (Le Grand Sambuc itself), its attractions include a genuine 17th-century chateau, an '18th-century' bastide – built in the 1970s, but few would guess it – and a 1.2-mile circuit, constructed at the same time by Régis de Fraissinet, who raced at Le Mans several times and was a successful competitor in hillclimbs. The property, in a remote part of southern France, near Aix-en-Provence, is bathed in sunshine for most of the year, with no neighbours to complain about noise.

The circuit is regularly used by car clubs and manufacturers: Porsche, Ferrari and Mercedes-Benz have hired it. Derek Bell tested Bentley's Le Mans racer on the track in 2002, the year before the team won *les 24 Heures*. Michael Schumacher and David Coulthard are among numerous famous racers who have driven there. I tried the circuit with a few gentle laps (especially because it started to rain and I could not find the windscreen wiper control!) in a De Tomaso Pantera kindly loaned by Monsieur Fraissinet.

The downhill start/finish straight has two kinks, taken flat even in very quick cars. The lap record was set in the early 1990s by a Grand Prix driver in 45.4sec – an average of about 94mph[3]. The car was clocked at 186mph at the end of the straight. A decade later, a friend, competing in a classic car rally, "struggled to reach 95mph" in his XK150 at the same point. This is followed by a long, constant-radius right-hander leading into the twisty northerly side of the circuit.

From there, the track climbs towards a tight, dipping S-bend. Again the road ascends, through a faster S-bend, to the highest point of the circuit, where a deceptive, double-apex right-hander leads back to the main straight.

All round the track, Armco barrier is close to the edges: there are no 'run-off areas,' because Monsieur Fraissinet became convinced in his racing years that the worst crashes occur when cars hit barriers at the wrong angle. The track is wider than many small circuits (between 30 and 39ft), but, if you get things seriously wrong, you are liable to scrape along the Armco, scrub off speed, and dent panels or damage suspension. No one has been injured in a car there: "Not even a broken finger!" However, this design is less suited to motorcycles and several riders have been hurt.

The chateau, used as a reception centre, is rectangular, with cone-topped cylindrical towers at each corner. It needs attention. The splendid bastide is on three floors, the ground floor dominated by a fine living-room with a stone fireplace. The top floor, with windows all around, has sufficient exposed oak beams to build a schooner. In one direction, you can see the Mediterranean, in another the Alps[4/5].

There are several springs on the land. There is a tennis court and a swimming pool. About 80 per cent of the property is fenced, with herds of wild sheep, deer, boar, pheasants, partridge and rabbits[6], plus 150 acres suitable for farming olives, almonds and vines.

I was all set to buy Le Grand Sambuc, until Émile Garcin, Ferrari-owning estate agent, told me that the asking price was nine million euros. If you are up for that, it might still be for sale.

---

[1] The top of the steep sledge run in white winters. But that's another story (and would be grounds for another charge of negligence).
[2] I visited it in 2002 for *The Daily Telegraph*.
[3] This is considerably faster than the all-time Rookwood record.
[4] The nuclear power station at Cadarache, to the north, seemed to be just out of view, however.
[5] And on shelves on three sides there were, perhaps still are, 1/43rd-scale models of every Le Mans-winning car since the first race in 1923.
[6] No wildebeest though, I think.

63 Measure for measure

ENGLISH PEOPLE BORN A few years before me exclusively used (and many still do) the imperial system for weights and measures. Those born a few years after me are fully metricated. My generation is more or less able to flit between the two.

Living in France, I am obliged to use the metric system, but I still think imperially for many things. I buy stuff in metres and centimetres and then use feet and inches for my astoundingly skilful DIY jobs. I calculate driving distances in miles, but have switched to litres for petrol. I think of beer in pints, but of wine in litres. Mostly, I do not find it confusing except for weights: if something reasonably small is stated to weigh Xlb or Ykg, I have to look at it and perhaps lift it, though, oddly, at the other end of the scale, for weights of cars, for example, I do not have a problem in either system. I do miss the hundredweight, however. Where did that go and why?

I wrote a column about this once, with the headline, "**Q: What's afoot? A: 30.48cm.**" I received a letter from an alleged scientist who claimed in a fat-headedly angry tone that some obscure organisation to which he belonged had ruled several years earlier that the centimetre no longer existed, and that every dimension would henceforth be measured in millimetres, metres or kilometres.

I replied, enclosing a receipt from a hardware store, a photocopy of a page from the annual Swiss publication *Revue Automobile/Automobil Revue* (published in French and German) and some sarcastic remarks, that this news would cause a stir on the mainland of Europe, where the centimetre blithely lives on, ignoring decisions made by English committees with too much time on their hands.

Incidentally, the English gallon is thoroughly European. It came from an old Norman measure, the *galon*. "Dad, what did they use before William the Conqueror arrived in Hastings?" "Just fill the bloody bucket and stop asking daft questions." The American gallon, 17 per cent smaller than ours[1], is based on the old English wine gallon.

The litre, which was invented by the French, is derived from the volume of 1kg of water at 4°C, under standard atmospheric pressure. Why did they not use claret and room temperature?

Similarly, you might think that the French would have based the centimetre on something interesting, such as some part of Napoleon Bonaparte's anatomy. The true story is far more bizarre. The length of the metre was finally decided in 1799, after years of heated debate. It was originally proposed that it should be one ten-millionth of the distance between the North Pole and the Equator, via Paris[2]. Only a French bureaucrat could think up something as spectacularly preposterous as that in the middle of a bloody revolution.

At the same time, these people, forerunners of the énarques[3], decided that it was an appropriate moment to change the names of all the seasons and the months of the year, for no obvious reason other than Professor Parkinson's Law that work expands to fill the time available. On that topic, they even metricated time: each day in the exciting new Republican Calendar was divided into ten hours, each new hour into 100 minutes, and each new minute into 100 seconds. They did not stop there, either: each month was divided into three ten-day weeks. It must have been infuriating to them that the Earth's motion around the Sun and the eccentric lunar orbit were stubbornly resistant to metrication[4].

164

It is rather as if a 21st century French government, instead of concentrating on the economy and all the important things that most people are worried about – unemployment, companies going bankrupt, the cost of living, housing shortages, energy, violent crime and acts of terrorism, cutting military budgets while increasingly engaging in foreign wars, the supply of clean water and so on – would choose to spend hundreds of hours debating, for example, whether or not homosexuals should be able to marry each other ...

The metric system is undeniably more logical and simple than the imperial. There might be some long-term savings to be gained if Britain went fully metric, just as there would if Britain switched to left-hand drive, which is generally more comfortable for the driver[5], but the costs of either change would be enormous, whether they were measured imperially or metrically. There are a few things, I would suggest, that require more urgent attention.

[1] This is not the only reason that American cars have traditionally achieved fewer mpg than cars from Europe and Japan.

[2] I am not making this up. Apparently they did not have a piece of string long enough to measure this. French joke ... Q: How long is a piece of string? A: Under 10,000km.

[3] Alumni of the École National d'Administration (ENA), memorably described by CAR magazine's French industry correspondent in the 1980s as "the world's most expensively educated idiots."

[4] None of this sophisticated *connerie* caught on with the general public, even though they greatly enjoyed watching other people's heads being lopped off by the dropping blade. However, metric clocks are still being manufactured, for reasons that are difficult to decipher. Perhaps they are given as retirement presents to annoy people who are greatly disliked, such as those who insist that the centimetre no longer exists.

[5] With LHD, the driver's right leg can lean comfortably against the centre console while cruising and the inside surface of the front wheel arch provides a useful bracing point for the left foot, except in Morgans, of course.

64 Testing, testing ... like so, jawohl!

THE HUNS WORKING ON motoring publications had – and probably still have – a particular method of testing cars. They had a set of test drivers and a set of road-test writers. The drivers did no writing. The writers did no testing, though they did drive test cars on the road and delivered them to the circuit for the testers to do their work. I was informed that this was the correct way of doing things.

In Britain, each magazine had its test team. Wherever possible, everyone drove every test car and, in each case, the road-test editor nominated a member of his team to be in charge of the test. That person would be responsible for recording all the figures at Millbrook test track in Bedfordshire: maximum speed, acceleration, braking, and so on, as well as having a blast around one of the handling tracks. Usually, two or three cars would be taken to Millbrook, and all tests were conducted two-up. It was sometimes a nice day out in the country, but also hard work. When the Huns bought the magazine I edited, I was informed that this was the incorrect way of doing things.

I was instructed to visit the Fatherland, to find out how to do things correctly. I was surprised when I discovered that *auto motor und sport* did its performance testing at Hockenheim[1], except for maximum speed, which was checked on the autobahns. I flew to Stuttgart, spent a night in a crap hotel and was then driven to Hockenheim, where I spent most of the day observing how German testing was done, learning the square root of nothing new.

Hockenheim in those days was still essentially the old ultra-high speed track, though it had been rendered somewhat safer by the installation of Armco barriers and of a chicane on each of the long straights (and later a third chicane at the Sudkurve, following Patrick Depailler's death there in 1980). The Germans did their acceleration runs on the stretch between the Nordkurve at the exit of the stadium section and the first chicane, which is where Jim Clark had his fatal accident in 1968 (before the advent of chicanes). This stretch was straight enough for the purpose, but was actually one long, blind bend.

I sat in for some acceleration runs in the quickest car available on the day. The driver was highly competent, as I expected. I noted that there was *just* sufficient room to hit 200km/h (124mph) before having to brake very hard indeed, as the track curved sharply to the right towards the entrance to the first part of the chicane. We stopped, turned round, and did the return run (acceleration figures are always the mean of runs in opposite directions). I noted that *a-m-s* had two fifth wheels and asked the tester if there had ever been any accidents with drivers taking off in opposite directions. The driver laughed and said, "Almost!"

Later, I watched in fascination as a test writer interviewed a tester, taking copious notes. Then I flew home and wrote a succinct report of what I had observed.

I wrote that whereas we were able to use Millbrook on almost any weekday, merely needing to make the booking the day before, *a-m-s* could go testing only on Mondays, which was inconvenient because the fortnightly German magazine often had a dozen or more cars to assess. Millbrook, I pointed out in detail, was far superior to Hockenheim in every respect, including safety, adding that if the Stuttgarters did not know much about it, they would certainly know of Opel's test centre at Dudenhofen, which is almost identical: both GM tracks have a high-speed bowl, an acceleration straight, a skidpan, several handling circuits and other facilities.

I mentioned that the Peiseler fifth wheels[2] used by *a-m-s* were very much like the one we used, except that ours was a more recent model. I could not resist adding that conducting slalom tests with parked cars nearby was an avoidable and unnecessary risk. I concluded by suggesting that selecting people with skills in both writing and driving seemed like a more cost-effective policy than assuming that those who write are unable to drive, and vice versa.

I sent this report to Horst, alias Geoffrey[3], with a copy to another unpleasant Hun in Stuttgart. As I was an unperson, there was no reply from either, but, from then on, there was no attempt to interfere in our testing. Harassment was redirected to other areas in which we were doing things wrongly. It was almost enough to drive a chap to drink.

[1] The Hockenheimring, in Baden-Württemberg, then a challenging high-speed circuit, later reduced by Herr Herman Tilke the circuit designer to a sort of kart track for modern Grand Prix entertainments.
[2] These were precision-manufactured devices from Peiseler GmbH of Dachau, near Munich, with its workshops just the other side of the autobahn from the infamous camp. The equipment consisted essentially of a bicycle wheel with lightweight twin forks, attached to the car, usually by rubber suction pads, and connected to an electronic magic box that recorded time elapsed and distance covered. This was the most accurate system available at the time, but has since been superseded by GPS-based devices.

Dr Peiseler himself was a clever engineer in a white coat who employed a weird woman in a black leather coat as a translator for English visitors. He seemed to understand English vernacular far better than she did, as he always laughed at my jokes, while she remained expressionless. Perhaps she found them unamusing. It's a free country, as they used to say.
[3] See Chapter 32.

65 Missed opportunities and creative fibs

"NON, JE NE REGRETTE rien," lied the warbling little sparrow. Well, there are lots of errors, both of commission and omission, that I regret. Also, sometimes one's friends tell you outrageous fibs without blinking. But Mickey Mouse's fickle index finger of Fate has moved on, and there is not a jot that I can do about any of that.

Some of my regrets relate to the thing that is closest to all our hearts: money, money, money. That's what we all want, if we are honest, which, out of politeness or for some more devious reason that we do not wish to divulge, we are usually not, to be honest. I shall come back to that.

One terrible missed opportunity was the failure to have a camera with me when I had in the frame of my mind's eye the shattered remains of the historic Citroën factory on what had once been called the Quai de Javel, as mentioned in Chapter 68. I could have sold that evocative image worldwide and made a lot of money, money, money. Also, it would be nice to have a large framed print of it on the wall.

But sometimes, it is not the cash that bugs us. It can be the frustration when you have a 'light-bulb moment,' too late. *Fast Lane*'s motorcycling correspondent in the 1980s was Ian Macpherson[1]. I had not planned to include motorbikes in the magazine, but Ian, whom I had not previously met, invited himself to the office and deftly talked me into the idea.

It worked out well: he wrote some excellent articles, possibly gave the circulation a mild boost, and certainly helped the advertising department to widen its range of prey victims. Although I am not a biker, the engineering of motorcycles fascinates me. For many years, the motorbike manufacturers were well ahead of the car makers in presenting technology as art.

Ian's most imaginative contribution to the magazine concerned a visit to the Nürburgring to test an unusual machine that went under several names over the years. At that time, there was a choice of Ecomobile or Oekomobil. This was a fully-enclosed motorcycle with retractable dolly wheels that were mechanically deployed by the rider at low speeds. If the rider neglected to deploy them when stopping for a red traffic light, for example, the dolly wheels were automatically lowered to prevent the machine from falling over with an embarrassing and expensive *kerrang*. Similarly, there was a system that prevented them from being lowered, with potentially catastrophic consequences, at speed.

The Ecomobile was the product of a Swiss engineer, Arnold Wagner. It was quite a clever invention, and well executed, but it never achieved commercial success, probably because of the high cost. Perhaps it was ahead of its time, the perennial explanation of failure.

Ian was part of a group of biking journalists who arrived at the Nürburgring early one morning, having had an explanatory lecture during a press conference in a nearby hotel the previous evening.

There were six Ecomobiles: Arnold Wagner's works demonstrator, and five privately-owned examples. The owners, for reasons unexplained, were all Swissair pilots. The journalists spent the morning riding pillion, while the machines were demonstrated in the villages and back roads near the circuit. So they were *at* the Nürburgring, but not *on* it, not even on the 'lite' version, the 3.2-mile modern grand Prix circuit.

The idea was that, after lunch, the Swissair pilots and Mr Wagner would take the hacks, still as passengers, for further rides around this short road route. Actually being permitted to ride them was not part of the plan, though this had not been explained in advance.

Ian sat next to Herr Wagner at lunch, switched on his tape recorder and asked a few questions while eating the first course. Then he said, "Excuse me a moment." He was gone for 20 minutes. When he returned he switched off his tape recorder and put it in his briefcase. Then he thanked Herr Wagner for his kind hospitality, and told him that he was going to order a taxi to take him to the airport. Herr Wagner was surprised, and protested that he had not had the benefit of the full day's instruction, and that he would miss the best part of the launch, riding around the Grand Prix circuit the following morning.

"Oh, that's all right," said Ian. "I've just done a lap of the Nordschleife[2]." In his feature article, he wrote that the key had been conveniently left in the ignition of the works demonstrator. Herr Wagner's expression changed from mild surprise to horrified astonishment. Well, this was what happened according to Ian …[3]

What, you will be wondering, was the missed opportunity in this? It came when the issue of the magazine was published. The spread looked good, but the moment I saw it, I uttered one word. "Bugger!" I said, rather loudly. A colleague asked what the problems was. I explained that I had just thought of the perfect headline, too late: "WAGNER'S RING CYCLE."

[1] Now Lord Strathcarron, Mk III.
[2] The real Nürburgring, 'The Green Hell,' all 12.8 miles of it.
[3] It was printed in *Fast Lane*, so it must be true. And in any case, it was a good yarn.

66 Polluted steering

THERE ARE MANY YOUNG people these days who have never driven a car with rear-wheel drive. This may explain why professional footballers, suddenly rich beyond imagination, so frequently crash their supercars during the first week of ownership, their previous driving experience restricted to front-wheel-drive cars.

It is not merely that those front-driven cars have less powerful engines: they do not respond in the same way to too much throttle, or to not enough.

I am one of those relics of the era when the vast majority of cars on the market were rear-wheel drive. Like many of my contemporaries I developed a strong preference for cars with driven rear wheels. I enjoyed driving cars generally (with occasional ghastly exceptions), and, in my early years on the road, I had had fun in various front-driven cars, such as Minis and Deux Chevaux, but I never found them as satisfying as cars with what the French call 'propulsion.'

I have retained this preference, even though I concede that, in small and medium-sized cars, front-wheel drive provides undeniable advantages in space utilization, and also generally delivers easier driving behaviour on slippery surfaces. I have considered only a few front-driven cars to have a serious fun factor. Three that stand out are the Alfasud, the Peugeot 205 GTI, and the Lotus Elan M100, with several others, notably various generations of the Golf GTI, in the Highly Commended category.

The Sud had been in production for seven years when its finest version, the 1.3ti, was introduced in 1978. I ran one for a year as my long-term car on *Motor* and, when that tenure ended, I was upset, to put it mildly, especially because the replacement was a Datsun Sunny 120Y Coupé, which provided conclusive proof that a rear-wheel-drive car can be nasty, just as the Sud demonstrated that a front-wheel-drive car can be nice.

What was it about the Alfasud that was so exceptional? It was a combination of dynamic elements. The flat-four engine had a wide power band, even if there was not much power, throttle response was impeccable, and the exhaust note was wonderfully rasping. The five-speed gearbox was slick. The brakes were efficient and smooth in operation. But it was the ride and handling, and, above all, what happened when you hit the apex of a bend with your foot fairly hard on the throttle, that really set it apart.

Problems often associated with front-wheel drive are steering kickback, torque steer and excessive understeer. The 1.3ti had none of these unpleasant characteristics to any significant degree. Although it tended towards understeer in tight bends, it was generally neutral, and would even edge towards oversteer under power, like the later Peugeot 205 GTI, at higher speeds. Also, despite its horizontally-opposed engine, the Alfasud, at least in early versions with relatively narrow wheels, had roughly the same turning circle as a Ford Fiesta.

Alfa Romeo achieved an unexpected but ephemeral sort of perfection with the 1.3ti. While build quality improved to some extent, later front-driven Alfas were not quite as good dynamically. Subsequent Alfasuds were fitted with wider, lower-profile tyres and stiffer suspension, in line with the buying public's misplaced conception of what constitutes 'sportiness.' The car was still very good, but much of the indefinable magic was lost. I am sure these changes lowered lap times around test tracks, but that is beside the point.

The steering of the 1.3ti was perfectly weighted, and you could feel exactly what it was doing. It allowed the car to enter corners with the same sort of precision that you get from a good rear-driven car. And the ride, though sometimes over-reactive at low speeds, was beautifully controlled at speed.

No other front-driven car of the period matched this level of excellence, and few have even got close since then. While the Alfasud was a masterpiece of applied engineering as far as its dynamics were concerned, it was a shame that the same was not true of its body construction. The steel started rotting, silently and – for a while – invisibly, even before the cars left the Pomigliano factory.

In passing, during my Alfasud year, we had a Chevrolet Caprice Classic on test at *Motor*. This was in the early days of emissions regulation, and it was the period of strangulated engines. Despite its five-litre V8, the American car could not match the Italian for acceleration or top speed. I shall not bother to mention fuel consumption, handling or braking, which had evidently not been of major importance to General Motors.

The Chevy was about 52 per cent heavier than the Alfa. It was 58in longer and 16in wider. Yet the little Italian car had more room inside for four people, and more luggage space. How the American manufacturers managed to survive was a mystery to me.

Returning to the topic of this chapter, 'Traction Avant' is what the French call front-wheel drive[1]. The French believe that they invented it. The French believe that they invented just about everything … but in this instance they may be correct. Moving on from snide stereotypical remarks, it is obvious that the more power that is fed through the front wheels, the greater the problems outlined above become, and you then have a pronounced lack of traction avant, which is a nuisance.

Sports cars do not have driven front wheels. That is the received wisdom. Therefore, when it became clear that the new small Lotus in the late 1980s was going to be driven from the front (unlike any other Lotus to leave the Hethel factory before or since), I was sceptical. I was not alone. *Everyone* was sceptical. Rightly so, it is generally believed, because the car was a marketing disaster, and led directly to Lotus being sold by General Motors. But it might have turned out differently. There is an interesting story behind that, which I think is worth telling.

I had been amused to discover that among the suspension development engineers for the M100 was John Miles, the former Grand Prix driver[2]. During the time he spent producing outstanding features as an overworked technical writer for *Motor*'s rival weekly *Autocar*, he coined a memorable phrase to explain what he disliked about front-wheel drive: "polluted steering."

I drove to Hethel early one morning in November 1989. Rain was descending in apocalyptic fashion. Soon after arrival, I found myself in the driver's seat of an Elan M100, with Chief Engineer Roger Becker[3] in the passenger seat.

---

[1] See Chapters 53 and 54.

[2] Son of the renowned ham actor Bernard Miles, John had a distinguished motor racing career which ended with the trauma of being Jochen Rindt's team-mate when the champion-to-be was killed at Monza in 1970. Later, he made a significant contribution to the excellent ride and handling of a long series of roadgoing Lotuses.

[3] Roger Becker (1945-2017) was one of the finest development engineers in the motor industry. He worked for Lotus for 43 years, becoming Chief Development Engineer and Associate Director, until his retirement in 2010. His successor in the job was a young engineer named Matt Becker – his son.

67 The conversion of John

IN THE PUBLICITY MATERIAL for the launch, it was claimed that front-wheel drive was chosen for the car because that would make it quicker from point to point on demanding roads. Many observers, including me, believed that the real reason was that GM did not have a suitable engine/transmission package in its range for rear-wheel drive in such a small car.

Up to a point that was true, but the full story was far more complex. A lot of things had been going on in the background, as has often been the case at Lotus. Before the new Elan M100, there was the stillborn M90. This was a front-engined, rear-driven sports car concept, and it was essentially like the original Elan re-invented, but better in every respect, except perhaps styling, but that could have been addressed before production.

All the major components in the driveline – four-cylinder 16-valve engine, gearbox and differential – were from Toyota, with whom Lotus had closely collaborated for some years, and all were aluminium alloy. It was going to be the definitive lightweight, low-cost sports car of the 1980s. If Colin Chapman had not died suddenly in 1982, the M90 project would almost certainly have gone into production.

A twin-test between the M90, which was going to be called Elan, and the Toyota MR2 (with essentially the same engine, but mounted behind the cockpit) would have been interesting. But alas, it was not to be.

Lotus has always needed stability and a parent company that understands the company's virtues and how to nurture them. But that has never happened[1]. It has also needed a capable and principled chief executive, preferably an engineer. Instead, it has had, at various times, David Wickins (a salesman), Romano Artioli (an Italian juggler), and Dany Bahar from the planet Tralfamadore.

During the Wickins period, the M90 became the X100, but never progressed beyond prototype stage. Wickins would not put up the money. Then Lotus was acquired by General Motors in 1985, and the moment had passed.

Without those nice, light Toyota components, it was time to move on. You might imagine that, considering GM's numerous worldwide parts bins, this would not be a problem. However, GM did not have any comparable kit for installation in a rear-wheel-drive chassis, so the bold decision was taken to make the a new 'entry-level' Lotus with front-wheel drive. Or at least, that is one interpretation. It has also been suggested that the hour had arrived for a front-driven sports car, because, as mentioned, a large number of drivers had driven nothing but front-driven cars. The objective was to build the best-handling front-driven car to date.

An unpromising four-cylinder engine of Isuzu origin was chosen, and Lotus' engineers did a fine job in tuning it for sports car use. Happily, it came with a rather good five-speed gearbox,

As with all car projects, the Elan M100 was a group effort. Ian Doble played an important role in engineering development, and Barrie Wills (ex-DeLorean, Reliant and Jaguar) was brought in by Lotus boss Mike Kimberley[2] to ensure that the launch deadline was met.

So there I was, with the famous Roger Becker as navigator. The rain was absolutely bucketing down. Roger gave me route instructions as we hacked around East Anglia for a couple of hours, followed by an Esprit Turbo driven by a Lotus test driver, who was accompanied by my photographer. Both the latter and I were worried about the weather, he, for obvious reasons, I, because I thought it would be impossible to draw any meaningful conclusions about the car's dynamics. It turned out that I was quite mistaken, and the downpour proved a blessing in disguise, for me if not for my photographer. Very few cars that I have driven have been as easy to control in such conditions.

In the heavy rain, the test driver in the Esprit Turbo had no chance whatever of keeping up with me. Nor would I have been able to keep him in sight, if we had swapped cars. Although some torque steer was evident in the wet (hardly at all on dry surfaces), the Elan's capabilities were quite astounding. I was especially impressed with the way it could traverse standing water without aquaplaning or kicking back through the steering wheel. Body roll and fore/aft pitch changes during acceleration and braking were all negligible.

In fact, I think on those winding, bumpy roads, the Elan might still have been the quicker of the two cars, if the weather had cleared and all the water had evaporated. As I discovered in later drives, it was often not obviously front-driven in the dry. Whatever the conditions, it was one of the quickest point-to-point cars I have ever driven, though I doubt that it would stand a chance against something like a Subaru WRX.

Strangely, the brilliance of the M100 had little to do with its steering, the directness of which had been such a notable feature of earlier Lotuses. It was surprisingly uncommunicative around dead centre, though it gave more feel as soon as lock was applied.

The key to the Elan's magic was in the front suspension. At a glance, this was a conventional layout typical of Lotus: unequal-length wishbones and coils over dampers. However, this apparent simplicity was deceptive. At the inboard part of this was what was described as a 'compliance raft,' attached at one end to the exceptionally rigid chassis and at the other to an 'interactive' lower wishbone. The purpose of the design, developed by Roger Becker, Jerry Booen and John Miles, was to limit castor angle loss compliant bushes.

The result was a car that went where it was pointed, which could be adjusted easily mid-corner without excessive lift-off oversteer, and which maintained outstanding body control over all surfaces[3].

Concerning John Miles' involvement in the project, I am convinced that, when he was given the assignment, he set out with typically fierce intensity to prove his own prejudice against front-wheel drive wrong!

When we returned to the factory, I was quizzed by a committee of five, including Mike Kimberley. There was an extensive discussion of dynamic behaviour, during which I praised highly the handling and brakes. John looked at me, raised a curious eyebrow and asked mischievously, "But was it fun?"

Well, it certainly was, but alas, that did not make it a success in the market. If Lotus had been able to widen its model range with a two-plus-two version, the M100 might perhaps have fared better. However, due to an extraordinary cockup during the design process, the chassis was a few inches shorter than originally intended and this was no longer possible.

But when people think of sports cars, they do not associate them with front-wheel drive, even if they have never been behind the wheel of anything with the rear axle driven. Not long before the M100 launch, the Mazda MX-5 had appeared. This was really a modern reincarnation of the original rear-wheel drive Elan, but with vastly better build quality. There was no way that it could have kept up with the M100 on those wet roads. However, it went on to become the best-selling sports car in automotive history.

After the failure of the M100, Lotus returned to making rear-wheel drive cars, the most successful of which have been the Elise/Exige. These are often used as trackday cars, and it is relatively easy to modify them to make them perform well on circuits. It would be far more difficult to tune an M100 for such use.

[1] Perhaps Geelong, the new Chinese owner, will provide that. It is too early to be sure.

[2] Kimberley, after ten years as a Jaguar engineer, joined Lotus in 1969. He became the boss of Lotus following the death of founder Colin Chapman in 1982. Subsequently, he worked for various other car makers, including Lamborghini, before returning to Lotus. He retired in 2009. Kimberley and Barrie Wills had first met as engineering apprentices at Jaguar.

[3] However, it could occasionally ground when asked to leap over a humpback bridge.

68 Plan A: a relaxing weekend in Paris

THE M100 WAS DELIVERED to my house in East Grinstead early one Thursday evening. The next morning I took it for a drive around the Sussex lanes. This was the first time I had tried the new Elan on dry roads and it was a revelation, just as it had been, for different reasons, on wet roads.

During this drive, I recalled John Miles' remark that it was often not obvious that it was front-driven. This was very true, and especially so in faster bends. I still preferred rear-driven cars, and still do, but this was really an impressive achievement.

My assignment was to drive to Paris with my wife, have a nice dinner and stay in a nice hotel at Lotus' expense and then deliver the car to Montlhéry, the old racing circuit to the south of the capital, before midday on the Saturday. There was a classic car race meeting that weekend, rather in the style of the Goodwood Revival, and Lotus had a marquee to present the new sports car to the French press and dealers. Then we were to fly back to Blighty on the Sunday. A nice, relaxing trip was in prospect.

We arrived at Dover in plenty of time to catch the 4pm ferry, which, in turn, would leave plenty of time to cruise to Paris. However, things did not go according to plan. One jetty was out of commission, having been seriously damaged by a careless captain, and there was a queue of ships waiting to disgorge cars and passengers and then be re-filled.

Our ferry, I discovered, was loitering in the Channel, waiting its turn. Then I discovered that there was a strike in Calais. Dockers were blockading the harbour and it was not clear when or if we would be allowed in. Eventually, we boarded and, at around 10pm, the ship edged out of the dock. Instead of an early-evening gourmet dinner with plenty of vin rouge in Paris, we ate in the ship's not-bad-but-not-great restaurant, and I was obliged to restrict myself to a couple of glasses.

The ferryboat then hung around the outside of Calais for some time, while negotiations apparently continued. These came to nothing and eventually the ship was redirected to Dieppe. We drove down the ramp at about 4am and headed for Paris, in drizzly rain and pitch darkness.

A couple of hours later, the rain had stopped and the light was brightening, though the Sun had not yet put his hat on. We stopped in an 'aire' for bladder-emptying purposes somewhere within greater Paris. As I was about to get back into the car, I noticed something strange in the near distance below us. It resembled a bombsite, with a large area of flattened buildings. In the centre of this devastation stood the remains of a tower, with a large red double chevron ...

I realized almost immediately that this was the old Citroën factory on what had been the Quai de Javel and which had then become the Quai André Citroën. The factory had originally been built to manufacture artillery shells for World War I. After the Armistice it was converted and expanded for building cars. The first car to roll off the line was the Type A, Europe's first mass-produced car. The last was a DS, on 24 April 1975.

And then I realized to my dismay that I had forgotten to bring a camera with me. This was a major opportunity missed. We pressed on, checked into our hotel about 12 hours later than scheduled, slept for a couple of hours, and then headed for Montlhéry under a bright blue sky.

At the Lotus reception behind the main grandstand, we had just got out of the car when a man with a walrus moustache asked my wife what she thought of it. "It looks like

175

a squashed toad," she replied. I introduced her to the celebrated designer Peter Stevens[1], who should have been knighted long ago.

Beauty is in the eye of the beholder, of course, and many people liked the look of the new Elan. I do not know anyone who has driven it who disliked it. It really did set new handling standards for front-wheel drive, and it was also almost certainly the most reliable car up to that point ever to wear Lotus badges. If it was so good, why did it fail?

That is a tale as complex as its creation. Mike Kimberley had been sent off to business school at Harvard. The management team that he had personally appointed to run Lotus in his absence had taken a radical decision to change from the company's traditional 'vertical' production process (building as much of the car as possible in-house) and had farmed out the supply of many components. If this had not happened, might the M100 have delivered a sufficient profit margin? Was the world ready for a front-wheel-drive sports car, however excellent?

Those are questions that will never find definitive answers. Perhaps the best explanation is that the car suffered small manufacturer syndrome: a large sum of money ($100 million in this instance) had been invested in the car's development. To make a profit, it was then essential to reach a certain volume. However, the Elan M100 arrived just as the market was going into recession and there was no chance that it would hit its sales targets.

This is a combination of events that has wiped out many small manufacturers, whereas larger companies, with wider model ranges, can more easily adapt to survive lean periods and even self-inflicted cock-ups. The Hethel survival strategy has for long been the Lotus Engineering division[2]. If that goes down the tubes, as it nearly has on several occasions over the years, that would almost certainly be terminal for Lotus.

GM, as parent company, took the decision to cease production of the M100. By then, nearly 4000 had been made. Having demonstrably failed to achieve whatever it had set out to achieve when it bought the Lotus group[3], GM sold it in 1993 to a Luxembourg consortium manipulated by an Italian businessman named Romano Artioli. A further 800 examples of the M100, called the series 2, were produced during the period of Romano Artioli's ownership, after a supply of surplus engines had been found in a warehouse!

At the end of this final Hethel run, in 1995 Kia bought the rights to the M100 and manufactured it in Korea. The original body tooling was used, but a new engine and transmission were installed, and there were various other changes.

Having produced around 1000 in three years, Kia then abandoned the model. Again, the reasons for this were complex. At that stage, the Korean company had insufficient experience in composite construction and the quality was not up to Hethel standards. The running gear was also woefully short of the original, and the engine was a buy-in, which caused cost problems in view of the low volume.

Kia's Elan (called Vigato in Japan) was severely criticized by anyone who had driven the original. Korean companies are hypersensitive to such things. Without significant investment, there was little chance of turning it round and then Kia, which was still struggling to establish itself, suffered major financial problems, as did the Korean economy as a whole. Investing in a non-volume product didn't make much sense. It was the wrong package, at the wrong time, for all the wrong reasons.

The greatest puzzle of all to me in this sad saga is that no other car manufacturer has used the compliance raft system pioneered on the M100. Perhaps they would say that they already have clever electronic traction control systems. But it is not the same thing. The Lotus Elan M100 set new standards for handling and steering response of front-wheel-drive cars, which, to my knowledge, have not yet been matched. I doubt that they ever will be.

[1] Peter Stevens, as Senior Lecturer at the Royal College of Art's vehicle design course in Kensington, trained a generation of designers, who went on to occupy senior posts in car manufacturing companies throughout the world. As a designer, he was responsible not only for the Elan M100, but also the redesigned Lotus Esprit, the McLaren F1 supercar, numerous other road cars, and several racing and rally cars.

[2] The engineering consultancy division has collaborated with numerous car manufacturers, in some cases developing new cars from scratch, in others working on specific components. These include lightweight body/chassis construction, suspension design and tuning, engine efficiency and electronics.

[3] When GM bought Lotus, it was widely feared that the American giant would interfere too much in managing the small British company. At the end, it was evident that it had not interfered enough. The same thing happened at Saab. It is astonishing that, at the time of writing, General Motors still exists.

69 Drinking and driving

DRINKING AND DRIVING CAN be enjoyable hobbies, but they should be savoured separately. I have always endeavoured not to indulge in them simultaneously. However, on one occasion[1], I was obliged to do so for professional reasons. If you have got this far, you might feel that an explanation is required. Here goes.

In 1977, my colleague at *Motor* Rex Greenslade had the idea, probably after several pints of Harvey's, of testing people's behaviour before and after consumption of different quantities of alcohol. We hired Brands Hatch, though we used only a section of the straight near Dingle Dell. We assembled early in the morning and set up a course containing slalom, lane-change, and reversing manoeuvre.

Taking part were a couple of *Motor*'s road testers, including me, and other drivers of varying degrees of experience, among them the neighbours of the deputy editor, specifically chosen as Mr and Mrs Average[2].

In attendance, we had a traffic policeman to breathalyze us, and a doctor and nurse monitoring blood/alcohol levels and checking urine samples at regular intervals (a tent was provided for privacy). A film crew was there to record the event for a television programme called *Top Gear*, which in those days was about cars.

As well as the medical team, Greenslade took the piss. He sat in on all the tests with clipboard and stopwatch. To evaluate our ability to concentrate, he kept up a constant stream of dumb questions that you might be asked on *The Weakest Link*, such as "Who wrote Beethoven's Fifth Symphony?"

We all had half an hour's practice, then began in earnest. While we testers set our best times stone-cold sober and steadily became slower and more erratic, most of the other drivers became marginally quicker after a couple of shots boosted their confidence, though they were still a long way off the par time.

We were given vodka mixed with orange juice; although it was carefully measured, none of us knew exactly how much we had drunk. I was amazed that although I felt totally unfit to drive after my second drink – and said so – the breathalyzer gave me a marginal result, but the blood and urine tests passed me street legal. At that stage, I had consumed two doubles on an empty stomach and felt as pissed as two parrots.

By mid afternoon, several people were disappearing into the Kent woods to do technicolour yawns. Mr Average was redefining morosity, while Mrs Average became stridently voluble or volubly strident. Divorce seemed inevitable.

Starting my final test, I had put away threequarters of a bottle. As we entered the slalom, Rex asked, "Which London station is named after a famous battle?" I replied, "King's Cross" and we both doubled up laughing. You had to be there. I lost control, and came to a squealing halt with three plastic cones jammed under the car.

I sat down on the grass verge, somewhere around 12.8 out of ten on the mellowness scale. It was then that I observed Chief Constable Barry Pain being interviewed by the BBC crew. It was time for action. I refer you to the Introduction for what happened next. I do wish I had that hat.

After that incident, the light seemed to fade. Uncle Maurice, the Chief Photographer, told me later that he had given me a lift home to Blackheath, and he made up some cock-and-bull story about me cackling with laughter all the way and periodically leaning across and beeping the horn. I awoke around midnight, in pitch darkness, fully clothed on my bed, wondering where I was and who I was and harbouring doubts about which species I was.

First I remembered Brands, then that I had to go testing at MIRA the next day. I set the alarm for 6am. I awoke, surprisingly feeling not too bad – it was 15 hours after my last drink – and headed north.

Our habitual rendezvous was Newport Pagnell services. I had breakfast and was surprised that nobody else had arrived by 9am. At 9.30 I telephoned the office. Jeremy, the Road Test Editor, answered. I asked him what the hell he was playing at.

After a long silence, he said that he had telephoned at 8 o'clock the previous evening to cancel, and that I had answered.

"You did seem rather monosyllabic," he added. I had never previously been *that* drunk and it has never happened since, even at Motor Shows.

[1] As suggested obliquely in the Introduction.

[2] The proposition was, of course, not put to them in those terms. They probably imagined that they were doing their friendly neighbour a big favour, rather than being used as guinea pigs in a scientific field experiment.

70 The mysteriously empty tureens

ON THE EVE OF the 1993 Geneva Motor Show, I was invited to an official dinner by Volkswagen at the Hotel Beau Rivage on the Quai du Mon-Blanc, near where the waters of Lac Leman (as in man-made) pass under the road bridge, to continue the seaward journey as the River Rhône.

Usually at these events, there is a set meal of three, four or five courses, or perhaps even more, but this was Volkswagen Germany and this was a big event with about 300 guests. They had decided to cut costs and have a buffet instead.

I introduced myself to the other people around my table. I knew none of them, and none of them seemed to be involved in anything that would interest me professionally (or indeed, in any other way). I expect that was mutual.

To dispel that 'What the fuck am I doing here?' feeling, I decided to try to extract something from one or two people at other tables and then spend the rest of the evening on the nearby Fiat Boat. But first I should take on some solids. I hate queuing for anything at the best of times, and I could see that a big queue would soon build up, so I headed straight for the buffet.

I recognized the face of the man immediately ahead of me in the queue, who had obviously had the same idea as me, but it took me a couple of minutes to identify him from the depths of my erratic memory. Then I got it – although I had never met him I knew for certain that he was José Lopez, the notorious José Ignacio Lopez de Arriortúa who was very much in the news at that time.

Mr Lopez had joined Volkswagen as head of production, having been personally head-hunted for the job by Ferdinand Piëch, after he had become famous for introducing Japanese 'just-in-time'[1] efficiency methods to GM. The Americans never forgave the Spaniard for jumping ship.

Mr Lopez lifted the lid of a large silvered tureen, only to discover that it was empty. He looked perplexed by this. He hesitated, as if he could not quite believe in the emptiness before him. Then, having decided that there really was nothing there, he moved on to the next tureen. That also was empty, as was the third, though they were all perfectly clean.

I leaned forward and said quietly, "It would appear, Mr Lopez, that on this occasion your cost-cutting techniques have gone too far." He looked round at me, fury blazing from his eyes. And then he burst out laughing, though he did not pursue the conversation. Further along the line, we both managed to fill our plates with reasonably appetizing comestibles.

While I was consuming this, and making a mild effort to maintain polite conversation with my neighbours, I noticed that Lopez pointed at me, said something to those around his table and they all laughed. I finished my food, got a story out of Volkswagen's PR chief, the amusing and amusingly-named Klaus Kocks.

Mr Kocks once said at a dinner for the British motoring press that in the UK, *Fawlty Towers* was regarded as a comedy programme, but the Germans had recognized it as a documentary about the psychological makeup of the English. On another occasion, he asked if anyone present knew the difference between an American and a yoghurt. Nobody did, so he provided the answer: a yoghurt can produce its own culture. He once told me that something I had written about his boss Dr Piëch was "the most libellous article I have ever read in a national newspaper." Then he added, "but it's absolutely true."

Klaus Kocks was later, somewhat improbably considering this apparently uncontrollable propensity for making rather good jokes that stuffy people found 'inappropriate,' a spokesman for the German government of Herr Gerhard Fritz Kurt Schröder[2].

On the way out, I wanted to have a word with Mr Lopez. But he was being interviewed by a German TV crew. He looked up and smiled. I headed for the Fiat boat and unfortunately never met him again. Like a number of high-fliers hired by Ferdinand Piëch, Lopez ended up being hung out to dry, and General Motors hunted him down with maximum vindictiveness.

It has often occurred to me that the best way to get on in life is to make bold remarks that knock people off their guard.

[1] An ingenious system whereby manufacturers transfer unwanted risk and unavoidable inefficiency to their original-equipment suppliers. It also massively increases road freight.

[2] Many misdemeanours may be listed against Herr Schröder. For a start, he is a qualified lawyer. While exercising that devious profession, he secured the early release from prison of the violent extremist fruitcake Horst Mahler. However, like Jacques Chirac (against whom many misdemeanours may also be listed), he opposed the stupid invasion of Iraq concocted by Bush Junior and Blair.

71 An inspector calls

MAKING A PROFIT IN the motor industry is difficult at the best of times. It is tough for companies both large and small. Simply consider this: in the early 1950s, over 60 separate companies were building motor cars in Britain.

Following all the bankruptcies and mergers and takeovers, today the largest remaining independent British car manufacturer is The Morgan Car Company. If you had suggested in 1950 that this might one day be the case, you would have been an object of ridicule.

The market is fickle; long-term planning always involves an element of gamble, which of course, is a far greater risk for a small-scale operation lacking the assets, flexibility and economies of scale enjoyed by multinationals. One moment you can be smugly apologizing for the long waiting list, the next everything may go ominously quiet, and suddenly you have severe cashflow problems, with overheads constantly mounting. And then, it's tits upwards.

In the 1980s, my friend Laurence Pearce ran a small business in Surrey, modifying Jaguars. Later, he became a manufacturer of cars for road and track and, for a while, was a successful racing team owner[1], before switching to the less commercially risky occupation of racing-car preparation for customers. The company was staying afloat, but was just failing to hit the big time, and was frequently on the brink of collapsing into insolvency.

One day, his premises were honoured by a visit from two members of the VAT division of Her Majesty's Revenue & Customs. The senior inspector said, "Well, Mr Pearce, if you would be good enough to show us around your premises, my colleague and I will then examine your books. After that we can sit down and have a little chat."

Laurence gave them a guided tour of his workshops, where a dozen skilled employees were busily working. One man was on the lathe, two men were installing an engine, two were changing suspension components, others were fitting replacement body panels, spraying paint and so on.

The VAT inspector asked a few questions as they walked around. Then he and his minion were shown into Laurence's office, where they were served with coffee and The Books. Meanwhile, Laurence and his closest assistant (his wife Fiona) sat in the secretary's office. He spent the time checking through his order book, making and receiving numerous telephone calls ... and worrying about what might come next.

After about an hour, the door dividing the two rooms opened and the senior inspector invited Laurence to go into his own office. The three of them sat down.

"Right, Mr Pearce," he began, "now, please correct me if I am in error, but it seems to me that your business operates in the following manner: brand-new cars are delivered from the Jaguar factory to your premises here. Your staff then remove certain parts from these vehicles – body panels, engines, transmissions, suspension components, wheels and tyres, brakes, internal trim and so on. Then you replace those parts with other components that you have either bought in from suppliers or fabricated on these premises. After that you sell completed, modified cars to customers ...

"Now what I want to know, Mr Pearce," – he paused and glanced to check that his young assistant was paying attention to The Master at work – "is this: what do you do with all the brand-new, unused, standard components that you remove from these motor cars?"

Laurence placed his elbows on the desk and leaned forward, staring intently into the inspector's beady little eyes. "It's none of your business," he declared casually after a few moments, "but I sell them for cash."

The inspector looked as if he had been smacked in the face with a damp haddock. His jaw dropped, his eyes opened wide. Then he suddenly burst out laughing, and laughed until tears rolled down his cheeks.

"That's very good, Mr Pearce," he said, "Very good indeed. I've never heard that one before. Excellent!" He glanced at his watch. Standing up and putting his papers into his briefcase, which he then snapped shut, he shook Laurence's hand and said, "Well, that's all in order. We must be going." With that, he and his assistant left the premises.

Laurence and the VAT man had understood each other perfectly. This had been a symmetrical transaction.'

The Lister Storm won the FIA GT Championship in 2000, with drivers Julian Bailey and Jamie Campbell-Walter.

72 Asymmetric, man

AKERLOF, SPENCE AND STIGLITZ sound like one of those earnest progressive rock bands from the Seventies. One can imagine Stiggy performing a 30-minute drum solo. But, in fact, George Akerlof, Michael Spence and Joseph Stiglitz are distinguished American professors of economics[1]. Where would we be without them? Frequently plunging into unpredicted recession, I expect[2].

However, these eminent gentlemen, who together formed the convenient acronym ASS, vouchsafed us an extraordinary insight to guide us into a new century, the one in which we are now stuck. And may the Lord make us grateful, etc ... After an intensive investigation, lasting several decades, into markets in general and the process of buying and selling cars in particular, they came up with the answer to a Big Question. It was such a finely crafted piece of work that it earned them, jointly, the Nobel Prize for Economics in 2001. It was all to do with informational asymmetries. Wake up at the back there. I may be asking questions later.

ASS investigated why the car-buying public dislikes car dealers. Apparently, according to the intrepid trio, this has nothing whatever to do with sheepskin coats, which was the first thing I thought of. The reason, they said, is that the car dealer knows more than the buyer about the product he is selling. The professors describe this phenomenon as *asymmetric information*. This can lead to *adverse selection*, which invariably causes distress.

The band had been banging the same asymmetric drum for three decades. In his classic 1970 paper, "Quality Uncertainty and the Market Mechanism," Akerlof analysed a market in which the seller had more information than the buyer, regarding the quality of the product, inventively using the term 'lemon' for a defective old car.

One cannot help feeling that this warped view of the car-buying process must have stemmed from an unpleasant personal experience involving the purchase of a used car. Perhaps, one fine spring day in 1969, wearing a predominantly purple tie-dye T-shirt, flared yellow trousers, mirrored sunglasses and red plastic sandals, young George Akerlof strolled absent-mindedly on to a used car lot in the suburbs of Los Angeles, intending to buy a rather nice-looking black Corvette Sting Ray that was on offer for $1000.

"Here comes one," said ace used-car salesman Herman W Lovechild III to his associates. "Just watch this, guys. Watch and learn."

Half an hour later, to his surprise and consternation, George found himself $1500 poorer, driving away in a lemon-yellow Corvair with contrasting lime-green vinyl interior trim and an imitation-leopardskin steering-wheel cover. That evening, reflecting with his friends Mike and Stiggy on this bewildering incident, George, scratching his beard, said "It was, like, asymmetric, man."

"That weird guy Ralph[3] says those things are unsafe at any speed," sneered Mike. "And they're seriously uncool, too."

"What we have here," said Stiggy, drumming his fingers pensively on the table, "is an adverse selection."

"Far out," said Mike.

Ever since that trauma, George has stayed awake at night thinking about the mesmeric intellectual power of used-car dealers. He even came up with a complicated algebraic formula to explain it all.

Not all the car salesmen I have met have given me precisely that impression. By examining the problem through the wrong end of the telescope, the three professors may have overlooked a crucial point: they make no reference to punters, of whom, in the popular expression, 60 are born, on average, every hour. In fact, there are far more than that being pushed out screaming and unready into the cruel world, otherwise there would not be enough of them to keep the used-car business rolling; not to mention the new-car business.

Joseph Stiglitz is a member of France's *Légion d'Honneur*. Other American recipients of this lapel accoutrement include Clint Eastwood, Arnold Schwarzenegger, Sharon Stone and Barbara Streisand. Michael Spence's big thing is Signalling Theory[4]; this is an offshoot of the asymmetric stuff. Talk to your boss about it, but my advice is that you should tell as many lies as you can get away with. George Akerlof is your man, if you want to have a long and serious talk about lemons.

Akerlof, Spence and Stiglitz could have gone on to investigate why people dislike professors of economics. Is this necessarily an asymmetrical problem?

Of course, there are some people who delight in asymmetry, Chris Bangle for example.

[1] Are there any *undistinguished* America professors of Economics? If so, what are their distinguishing features?

[2] So there would be no discernible change.

[3] Ralph Nader (born 1934), professional troublemaker, failed presidential candidate, president of the Chevrolet Corvair Owners' Club. In his favour, votes for him prevented Al Gore from becoming US President. On the other hand, this allowed George W Bush to become President of the US. Rather a negative record, then.

[4] You can cut out those dishonest signals, thank you very much.

73 The High Priest of Asymmetry

IN 1992, THE PIOUS American beardie Chris Bangle arrived at BMW as Director of Design. Many observers believed that the company then had the best-looking range in the business. Many observers worried about what he would do about that. Several years later many observers felt that their worst fears had been justified.

New Edge[1] was already old hat; the latest trend in car design was Flame Surfacing, in which body contours were designed to look as if they had been shaped from a wax block by an Irish drunk with a blowtorch. Like 'New Edge,' mostly a Ford thing, this was, in essence, a way of describing something that had been around for ever.

Also, it allowed trendy designers to tell the stuffy men in suits, "Hey! Look at this brilliant new idea." By signing off the budget for this type of tomfoolery, the stuffy men in suits feel that, by association, they are *cool* or *hip* or *funky* or *bad* or *evil*, or whichever adjective is currently in favour to denote exceptional cleverness.

The other big design trend was that symmetry was out. Not *far out*, just *out*. Bangle was the High Priest of this new sect. He suggested that the human eye prefers asymmetrical "more natural" shapes to purely mathematical, symmetrical forms. Making one side of an object a mirror image of the other was banal. Bangle was in good company: Victor Hugo said precisely that in *Les Misérables*. By implication, Vincent van Gogh was of the same opinion.

This idea was not entirely new in cars. I once noticed that the two sides of a 212 Inter one of the earliest Ferrari road cars, did not match: wheel-arch gaps varied substantially and slightly different trim designs were used from side to side. The first owner of that car, visiting the factory in Maranello in the early 1950s, was granted an audience with *Il Commendatore*.

Through an interpreter, the Englishman inquired about this discrepancy. The great man/evil old bastard[2] replied casually that *of course* the two sides were different: they had been made by two different craftsmen. Now *that's* the way to treat troublesome customers with too much money who come to your factory and have the effrontery to ask silly questions about your five-star product.

Bangle turned his philosophical view into three dimensions. His BMW X coupe concept car had two especially irritating features. One was that the 'e' had no accent the other was its wraparound rear window. Well, it wrapped around on one side, but not the other. When the hatch, hinged at the rear valence, was opened, taking one tail-light cluster and part of the right rear wing with it, luggage could be loaded from what was the nearside in left-hand drive versions. This made production of right-hand-drive X coupes highly improbable. Besides, what was the point?

Rather lamely, Bangle pointed out that cars are already asymmetrical anyway because they have a steering wheel only on one side (except, he might have added, for the McLaren F1, which had a central driving position, being let down only by details such as the position of the gear lever). BMW's suits sportingly signed off this asymmetric show car, but would not go further than that, and Bangle seemed to forget the whole thing after a while. I do not believe this was because of a column I wrote suggesting that, if he were so desperately keen on asymmetry, he might consider shaving off one side of his beard and snipping away half his bow-tie.

At around that time, I also wrote, "Looking on the bright side, at least the X coupe is a step forward for Chris Bangle. One of his previous creations was the Fiat Coupe[3], which

186

ooked wrong from both sides, whereas the X coupe looks wrong only from one side. As et, I cannot decide which."

When you interview someone senior in the motor industry, you can be sure that there as been a full briefing, that the person you are interviewing has read *everything* you have written about him or her, or possibly it. So I was mildly apprehensive when I travelled to Munich for *The Daily Telegraph* to interview BMW's Director of Design. It did occur to me, s the symmetrical train pulled out of the Gare de l'Est in Paris, that I was on the same nes that led to concentration camps such as Dachau, just outside Munich, some 60 years earlier.

If you are really interested (though I cannot imagine why), look it up.
Delete as you think applicable. I am inclined to say, "Stet."
Also without an accent on the 'e.'

74 Shadow boxing with Mr Bangle

CHRIS BANGLE[1], FULLY BEWHISKERED, but tieless, was approaching his 46th birthday and his 10th anniversary as BMW's head of design. At his invitation, I sat in the driver's seat of the CS1 concept in BMW's design headquarters. He did not mention that, after this tiny open tourer was unveiled in Geneva, I had written that it might suit Noddy in the new millennium. (If he had, I probably would not have said "Parp, Parp, Big Ears!")

Neither did we discuss any of the other sarcastic things I had written about him. I guessed correctly, however, that he was waiting impatiently for me to utter the word "asymmetry." When I did, he spoke to an assistant and a huge aluminium door opened in the hangar-like, air-conditioned studio where BMW board members evaluate the design team's work; the X-coupe concept was wheeled on to one of three turntables.

We discussed asymmetry. We also discussed his 'E65' 7-series, the design of which had recently been mauled in *Forbes*, the American magazine for plutocrats. There was even a 'Stop Chris Bangle' internet campaign, that evidently irritated him enormously.

I asked about Bangle's mission to change BMW. He replied, "What I said was, hopefully you won't see the changeover point. I was very careful, when I came here, to respect BMW's design tradition. I never said I have come here to change things." I decided not to say that a lot of people thought they could see the changeover point, very clearly.

Fine. But how had he changed things? Wrong question again. "I look at my role here differently. Design is a culture at BMW: you should ask what is my role in it." I said that was what I was there to find out, so he told me, at length. He talked about staff numbers, budgets, the MINI, the challenge of making profits from smaller cars, motorcycles, Rolls-Royce, "team building," and so on.

We spent the whole time in a sort of shadow-boxing display. In Bangle's defence, I go back to the point that, when he arrived, the company's product range looked *really* good. Ideally, if you are a designer, engineer, chief executive or whatever, it is useful if your predecessor was a bit crap. He did not have that advantage. The 'E38' 7-series (1994-2001), for example, was possibly the best-looking large four-door saloon ever produced, and the smaller models were also standard setters. So how do you follow that?

There is a funny thing about car design chiefs. Because of the way that model cycles work, an incoming chief designer will usually have to introduce several models over which he has had little or possibly no influence before his own work can be presented. That had been the case with the E38.

He spent a long time, explaining in quite interesting, technically complicated detail how the design of his 7-series, the E65, had come about. He used the word "dogma" several times and he chucked in a bit of weird stuff, such as, "It's post-modern in many ways, implying that you are integrating multiple concepts into one totality." I prevented myself from saying, "Whatever."

However, most of what he said made sense, even if one did not like the end result. But an interesting point that I was unable to make at the time is that all the elements that made the E65 so controversial do not apply in the case of the more elegant car that followed it, with the code F01[2].

We moved back to asymmetry. "There's an interesting dogma," said Bangle.

"Where does symmetry come from? BMW has a very strong design philosophy – you could call it Form Follows Function; we call it authenticity. That's what the car is, so that's how it should look." He then explained the way the X-coupe's asymmetric design had evolved, and that made sense too, sort of.

Mr Bangle did not actually shout at me at any point in the interview, but, unsurprisingly, he was on the icy side of cool towards me. Towards the end, I asked some more wrong questions such as, which designers past and present did he admire? He refused: "I'm not the guy who comes up with a list of names, so you can print three next to mine." I considered asking for amusing anecdotes about spoons, but I thought Bangle was probably not a *Private Eye* reader.

When the Vatican buys a Popemobile, is that a symmetrical transaction?

[1] After training as a Methodist priest, Bangle was lured into the material world of car design, obtaining an honours degree at the Art Center College of Design, Wisconsin. He worked on interior design at Opel, then joined Fiat, becoming design chief, before joining BMW. He left the company in 2009.
[2] For some reason, BMW chose to abandon its long tradition of E-numbers with this car.

75 It's The Pope, virtually[1]

IT WAS WHILE IDLY watching the then Pope, that old Polish bloke, on the haunted fishtank, and having recently considered the GM 'platooning' concept (see Chapter 98), that I came up with an idea. It was as if a 150-watt light bulb[1] had been switched on inside my head.

Pope John Paul George Ringo, who had given up a promising career as a professional golfer when he entered the priesthood, was in foreign parts somewhere. He had done that kiss-the-tarmac number and was now stooping in the back of the latest Popemobile. As the camera angle was from the rear threequarters apart from closeups of his face, I was unable to discern the make of vehicle upon which his Holiness's conveyance was based.

From the 1930s, and particularly since the first bespoke Popemobile (based on the dreadful 230G) was made in 1980, the preferred papal marque has usually been Mercedes-Benz, though there have been Range Rovers, some enormous modified lorries, and even, at the other end of the scale, a Seat version of the Fiat Panda that rather resembled a golf buggy.

His Holiness had a very mechanical look, his body remaining rigidly immobile, one frail hand holding onto a bar, the other waving feebly at intervals, his head nodding occasionally, on his face an expression of beatific serenity, which some may have mistaken for an expression of imbecilic senility, or the consequence of the ingestion of sedatives.

It seemed to me that it was cruel to subject that elderly gentleman to his gruelling schedule of global travel, and the same holds true of his successors. Does the Pope really need to be on the spot in person to deliver his message to the starving masses in 'the Third World'? I do not believe so.

It occurred to me that there was an opportunity for a car manufacturer, in association with a software corporation such as Microsoft, plus Madame Tussaud's, to introduce a limited-edition niche model, the Virtual Popemobile.

Every manufacturer needs a 'loss leader' or in Fordspeak a 'halo-effect' model. This means a model that excites people's imagination: though they may not be able to afford or even want that special version, it draws them into the showroom, and that is halfway towards extraction of the punter's cash.

There could be a production run of a couple of dozen examples, each with a numbered brass plaque on the facia. Once these had been delivered, 24 identical, virtual popes, remote-controlled by specially-trained cardinals via satellite link from the Vatican, could be simultaneously spreading the good word all over the world, with huge savings in air fares, accommodation and security arrangements. These virtual popes would nod and wave at appropriate moments and say a few words in Latin from time to time.

Standard equipment would include a Host dispenser, Communion wine goblet-holders, a Holy Water reservoir (with font), and switches for sanctification and excommunication. Everywhere the virtual Pope went, he would leave a sweet aroma lingering in the air as he wafted past, thanks to a special incense additive in the fuel.

The virtual Pope, being infallible, would never crash[2]. The advertising campaign would have the slogan, 'The Virtual Popemobile – with Windows.' And bulletproof windows, at that.

Incidentally, I wonder what happens to old Popemobiles and how much they are worth. They certainly redefine the expression, 'one careful owner.' They are not listed in *Glass's Guide* or its rivals, and I have never heard of one passing through British Car Auctions or Bonham's, the upmarket auctioneers. Nor have I ever seen one advertised in *Exchange & Mart*.

With space in the back to stand up and wave at one's ecstatically cheering supporters from behind the comforting security of bulletproof glass, a re-liveried, deconsecrated Popemobile would be the ideal conveyance for whichever clown is playing the role of Mayor of London, once the virtual Pope had been detached and put in storage. However, I do think that the mayor should be dissuaded from buying a fleet of mayormobiles. One mayor is surely sufficiently artificial without the need for electronic assistance.

After JPII popped his clogs, the world had Pope Benedict, whom the Italians nicknamed Il Pastore Tedesco. When he retired, the cardinals asked Jorge Maria Bergoglio if he wanted to be Pope, he quipped, "Can I be Frank?"

Well, that's enough of the Pope jokes. Let's move on to the future, as imagined by Automobiles Matra[3].

[1] This chapter is adapted from a column that I wrote for *The Daily Telegraph* in 1998. It was spiked because the saintly Charles Moore, Editor of the paper at that time and a devout candlestick, did not wish to be excommunicated. Well, not really; it was rather that the Motoring Editor did not wish to be crucified.

[2] This would be the most difficult part of the assignment for Microsoft.

[3] RIP.

76 Avant-garde? Says who?

WHEN I FIRST SAW the Renault Avantime prototype at the 1999 Geneva Motor Show, I was sceptical, for two reasons. First, the concept was a trifle weird – take a large 'people-carrier,' remove two doors, and turn it into an upmarket coupé. Second, I have an in-built resistance towards anything or anyone described as 'avant-garde.' It is conceited, pretentious and presumptuous.

I thought about it further and decided it might just work. The show car had some exquisite details, in particular the aluminium cylinders on which the ingenious double-hinged doors were hung, a wonderful fusion of art and engineering. Also, I could sense that this was Matra's last stand. If the Avantime succeeded, the company, which had lost its contract to build the Espace for Renault, might survive; if it failed, that was curtains.

I really wanted the Avantime to succeed. By then I had forgiven Matra for its three-seat Bagheera, which had powerful ventilation, but feeble air filters, leading – some 30 years previously – to the most violent attack of sinusitis I have ever suffered.

However, I did feel that the name chosen for the car was not just presumptuous but a hostage to Fortune. The vast majority of those who proclaim themselves to be 'avant-garde' do not even make it as historical footnotes and end up grumpily performing menial tasks badly.

There were numerous production delays, which is often a bad sign. Eventually, in June 2001, I was invited to the launch, in Berlin. Renault's first choice of location had been Bilbao, where we were to have had a press conference in the Guggenheim Museum, because Renault's Chief Designer Patrick Le Quement was a great admirer of its architect, Frank Gehry. But, because of the delays, that was no longer possible. Instead, in a somewhat tenuous link, the conference was in Berlin's DZ Bank, another Gehry building, close to the Brandenburg Gate.

Berlin seemed an odd location, but actually it was very apposite. A team of drivers had been hired to cruise Avantimes around the city all day and, even in the new, dynamic, united Berlin – almost entirely unrecognizable from the divided, paranoid city I had last visited in 1970 (a few days after the evil Andreas Baader and Ulrike Meinhof[1] had escaped from jail) – the car looked startlingly modern.

My first disappointment of the test drive was when I opened the door. Those lovely aluminium cylinders had been axed by Renault's bean counters. The hinges, which still operated in the same way, were now hidden behind a strip of naff leatheroid, because they were not a pretty sight. My second disappointment was when I closed the door, which caused a nasty, hollow clang rather than the whispery clunk of an upmarket limousine. The third was when I sat in the back, which I found cramped and claustrophobic.

It was no surprise to find that, as a driving machine, the Avantime was much like an old Espace, which is to say, comfortable, easy and just a bit dull. In the end, I came back to my original instinct, of not seeing what the point of it was. As a fenestrated van, the Espace was a far more practical vehicle. If you wanted a slightly impractical coupé, the competition was fierce, and there were plenty of rivals that offered superior dynamics, performance and value for money.

If I had been a squillionaire looking for a chauffeur-driven motor at the time, and it had to be French, I would certainly not have chosen an Avantime. Instead, I might have opted for the Vel Satis, another of Renault's sales duds, on the de Maupassant principle[2], rather than either the Avantime or the Espace. The Vel Satis was not a bad car in any respect except external appearance, and the interior was gorgeously finished and spacious for tall people. It attracted far less attention from resentful ne'er-do-wells than the German opposition. The occupant was usually some middle-grade fonctionnaire.

The Avantime eventually limped onto the market, failed by a fat margin to meet its ambitious sales targets, and was quietly knocked on the head. Fewer than 9000 found buyers in two years of production. Matra's car division sadly went down with all hands. As is sometimes the way with these things, the Avantime almost immediately became a 'collector's car.'

The driving route on the launch turned out to be more interesting than the car. This was, I believe, the first international car launch that took in roads which, until the fall of The Wall, had been in East Germany.

We headed west from Berlin on a crowded autobahn, past Spandau (now there's a mystery wrapped in an enigma, Mr Churchill ...), and then turned south and began a long anticlockwise loop, passing through some quite attractive countryside and many villages, most of them unremittingly grim. The Germans seem to specialize in unremittingly grim villages. The few, unremittingly grim villagers we saw stared at us with suspicion. We were the shock of the new, on four wheels ...

My co-driver and I pulled onto a grass verge in a wooded area to swap places. Suddenly he said, "Hey, look at that!" It was a dilapidated concrete watchtower, disappearing beneath grasping ivy. I looked at the map: we had stopped at the edge of the Sachsenhausen extermination camp. That is where, among many other brave and unfortunate men, Robert Benoist[3], one of the leading racing drivers before the war, met his grisly end.

The gap between success and failure is often narrow, for special agents as for the motor industry. It is a harsh old world.

[1] Their demented disciples were responsible in 1986 for the cold-blooded murder of Georges Besse, a fine man who began with vigour and imagination Renault's slow emergence from being a rotting symbol of State ownership.
[2] Asked why he dined every day in the restaurant of the Eiffel Tower, after having denounced the structure as a blot on the landscape, the great writer replied that it was the only place in Paris from which one could not see it.
[3] See Chapter 60.

77 The real Mona Lisa, allegedly

SHORTLY AFTER THE EPIC round-Europe drive described in Chapter 43, I attended the *24 Heures du Mans* in June 1984 as part of a 60th anniversary celebration of the first Bentley win there, organized (if that is not too strong a word) by 'Pluspenis,' legendary Press Officer of what was then an all-British Vickers subsidiary company, Rolls-Royce/Bentley.

I was recruited to drive some local notables for a couple of laps of the circuit on the morning before the race, in a Bentley Mulsanne Turbo, then in the early stages of its development. Starting the second lap, we came past the pits and over the brow under the Dunlop Bridge flat out (this was before the chicane was installed there), reaching about 135mph, when I had to apply emergency braking to avoid a boxer dog that ran across the track. We missed it by a fissure in the Time-Space Continuum. My passengers seemed to think that I was extraordinarily skilful. I thought that they and I, not to mention the dog, were extraordinarily lucky.

While taking tea that afternoon in a special enclosure for alleged VIPs, I asked Pluspenis who was the elderly cove sitting alone, wearing an enormous sunhat. I was amazed to be told that it was Amherst Villiers, engineer of the famous 'Blower Bentley'[1]. I knew of him, but had no idea he was still alive. He was then 83 but full of beans. I introduced myself and we chatted about what Bentley had once been, was then and might be in future.

I got to know Amherst quite well following that initial conversation. I tried to produce a magazine feature with him. My desire was to extract from him what a modern interpretation of WO's sporting Bentleys might be like. I still have some sketches he produced, showing a front-mounted, twin-turbo V12 (set well back in the chassis), with four-wheel drive, transaxle and inboard rear discs. I thought his concept was absolutely on the right lines. As for the engine, perhaps Mystic Meg[2] gave him the nod that Rolls-Royce and Bentley would be acquired by the Huns, and that, however it was split, a V12 would be available, one way or another. *Aum*, or something. *Aumherst*, indeed.

Amherst was charming and funny, but rather illuminated and often simply impossible. I first sensed this when I received an absurd letter from him suggesting that he should set up a small studio at IPC's expense, adding that in the early stages he would "probably require only one part-time assistant," but that "this might need to be adjusted as the project progresses." He seemed to think that the idea was actually to design a car, perhaps even build a prototype. I had to explain carefully that I had no budget for that, and that IPC was not about to provide one in the next million years. As Amherst's biographer Paul Kenny[3] aptly puts it, Amherst was "always on 'Send' and never on 'Receive.'"

Amherst and I were strolling up Kensington Church Street towards his flat one day, when he pointed to a large house on the corner of a side street. It had barred windows. He said that the original of the Mona Lisa was in there. "What about the one in the Louvre?" I asked. "Oh, that's a copy," he said casually.

That Bentley feature was never completed. Amherst was not greatly interested in the condensed format required for magazine articles, even though I tried to persuade him that it might lead to interest from Rolls-Royce/Bentley (which continued as a single company until 1998).

194

We remained on friendly terms and kept in touch, however. Like several other people, I tried unsuccessfully to dissuade him from pursuing his protracted and complex lawsuit against Rolls-Royce (involving a Phantom III modified to his design). This almost certainly hastened his death, in January 1992. On the other hand, this was a month after his 91st birthday.

In addition to automotive work, Amherst Villiers was a NASA rocket scientist, an aviator, a portrait painter (Ian Fleming and Graham Hill were among his sitters) and a mystic. His life might be regarded as a catalogue of brilliant ideas, most of which (including the Blower Bentley) did not quite come off.

Nevertheless, he had vision. The Continental GT and the Flying Spur and subsequent models produced under Volkswagen's ownership of Bentley, are virtually identical in their engineering concept to the sketches produced by Amherst 20 years earlier.

There is no doubt that Amherst Villiers was a brilliant man, but, if he had made the most of his talents, he might be remembered as a genius. That is true of many people with exceptional talent, of course.

Amherst was, just, a survivor of the Victorian era. And now for a Georgian relic with a Victorian connection.

[1] The supercharged version of the 4½-litre model, commissioned by Sir Henry 'Tim' Birkin, against the wishes of WO Bentley. It was fast but unreliable. It had some competition successes, but it did not win The Big One, the Le Mans race, though it might have done, with a bit more development and if Bentley Motors had not gone bust in 1931.

[2] Born Margaret Anne Lake on 27 July 1942 in Accrington, Lancashire (of Stanley fame), 'Mystic Meg' is a British astrologer who churns out fanciful bollocks to comfort the intellectually feeble in their rough passage through life. Even Wikipedia, with uncharacteristic caution, describes her as an 'alleged psychic.'

[3] This is an extract from Paul Kenny's excellent book, *The Man Who Supercharged Bond* (Haynes Publishing, 2009): "... while at Douglas, Amherst designed his own heavy lift launch vehicle, clustering four Saturn V rockets together. Piers Carlson recalls seeing a drawing Amherst had made of the design, and querying what a small spike alongside the vehicle signified. Amherst replied that it was a representation of the 555ft-tall Washington Memorial, drawn to scale. Piers concluded that, were Amherst's HLLV to take off, it would obliterate not only Cape Canaveral, but most of Florida too. His wife Eleanor recalls Amherst 'was quite disappointed when they rejected it.'"

78 The royal milk float

IN 1988, I ATTENDED a book launch in an office in Smith Square, Westminster. We were instructed to be there at 6pm at the very latest and informed that Prince Philip would arrive at 6.30pm on the dot and stay until about 7. So we all got to Smith Square before 5.45, and stood around chewing some rather good nibbles, having a drink and chatting about this, that and, of course, the other.

Time flies when you are talking shop and gossiping maliciously, especially when you are within a few paces of a well-stocked bar without a till and not planning to drive anywhere until the next day. By the time HRH arrived, it was past 8 o'clock. While sipping my third generous g and t, I looked out of the first-floor window as a Transit van bearing the logo of Lucas, Prince of Darkness[1], pulled up on the pavement below.

I had studied all the details of that unique vehicle, and written a rather unflattering appraisal of it. I was surprised to see it in the heavy metal for the first time. I presumed its driver to be a hack, arriving extremely late, and thought, there'll be a wheel clamp on that before you can say pour me another drink, barman, though I wondered whether the cranes on the lorries used to tow away illegally parked vehicles would be strong enough to lift it. However, the small, dapper, balding man who climbed out from the driver's door was not a hack. There he was, HRH himself, in person, the Prince, of Edinburgh rather than Darkness, a light man emerging from a heavy van.

HRH entered the room to a round of applause, for reasons unclear, but most people become more generous after the drinks have been served for a couple of hours. He was ushered around by the publisher's unctuous PR man. "And here, Sir, we have a select group of motoring journalists," he exaggerated wildly, arriving at the small, convivial gathering of hacks that included me.

HRH launched, without preamble or invitation, into a passionate speech about the excellence of the vehicle in which he had just arrived, how it was going to revolutionize transportation, energy use, and this and that and whatever. Then he paused, generously allowing everyone the opportunity to agree with the wise opinions he had just expressed.

"Tell me, Sir," I asked, plunging into the polite silence with a slightly raised eyebrow, "how much does that van weigh?" HRH replied that he did not know, so I gave him the exact figure. His eyes narrowed.

"What is its range on a full charge?" HRH did not know that either, so I helpfully filled him in, adding that, of course, that would diminish greatly if one did not run it on the flat and level, or if one fitted a heater or other electrically-operated equipment, or if one drove it 'aggressively'. Fortunately for HRH, it was a very warm summer evening and the steepest incline he had encountered between Buckingham Palace and Smith Square was probably when he mounted the kerb.

I had started, so I thought I might as well continue. "How long does it take to charge?" Fixing me with a steely glare, HRH said between gritted teeth that he did not have the slightest idea. I smiled and helpfully filled in this further gap in his knowledge, and added that, if everyone had a vehicle like that, nobody would be able to boil a kettle and the entire country would grind to a halt[2].

"To summarize, what we are considering here, if I may say so, Sir," I concluded, "is a variation on the milk float, rather than the answer to the personal transportation requirements of the masses[3]." I added, imagining incorrectly that this would bring a

196

smile to his face, as he was a horse enthusiast, "The milk float is a very practical solution for local distribution of dairy products, though I personally preferred it when they used horses."

The oily PR man, with sweating brow, steered a still-glaring HRH towards a more obsequious group of his lady wife's subjects. The Duke and I had engaged in an asymmetric transaction[4].

"Well, that's your knighthood up Shit Creek," said my friend Ray, who had remained silent throughout the conversation.

"Oh bugger. You are quite right. Shall we take his van for a joy ride?"

"No thanks. I have an irrational aversion to being shot at by marksmen in the Special Forces."

"Good point. Well, I'm off then. Have you read the book, by the way?"

"Yes."

"What did you think of it?"

"Unadulterated crap."

"Yes. So did I. Pip pip."

"Toodle-oo."

"That as well."

We may now continue on the theme of crap vehicles.

[1] This was the unkind, but apposite, nickname given to Lucas Industries by north American Jaguar dealers in the 1980s.
[2] As it will one day not far into the future.
[3] There are still a few people who disagree with this assessment of the "pure" electric car. But it is about as likely as phlogiston to succeed as the power source for the masses.
[4] See Chapter 72.

79 An Adequate Product Solution

ONE GROWS ACCUSTOMED TO being fired as a journalist, whether one is on the full-time staff[1] or freelance. It happened to me a couple of times. Irritating though it was to be dumped abruptly as a columnist for the doomed publication, *Carweek*[2], this led indirectly to me working for *The Daily Telegraph*, my major client for the next 15 years, which might otherwise not have occurred.

I returned from a New Year holiday in France in January 1995 to find a Christmas greetings good news/bad news fax waiting for me from Whispering Gavin[3], informing me, apologetically, that I had become surplus to requirements on his fading organ. This was inconvenient for a number of reasons, not least that I was due to board a flight the following day to attend the Detroit Auto Show.

Well, bugger it, I thought, I'm going. I had the flight ticket and a hotel room for four nights, courtesy of the Ford Motor Company. I went round the show as if reporting on it, but in a hurry, picking up rumours here and there. Somebody from GM said there was an opportunity to visit the Saturn factory in Spring Hill, Tennessee[4]. I jumped at the chance and was on an early flight the next morning.

The first time you visit a volume-production car factory, you can hardly fail to be astonished by the complexity of the construction of that depreciating mobile steel box outside your house. But, after that, unless you are a professional manufacturing nerd, one big car plant is pretty much like another. I had been dragged around so many huge car-making facilities that they had all more or less blended into one cacophonous, sole-destroying amalgam in the addled memory, with one notable exception[5]. I had a feeling, though, that the Saturn operation might be the second exception to this rule that I had encountered. It was, indeed.

For anyone accustomed to surly European car workers – at one time it was advisable to wear a hard hat when inspecting French car plants in case disgruntled Trotskyists decided to hurl ball bearings at visitors – a guided tour of Spring Hill was surreal.

The workers *smiled* at us. Some even waved and said "Hi!" It was like being an extra in some ludicrous Hollywood horror movie, *The Stepford Auto Workers*, perhaps. We met engineers, designers and product planners. More time seemed to be spent on 'Being Nice' than on engineering, designing or planning. All employees had to undertake *92 hours* of training per year to improve their "inter-personal relations." It seemed more like an offshoot of the Church of Scientology than a branch of General Motors.

We were repeatedly told that the unique, mould-breaking feature of the Saturn was the relationship between the company and its customers. Research had shown that Saturn's target buyers sought nothing more elevated than what was proudly described as an "Adequate Product Solution."

Far more important than performance, economy, dynamics, comfort or value for money, our hosts explained, was the way customers were treated before and after purchase. All volume manufacturers have made boring cars from time to time, but here was an innovative concept: Saturn set out deliberately to present blandness and mediocrity as primary virtues, rather than as the regrettable, but inevitable, penalties of low price and running costs.

After our tour, we were allowed short test drives of the Adequate Product Solution. The Saturns were even duller than Japanese saloons of a couple of decades earlier. Then we were shown around what is normally the sharp end of the operation: a sales outlet. At the Spring Hill Saturn dealership, we encountered another set of intense, smiley people. One said mysteriously, "We don't dicker with the sticker." A translator explained that the price on the windscreen was the price that would be paid: there would be no messy, divisive haggling.

Without irony, someone boasted that every Saturn dealership was identical, down to the precise location of the water dispenser. Unembarrassed comparisons were made with McDonald's hamburger outlets.

On return to Blighty, I contacted Eric Bailey[6], then *The Telegraph*'s motoring correspondent, whom I had recently met on a launch. He was in the process of setting up the new *Motoring* section. I had a new client.

I cannot say that any of my sackings were on the Wagnerian scale in which they do it in the German motor industry. A master of the art was Eberhard von Kuenheim[7]. Anyway, one should never get in a flap about it.

[1] As in Chapter 32.

[2] A weekly motoring paper published by EMAP (East Midland Allied Press), launched amid much ballyhoo in 1993. It began in a large format, 370mm by 280mm (nearly A3 rather than the conventional A4 format). When Whispering Gavin (see note 3 below) showed me a pre-launch 'dummy,' I asked how that would fit on newsagents' shelves. "Don't worry, mate," he whispered, "EMAP's done a smart deal. They'll all be on special display near the counter." I walked into my local WH Smith on the first Wednesday of publication and, after a prolonged search, eventually found copies of *Carweek* strewn around the floor among the motorbike and fishing titles. The paper gradually downsized and then folded after only 18 months, losing an estimated £10 million, which were more than pin money in them days.

[3] See Chapter 35.

[4] Saturn Motors, founded by General Motors in 1985. I don't know why they chose that planet for the name, but I suppose Mars was taken and it was better than Uranus. After poor sales, General Motors terminated the brand in 2010.

[5] The exception was the Alfa Romeo factory in Milan in the late 1970s. It contained a splendid, Manhattan-style cocktail bar. The Italians evidently understood that the painless way to tackle such an ordeal is to be mildly anaesthetized.

[6] One of the characters of what used to be called 'Fleet Street.' Later, he moved from *The Daily Telegraph* to *The Daily Mail* [8] when almost all the traffic was in the other direction. Some may regard that as eccentric, others as shrewd, perhaps even sarcastic. I think Eric was just looking after his pension fund.

[7] See Chapters 2 and 3.

[8] To judge from readers' remarks in the electronic *DT*, many are puzzled as to why *The DT* is now much the same as *The DM*, when the answer is fairly obvious.

80 Sequiturs and bungarolas

WHEN I WAS WRITING a weekly column in *The Daily Telegraph*, I was acutely aware that people in the newspaper's hierarchy (not including those with whom I dealt directly) based their judgement of the success of columnists on the size of the postbag that they generated; today it would be the volume of e-mails. I recall reading a perceptive exposition of this rule, written by Joan Bakewell[1].

It is improbable that the allegedly saintly Charles Moore[2] ever read my column in the Motoring section. Only two pages of the entire voluminous multi-section newspaper of that era, apart from the front page, were of more than the slightest interest to him, provided that they did not attract a libel suit: the pages that attracted his attention were what is known in the industry as 'Ed' and 'Op-Ed'[3]. It is not very likely that anyone else above the Motoring Editor read my stuff either, but some of those people whom I never met probably weighed readers' letters to me on a scale, imagining that they were carrying out a scientific experiment. Obviously, they did this without reading them, because that might affect their judgement.

I used to receive a lot of intelligent and interesting letters from *Telegraph* readers, as well as the occasional unpleasant abuse. For the latter, I generally adopted the 'sticks and stones' philosophy. I absorbed the Bakewell theory of columns and followed it carefully. Without much effort, I discovered a surefire method of keeping the letters rolling in.

Living in East Grinstead, in West Sussex (just), was what gave me the idea. It is an attractive town, in parts, but it is a town that strangely over the years has attracted loony sects like flies to a cowpat: Mormons, Moonies and Scientologists, to name but a few. And The Caravan Club has its headquarters there ...

In my first application of the Bakewell theory, I suggested in a column that the use of public highways by caravans and motorhomes should be restricted to the hours between two and four o'clock in the morning, so that they would not inconvenience the majority of the motoring population. This prompted an encouraging response.

The Motoring Editor, Peter Hall, pleaded with me to desist, because he did not wish to be deluged with mail from deranged people whose fountain pens were filled with green or mauve ink. However, I explained that I had to find a survival system as a columnist, and if it was not this, it would be have to be that, so it might as well be this. He understood my point of view, especially after I suggested that he should simply get his secretary to pass all the hate mail directly to me. I continued on my mission.

From then on, whenever I felt that I was getting insufficient feedback, or even if I was simply running out of ideas, I would return with great pleasure to my specialist topic. This always worked perfectly; caravanning is a religious cult and its swivel-eyed adepts are very much like Mormons, Moonies or Scientologists, with a sprinkling of Spanish Inquisitors among them.

On one occasion, I had the inestimable pleasure of responding to a suggestion by a Mr Rupert Pontin, then the Editor of *Glass's Caravan Guide*, a publication for caravanning enthusiasts, that there should be a new term for 'motor caravan.' For some reason that I forget, he felt that it gave a negative image of the damned things, as if it might be possible to provide any other image of them.

Mr Pontin had pressed all the buttons for me. He had written a ferocious tirade against callous journalists who made fun of caravans, motor caravans and their users. He had even suggested that the police were attempting to suppress his sect: "Unfortunately there are a few police forces that would clearly like to see touring caravans off their roads," he wrote, in hilariously fractious mood. He took issue with "typical tabloid reporting" which, in his view at that time and perhaps still now, "frightens the public away from investing in a new Tourer." I relished the use of the verb "to invest" and also the capital T for "Tourer."

I wrote in response to this that he was absolutely right and that caravan people had no need of an unfair, harshly critical approach accentuated by airhorns and offensive gesticulation.

What they really needed, rather than that type of rudeness or the ruthless sarcasm of metropolitan sophisticates, was some tender loving care. They needed a counsellor, preferably gorgeous and pouting, to direct them back onto the right road with a kind word and a cuddle, to dig out and soothe the insecure, and slightly cracked tortoise that lurks within the id of every caravanner.

Mr Pontin, who had clearly thought this through during the dark winter months, and they can be very dark, when your pride and joy is moored in its home berth on the front lawn, conceded that the caravan industry "needs to respond by improving its image."

He came up with an intriguing suggestion: "One thing that the caravan industry could and should do is to rename the Touring Caravan as a Touring Home. This would complete the leisure industry's image, with products named Touring Home, Holiday Home, Park Home and Motor Home ... A change of name, marketing style and price will go a long way to improving the image and boosting sales, which are at their lowest level for many years."

I have no idea what the distinctions were between those various type of 'home' on wheels. However, I thought that, if Mr Pontin's renaming suggestion got off the ground, at least people would stop saying, "I was stuck behind a bloody caravan for miles on end."

We held a competition for readers of *Telegraph* Motoring to think up a new name for the benefit of Mr Pontin. The winning entry was "bungarola" (ie rolling bungalow) which I thought was brilliant. In a later act of deliberate provocation, I suggested that the traditional towed caravan should also be renamed, as "sequitur[4]." Sadly, neither of these descriptive terms has yet passed into common usage. Nor has 'Touring Home,' as far as I am aware.

I wrote that sequiturs and bungarolas flourished "like magpies, though all you who suffer from active caravanning have my sympathy, and you probably know where to find that in the dictionary. Cue more outraged letters from The Sequitur Club of East Grinstead." It worked a treat, every time. I suppose that they will hunt me down one day.

[1] 'The thinking man's crumpet' or at any rate Harold Pinter's regular extramarital shag.
[2] Born 1956, Eton, Trinity College, Cambridge, and so on. Editor of *The Spectator* (1984-1990), Editor of *The Sunday Telegraph* (1992-1995), Editor of *The Daily Telegraph* (1995-2003). Biographer of Margaret Thatcher, renowned candlestick, and so on.
[3] He hired the obnoxious Sarah Sands as his deputy and allowed her free rein to do whatever she wanted with the rest of the paper. That was the beginning of its decline.
[4] One of my Latin teachers, the late Mr Jimmy Hetherington, might have been proud of me, perhaps, though I am not certain that it carries the exact meaning that I intended: "It follows." When I was 15, Mr Hetherington sagely observed in an end-of-term report, "He still does not appear to use much Latin in his dream world."

81 Getting in a flap

WHEN WINSTON CHURCHILL WAS showing off what he regarded as his effortless fluency in French, to a French audience, in France, he wished to explain that his past could be divided into two parts, the first military and the second political.

"Mon derrière," began the great orator, pausing for effect, "est divisé en deux grosses parties." His audience remained respectfully silent, either because they considered that he was stating the obvious, or because they were wondering how that differentiated him from anyone else of heavy build[1].

I have made no major contributions to the defence of the realm, and none to the advancement of civilization, as far as I can recall. However, I have twice had an effect on the motor industry. These can be divided into two rather small parts.

The first began at a dinner on the eve of the 1982 Paris Motor Show. Around the table were Ron Mellor the Ford engineer, Rex Greenslade the recently-appointed Ford PR man and former Technical Editor of *Motor* magazine, which I was representing, and Michael Scarlett of our rival *Autocar*.

Mellor was a clever engineer and a hard man within FoMoCo; you had to be tough to survive there. He never minced his words. We discussed the new Sierra, which Ford was officially launching at the Salon. Michael and I had driven it and were asked for our opinions. We were both mildly positive.

After we had gone over various aspects of the car, Mellor gave me a fierce look and mentioned something I had criticized: as soon as you adjusted the temperature setting for the footwell, I had said, it was not possible to have cool air at face level. Mellor adopted his habitual aggressive-defensive act, remarking in the, er, heat of the argument, "What do you know? You're only a fucking journalist[2]."

Michael and I laughed, while Greenslade looked uncomfortable, especially when I said, "I'm sure *you* agree with me, Rex ..." It was a point he had drilled into my brain when training me as a road tester.

We changed the subject. Several days later, back in Blighty, I was telephoned by Ron Mellor's secretary who asked, "Which day next week do you wish to fly to Merkenich?"

I said, "Er, what?" or something like that. I was summoned to Ford's test centre near Cologne, specifically to the climatic wind tunnel, in which the temperature could be lowered to the level at which Captain Scott and his companions had turned into jabbering stiffs. I was kindly advised to bring some warm clothing and it was just as well that I had the full kit from some visits to the Arctic Circle.

So there we were, on two consecutive days, at some ungodly hour, as if any hours are not, inside the wind tunnel. It was sparrows' fart, except that sparrows would never fart in those circumstances, for fear of losing body temperature. It was like being within the bowels of a huge frozen anaconda.

The first day, we sat inside a Ford Cortina, the outgoing model. The second day, it was the new Sierra. We went through an identical routine both mornings, each car having been kept in the freezing cold all night. We set the fan, heater temperature and windscreen demister controls to maximum and then I turned on the ignition, simultaneously clicking a stopwatch.

I made detailed notes about how long it took for the windscreen to clear, for the side windows to clear, for the internal temperature to rise to an acceptable level (a thermometer indicated that), and so on.

I wrote that the Sierra was superior to the Cortina in all these tests. However, I added, this answered questions that I had not asked: once the two cars reached normal operating temperature, the Cortina performed better, in my opinion. Numerous readers sent letters expressing agreement with this.

Some time later, I had lunch with Ron Mellor. He said that, following that exercise, Ford's engineers had modified the system, introducing a piece of plastic that reduced the amount of heated air that could come through face-level vents. "We call this the Dron Flap," he said. "A bit like a cat flap."

He asked – with a sarcastic look – if that satisfied me.

"No," I said drily. "I want ambient air at face level[3]." Mellor, may he rest in peace, and I got on very well after that. On this occasion, my readers supported my point of view, but it is not always so.

[1] But more probably they thought, "Ces *rosbifs*, they have to make a joke of everything."

[2] Mellor's father had been Editor of *The Daily Herald*. William Mellor (1888–1942), a conscientious objector in the First World War, was a lifelong Leftie, and spent many of his recreational hours in his final decade shagging Barbara Castle; somebody had to. Some elements of this may perhaps explain why young Ronald Mellor developed a lifelong distaste for journalists and politicians. Part of a ring road in Blackburn, Lancashire, the town of 4000 holes, is called Barbara Castle Way.

[3] Modern Ford owners will find that they can grill their feet while simultaneously freezing their noses, or almost vice versa if they are so inclined.

82 Iron slugs

I HAVE A MINICHAMPS 1/43 scale model of a 1961 Lincoln Continental drophead. It is six inches long. This is not based on any old 1961 Lincoln Continental drophead, but *that* one, which had been transformed to special order into a six-seat, 21ft-long[1] presidential car by specialists Hess & Eisenhardt of Cincinnati, Ohio. It was known as 'X-100.' The model recaptures the early part of the famous presidential 'motorcade' through Dallas, Texas, on that sunny November day in 1963.

If you are still stuck (and I confess that I have no idea what I was doing on the 22 November 1963), the list of occupants sitting behind the chauffeur and bodyguard may remind you of the event in question. In the second row are Texas Governor John Conally and his wife; and in the back row, President JF Kennedy and the 'First Lady,' Jacqueline Kennedy.

They are all smiling and they look as if they are having a nice day out. Yes, this is the only car to bear the names of two presidents. It is, indeed, the Kennedy Lincoln, though its full name should be almost as long as that of Prince Friedrich von Thurn und Taxis). Minichamps omitted to include a figurine of Lee Harvey Oswald. That would be in bad taste, I suppose.

The most curious thing about the actual car on which this model is based is that, following the regrettable incident, it did not go into immediate retirement or to the crusher. Instead, after forensic tests and thorough valeting, it was sent back to Hess & Eisenhardt for an extensive rebuild, which was completed with impressive rapidity, the modified car being delivered in May 1964. The alterations included a bulletproof glass dome and full armour plating. Now more than a ton heavier, at 7800lb, it served as presidential limousine for another 15 years, and was used by Presidents Johnson, Nixon, Ford and Carter. The last-named perhaps decided that superstition was the better part of valour and commissioned a replacement.

In 1978 the Kennedy-Johnson-Nixon-Ford-Carter Lincoln left Washington and now resides in the Ford Museum in Detroit, which is worth a visit if you are in the area.

Ford generously leased X-100 to The White House for a mere $500 per year. Mind you, that was better than the deal that the Blue Oval got from The Kremlin several years later.

I once tried to persuade a man who had worked in the Press Office of the Ford Motor Company for several decades that, since he was approaching his retirement, he should write his memoirs, because he knew, as the saying goes, "where all the bodies were buried." He was not at all keen on the suggestion[2].

However, he did tell me a few interesting tales. One of them involved the visit to The United States during the Cold War of Leonid Brezhnev, in the middle of his long stint as General Secretary of the Communist Party of the Soviet Union[3].

While their respective bosses engaged in mental arm-wrestling, one of Brezhnev's minions behind the scenes mentioned to his counterpart, one of President Richard Nixon's lickspittles, that the man with the out-of-control eyebrows would very much like to have a Lincoln Continental in his enormous and well-stocked garage, and requested that arrangements be made for him to buy one.

Reagan's lickspittle made the appropriate investigations with the Ford Motor Company, of which Lincoln is a division, and came back to Brezhnev's minion the next day with the message that the Ford Motor Company declined to sell a Lincoln

Continental to the visiting potentate. However, it would be proud and honoured, as one might say, give him one.

The following day, having consulted with his superiors, the Russian minion said to the Yankee lickspittle, "In that case, Mr Brezhnev would like to have *two* Continentals." would have responded, "In that case, we have changed our minds. Mr Brezhnev may buy one of our cars if he wishes. By the way, the price has just doubled." I was perhaps not suited to a career in diplomacy.

Probably, to a 1970s Russian leader, a Lincoln Continental seemed like a nimble little lightweight runabout in which to be chauffeur-driven along the centre of the road. It was less than 20ft long and it weighed a mere 4834lb. The Russian ZiL limousine of that era weighed almost 6400lb even in short-wheelbase form, and that was before the installation of essentials such as bullet-proofing and cases of vodka.

Mr Brezhnev was an automobile enthusiast, one of the few Russians of his generation to own a collection of cars. No doubt Joseph Stalin would have denounced him as a "rootless cosmopolite" who should be liquidated. But he would surely have admired how cunningly Brezhnev had taken those capitalist imperialists for a ride. What would 'Uncle Joe' make of the current Russian head of state, Vladimir Putin?

I am not sure of the current state of ZiL or of whether it can survive. When the USSR collapsed, that was a crisis for ZiL, which was so associated with the Politburo elite. Yet it was not the first such crisis. The company had been founded in 1916 as *Avtomobilnoe Moskovskoe Obshchestvo* (Moscow Automotive Society), shortly before the Russian Revolution. Soon after the Revolution and the end of the First World War, it was nationalized and its chief activity over the years has mainly been the manufacture of lorries. Some years later, it was renamed ZiS (Zavod imeni Stalina).

Its car production was always in low volume and exclusively aimed at those animals who were significantly more equal than others. An amusing episode was when Nikita Kruschev, in one of those pot and kettle moments, denounced his predecessor's "cult of personality." The car maker felt understandably obliged to change its name to avoid guilt through association.

The new name chosen was Zavod imeni Likhachova, from the former director Ivan Alekseevich Likhachova. This could be described as the cult of a less important personality. It is surprising that it is not now called ZiP.

A ZiL, with chauffeur, was one of the rewards for having reached the top of the greasy pole; it and the chauffeur remained yours until you were liquidated by a chap with a trick umbrella, or promoted to manage an asbestos factory in Outer Mongolia. Among the perks of ZiL ownership was the right to drive down the middle of the road (in what were called ZiL lanes') and ignore any of the plebeian traffic regulations that seemed inconvenient[4].

The difficulty for Russian manufacturers is that wealthy Russians and high officials these days want the elite vehicles produced by BMW and Mercedes-Benz, in other words, Rolls-Royces and Bentleys. I doubt that Putin would be interested in conning the Yanks into giving him a Lincoln or a Cadillac, but plans keep appearing for allegedly indigenous super-powerful huge limousines. These will allegedly be capable of withstanding just about everything, perhaps even including strikes from tactical nuclear weapons.

A few years ago, Russian car company named 'a:level'[5] began work on a Mercedes-based limousine appropriately called BIG. From the press release, it seemed to be the ZiL for the 21st century, fulfilling all the requirements of a vehicle designed for a Russian president:

"This car is designed to fly over the highway like an iron slug. At 300km/h (186mph) it is going to sweep away everything on its way … It is no accident that the word 'iron' is used here because a fundamentally new coating called 'dim iron' has been specially developed for the BIG. It is this paint job that gives the BIG a menace which is so very true of its aggressive behaviour." Move aside, proles …

[1] Adding 42in-between the axles.

[2] I suspect that this was because his pension fund had been topped up after he had signed a non-disclosure agreement.

[3] This reminds me of the old joke about why Glasgow Rangers football club has more supporters than Glasgow Celtic.

[4] In 2016, Vladimir Putin's favourite chauffeur was killed in a head-on collision while hammering along the centre of the road, in a BMW. The President was not in the car at the time.

[5] a:level had early produced the coolest Russian car of all time. This was inspired by the four-door 1957 Volga (the car of choice of the KGB). The a:level version was a low-slung two-door coupé fitted with a V12 engine and wide wheels and tyres. It had elements of Studebaker in it.

83 Wheeler dealer

HE FIRST TIME I met Alejandro de Tomaso was in 1981. I was with Tony Curtis, then editor of *Motor*, and photographer Maurice Rowe. The four of us had lunch in the Canal Grande, a magnificent 80-room hotel in the centre of Modena which he owned and lived in.

It was a somewhat tense encounter. This was a year or so before the Falklands conflict. Although de Tomaso had lived in Italy for many years, he was of Argentine origin and far from Anglophile. I observed in silent, expressionless amusement the fierce look in his eyes, as Mr Editor Curtis, a patriotic Englishman, unwisely began to explain why Argentina's claims to 'Las Malvinas' were entirely spurious.

In the 1980s, De Tomaso was Italy's Number 2 automotive industrialist, albeit a long way behind Gianni Agnelli of the Fiat empire, and he made more cars than Ferrari, Lamborghini and Aston Martin combined. According to his own estimate, he produced more than 182,000. Two thirds of these were Innocentis, which were rebodied Minis. He made about 50,000 Maseratis during his 18-year ownership of the marque.

The remainder, around 12,500, were de Tomasos, the vast majority of them Panteras. Perhaps he never produced a great car, and his Maseratis were disappointing, but the Pantera was not bad, if excruciatingly cramped. At the time of writing it looks like the bargain classic supercar for drivers under about 5ft 10in tall. I am about 5in taller than that. I can fit into Panteras, but I would not like to drive one every day or for a long distance.

There is a Pantera in the Petersen Automotive Museum in Los Angeles. It has bullet holes in the door. The car's first owner, Elvis Aaron Presley, supposedly shot the car because it refused to start when he had hoped to demonstrate a 'burn-out' start on his driveway to a girlfriend.

Before the Pantera, he had produced a series of design concepts, some of them quite interesting, for the biennial Turin Motor Show. None of them came to anything much until the Mangusta[1] which went into production in 1967. It was designed by Giugiaro while he worked for Ghia, which was then owned by de Tomaso. It was a beautiful car and very fast, but its handling was never properly sorted and it was very expensive to build.

In 1975, de Tomaso bought Maserati for 210,000 lire, then the equivalent of about £65, Citroën having written off £3.5 million of debt. He eventually sold the trident marque to Fiat, for a vast profit. He acquired several other ailing Italian companies at knockdown prices: Benelli in 1971, Moto Guzzi in 1972, and Innocenti in 1976. He acquired both Ghia and Vignale in the 1960s before selling them to Ford, again for a vast profit.

Even years later, men in suits at Ford and Fiat winced at the mere mention of de Tomaso. The brazen way in which he repeatedly outwitted the big corporations is impressive. He was such a consummate wheeler dealer that it is surprising that he never entered politics. Perhaps his wealthy American-born wife, who influenced many of his decisions, prevented that.

De Tomaso was also a Formula 1 constructor. Like Enzo Ferrari, he had been a second-rank racing driver. He built several Grand Prix cars for wealthy amateurs in the early 1960s, joining Ferrari and BRM as the only remaining companies making complete cars – chassis, engines and gearboxes. With limited funds, he made no impact on the established teams and faded away.

In 1970, he returned, but this time on a simpler basis, with a chassis designed b Gian Paolo Dallara[2], using the standard 'garagista'[3] kit of Cosworth engine and Hewlan gearbox.

The team manager was a penniless Englishman named Frank Williams. The though of de Tomaso and Williams working together is either chilling or comical, perhaps both.

After being well off the pace in earlier races, the car was lightened by extensive us of magnesium. Piers Courage then qualified the de Tomaso Type 505 a more respectabl ninth out of 20 for the Dutch Grand Prix and was running well, when there was catastrophic failure of the front suspension, the steering or a tyre. He crashed heavil and was undoubtedly dead before the car exploded into unsurvivable flames. This wa a traumatic event for de Tomaso, who evidently lacked the ability of Enzo to shed a fev crocodile tears and 'move on.' The team plodded through the remainder of the seasor with Brian Redman and then Tim Schenken, and then quietly disappeared, the bos having lost interest. As is well known, Frank Williams, though deeply upset (Courage ha been a close friend), carried on.

The old De Tomaso factory in the outskirts of Modena was still operating when I wa there in 1996. There were ambitious plans for the Guarà and Biguà. The former was bette looking, but had no luggage space whatever, and apparently had knife-edge handling. Th latter, with Gandini designed body, morphed into the Qvale Mangusta and then becam the MG Xpower SV.

In the factory at the time of my visit, there were several of the company's one-of prototypes from the early years and also the sole surviving Tipo 505, which looked tin and fragile even compared with some of its contemporaries, not to mention more moder Formula 1 monsters. Redman and Schenken (and the unfortunate Courage) were brav men indeed, especially since they must all have known how magnesium reacts to flames.

The last Biguà was made in 2004, the year after the old man died. That was the en of de Tomaso production cars, or at least of de Tomaso cars built in Italy. The brand i now owned by a Chinese company, so there may be a 21st century Pantera, or something I wonder what the fierce old Argentine would think of that.

There used to be a De Tomaso Museum in the centre of Modena. It was small, bu there were some interesting exhibits, including that Tipo 505. There was a Mangusta, tw Panteras and two Vallelungas[4].

All have since been sold, I think. The Tipo 505 has been expertly restored by Hall & Hall and appears in historic events, such as the Goodwood Festival of Speed.

When de Tomaso sold Maserati to Fiat, he had retained 18 classic Maseratis (all from the period before his ownership). In 1996, the cars were transported to London to be sol at auction by Brooks (which now trades as Bonhams). There was a great outcry in Ital from politicians local and national, journalists and car enthusiasts. Strings were pulled wads of cash changed hands in mysterious ways, and the classic Maseratis, includin the last 'Birdcage,' were transported back to Modena, where they are now on display in specially-built museum.

The de Tomaso brand does not enjoy the same 'recognition' as Maserati, but, if th Chinese make a success of the new Pantera or whatever, all those old de Tomasos may ris in value, and perhaps there will be a *Museo de Tomaso* in Beijing.

The de Tomaso factory is still standing, on the outskirts of Modena, but it ha been pillaged and vandalized, and is gradually rotting away and disappearing into th undergrowth.

The last time I met de Tomaso was again in the Hotel Canal Grande, in 1996. I wa there for *The Daily Telegraph*. I think this may have been the final interview he ever gav

This time it was not a tense encounter, but it was weird and disturbing. The industry mogul had suffered a near-fatal stroke three years previously and was no longer in control of his business.

He looked more like 80 than his 68 years and was obviously in a desperate state. Yet there was still a lively look in the eye, even if it had lost its ferocity, and he proved that he remained mentally alert at the end of the interview. He could communicate only by making strange gurgling sounds that I would not have understood even with fluent Italian. A nurse and a secretary were there.

I had been instructed to ask only 12 questions. I had supplied my list, by fax, in advance and we went through them, one by one. I would read out the question, he would listen intently and then make gurgling noises, which the secretary, sometimes with the assistance of the nurse, would interpret and translate.

At one point, I asked what seemed a vital supplementary question. Having asked all the others, I then thanked him for his time. He gurgled something to his secretary, who laughed.

She said, "Mr de Tomaso says that you have asked him 13 questions. He says that this is unpropitious and that you must ask him another."

I asked if it was true that, shortly after his stroke, that one of his subordinates had shown him some renderings for the Biguà and that, after looking at them carefully, he had hurled them across the room and shouted, "Bring me Gandini!"

He replied that it was partly true, but that he had not thrown them across the room. "I merely said that I did not want them."

[1] Italian for mongoose, a joke not greatly appreciated by Ford, which was at that time involved with the AC Cobra.

[2] Before this, Dallara had been Chief Engineer at Lamborghini, where one of his projects was the Miura. And before that he had worked for Ferrari and then Maserati. He founded his own engineering company, which is still in business, and became a major manufacturer of racing cars. These have won races and championships all over the world, but mainly not wearing a Dallara badge.

[3] Enzo Ferrari's dismissive term for all his rivals except BRM.

[4] The Vallelunga, predecessor of the Mangusta, was built in small numbers for four years from 1964. Designed by Giugiaro, it was a pretty sports car, but apparently the chassis had barely sufficient rigidity even for its relatively low-powered Ford Cortina engine.

84 Max Power

IN 1996, A YOUNG driver was arrested in Eastbourne for winding the volume of the boom-boom 'music' in his car up to public nuisance level. The case went to the magistrates court, where a fine of £350 was imposed. Some controversy was caused when a magazine called *Max Power*[1] paid the fine.

I wrote a column about this in *The Daily Telegraph*, making a few sarcastic remarks about the magazine and its readers. I described *Max Power* as "essential reading for pubescent ram-raiders." It seemed unlikely that anyone on the staff of the magazine was a *Telegraph* reader, let alone among *Max Power*'s readers. However, I had poked a stick into a wasps' nest and trouble arrived soon. Someone drew the attention of *Max Power*'s editor to my column.

An irritating fellow with an uncouth Scouse tone of voice telephoned twice at around midnight. The first time (on a Saturday, just before Christmas), he asked to speak to "Pete." When I asked who he was, he replied that he was a reader of *Max Power*, and he added, "I think you're a sad old man, and you don't know what you're talking about."

I was about to produce some variation on the standard Kingsley Amis response, along the lines of, "What makes you think I should be interested in the half-baked opinions of vulgar oik?" or the Pee-wee Herman retort[2], but he put the receiver down. When he called the next night, my wife answered and spoke entirely in French. He rang off after a while.

On the Monday, I received a call from *UK Press Gazette*, informing me that *Max Power* had published my phone and fax[3] numbers.

The oik called again, uttered a few abusive remarks, ending in "... you prat" and put the phone down. A well-spoken man claiming to be manager of a printing company called, offering to print new stationery and business cards, saying that "One of the lads" had shown him the piece in *Max Power* and he assumed that I would be changing my telephone number. I think this was a genuine call of sympathy, mingled with amusement and a touch of entrepreneurial flair, but he may have been merely a piss-taker. Another oik called, making screeching noises. Highly satirical, as Willie Rushton, who had died the week before, used to say.

One caller left the following message on the answerphone at 6.30am: "You're the biggest fucking knob in the world." I thought it might be worth having a lapel badge fabricated or new business cards printed merely to have that added, in quotes, like those play reviews outside theatres.

These nuisance callers could not know that I had immediately taken to switching the telephone and answerphone to silent mode from 6pm to 8am. They may have maliciously imagined that their calls were disturbing my sleep, but they were received silently in the darkness of the night. It was their sleep that was pointlessly delayed, rather than mine.

A five-minute-long recorded message from one night prowler began, "I am a *Max Power* weader, and I am not a pubescent wam waider." I thought, maybe not, sunshine, but you are something else beginning with W, and it's not witty. I suppose I introduced a significant proportion of an entire generation to the word 'pubescent,' which may well have been their first word containing three syllables. Well, it is part of the growing-up process.

For a while, I was infuriated enough about this bloody *Max Power* affair for it to be difficult to get any work done. I investigated possible means of legal redress, but it turned out that none existed. I also contacted the 'chairperson' of MIPAA (Motor Industry Public Affairs Association), a friend of mine, but she told me, borrowing a Billy Connolly joke, that *Max Power*'s hacks were already about as welcome on press trips as a fart in a spacesuit. She added that from that point on, they may not be invited anywhere. "We have a very efficient 'grapevine' ..."

In the end, there were fewer abusive calls than I had expected, only about 30 in all, plus two faxes. And then they stopped altogether. One can reasonably assume that *Max Power*'s readers had an attention span similar to that of a goldfish, so after the New Year, they may perhaps have had other things occupying their bleak little minds and have forgotten all about me.

I had a long telephone conversation with one of *Max Power*'s shiny suits[4] about this affair, trying unsuccessfully to explain to him something that seemed obvious to me: that it was perfectly all right for the alleged journalists in his employ to write whatever they wished about me: they could be as rude as they wished, provided there was nothing libellous. To me, this was all as piffle before the wind, as Daisy Ashford would say.

However, I felt strongly and still do that printing my telephone number was irresponsible and unfair, a step too far. I pointed out to smug Mr Shiny Suit that if I still lived in England, one of his publication's more deranged readers might have thrown a brick through the window of my house or car. This seemed to make him pause for a moment.

The fellow did at least undertake not to publish my number again, and also that the magazine's staff would not do the same to other journalists with whose opinions they disagreed. He kept the first promise, but not the second.

A year or two later, a well-known television hack who specializes in the secondhand car market said casually on air that any customization[5] of a car considerably reduces its resale value. This is demonstrably true and not a controversial statement, one might think, but *Max Power*'s editorial staff disliked it being said and detested anyone who did not share their point of view. So they published his telephone number and invited readers to call him and express their disagreement.

Unfortunately, the chap was in the process of going through a difficult divorce and had moved out of what had been his family home. His soon-to-be-ex-wife, already on the edge of a breakdown, received a stream of abusive calls.

In anyone's life, there are ups and downs and this episode was mildly depressing, but most of my working life was either interesting or fun, and usually both. However, I have remembered the names of some of those involved.

[1] A monthly title launched in 1993 by the sinister EMAP corporation, with offices in Peterborough, the most unpleasant town in Britain. It was aimed mainly at the sort of young men who at the time wore those low-crotch I've-shat-my-pants jeans. For some years, it had a surprisingly high circulation – several hundred thousand at its peak – and then it gradually withered to nothing and was terminated in 2011. If *Max Power* was a motoring magazine, then it was the only one that EMAP ran successfully, for a short period, having failed dismally with *CAR*, which it bought in 1992 and sold in 2007; *Performance Car*, bought in 1990 and closed in 1998; and *Carweek*, its biggest, most costly and most embarrassing disaster.
[2] "I know you are, but what am I?"
[3] A means of communication that was briefly widespread in the 20th century.
[4] A derisive term for Publishing Directors, widely used by magazine journalists.
[5] Tuning of the engine or modification of the standard bodywork.

85 The largest pilot of all times

HE HAS WON MORE than 30 Grands Prix and he has been Formula 1 World Champion five times; he has also won the Le Mans 24 Hours five times, the Indianapolis 500 twice, and the Paris-Dakar and Monte Carlo rallies once each, among numerous other victories in various forms of motor sport. He is the only driver to have raced against both Graham and Damon Hill, and both Gilles and Jacques Villeneuve. His family has been involved in the manufacture of high-performance road and racing cars bearing their own name since the 1950s. Who is he?

His name is Michel Vaillant. You have probably never heard of him, but in the Francophone world he is as famous as Tintin, and like Hergé's little reporter, he is a comic-strip character; his first appearance was actually in Tintin magazine in February 1957. Since then, more than 70 albums of Vaillant's adventures have been published. In the past, there have been television series, some animated, others woodenly acted and directed. In 2003, a feature film (not animated) was released in France and Japan; starring Sagamore Stévenin, it was written and produced by Luc Besson (director of *Nikita*, *Léon*, *Le Grand Bleu*, *Taxi 1/2/3*, etc) and reportedly cost 25 million euros to make.

Square-jawed like David Coulthard, as dark-haired and clean-cut as Barbie's boyfriend Ken and as tough as Bulldog Drummond, Vaillant is heroic, brilliant, incorruptible and humourless, if a bit moody. He is married, and although sometimes tempted, is never unfaithful, as far as one can tell.

The creator of Michel Vaillant, Jean Graton, was born in 1923. He does not remotely resemble either David or Ken, let alone Bulldog Drummond, and never did, and (unlike Michel Vaillant and Peter Pan) he does not appear to have discovered the secret of eternal youth, a means of resisting the greying of the follicles, or, indeed, baldness.

Graton's father was a police chief in Nantes, who organized motorcycle races (and who was interned by the Germans during the war). In his early career, Jean Graton worked on a variety of other comic-strip characters, and also produced the kind of informative illustrations that used to appear in *The Eagle*, before he hit gold by creating Michel Vaillant.

At first, although all the cars except for the Vaillant (sometimes feminised as Vaillante) were based on real machinery, all the drivers were invented. But gradually Michel Vaillant, and his friend and rival Steve Warson, began racing against real grand prix drivers. Occasionally, other 'real' people appear in the stories, such as Jacques Chirac during his stint as Mayor of Paris, in the 1982 yarn, *300 à l'heure dans Paris* (that's kmh – 186 in mph); in that adventure[1], Vaillant is depressed because someone is trying to blackmail him for being unfaithful – of course, he is not – but nevertheless he overtakes Alain Prost to win the first-ever Paris Grand Prix.

It has been claimed that the greatest inspiration for Vaillant was the Belgian driver Jacky Ickx – though evidently not the original inspiration, as Ickx was only 12 in 1957. However, there are certain similarities, apart from facial bone structure: Ickx is the only man so far to have won grands prix, Le Mans (six times) and the Dakar Rally; he has also competed on motorbikes, like one of Graton's other creations, Julie Wood, a sort of Barbie on a bike …

Graton wrote all the stories and drew all the cartoons entirely by himself for the first 12 years, but since 1970 his studio has steadily expanded. Then his son Philippe, working with a team of illustrators and story-writers, took over. The plots remained engagingly less than fully baked and the illustrations a touch crude: just in case you thought grand prix cars were silent, you get 'visual sound effects' in the strips: 'VROOAAW' for full acceleration, 'RROAAOOOAAW' for flat-out in top gear, 'ROOAP ROOAP' for changing down twice, 'TSHIIP' when two cars rub wheels together, and so on. That does not seem to put off readers.

For the feature film, one car (a Lola-Judd) was actually entered under the Vaillante banner for the 2002 Le Mans, and another (a Panoz) as a Leader (Vaillant's great rival). They lined up 21st and 23rd on the grid, and the 'Vaillante' managed to finish the race, 27th and last. The Leader team are the baddies, and it is amusing to note that one of the car's drivers was Perry McCarthy, the original 'Stig' on the children's motoring programme *Top Gear*. It is always easy to tell the good guys from the bad guys in a Michel Vaillant strip: the bad guys all look like Perry McCarthy, or Ernest Borgnine.

It used to be a joy to read the English version of the Michel Vaillant/Jean Graton website, but alas it has been tidied up in recent years. I particularly enjoyed the statement that "Michel Vaillant really well is the largest pilot of all times." I had previously thought that really well was Froilan Gonzalez …

Among many other gems that would have appealed to Gerard Hoffnung, was: "Judge rather: in 40 years of career (which longevity!), he achieved exploits in all the disciplines, weight-heavy or even outboard motor boat! With through this exceptional career, Jean Graton makes us discover at the same time the dimensions spectacular one and the slides of these sports."

When you had recovered from these dimensions spectacular and slides, you could buy Michel Vaillant T-shirts and baseball caps and all manner of other merchandise, or vote for your favourite Vaillant album; Graton even allowed you to vote also for your least favourite album, and listed the results.

He also published some hilarious parodies of his work by various other artists. In one of them, entitled *Michel Braillant* (brailler is French for to bawl like a child), Michel's grey-haired mother says to his father, "I've been worried about our little Michel ever since the team has been sponsored by that big Vaseline company." However, in the race, all goes well: Braillant wins, thanks to his "superior penetration."

In one of Michel Vaillant's 21st-century comic-book adventures, *L'Épreuve*, our hero took on a number of famous drivers – among them Michael Schumacher, Gilles Villeneuve, Giancarlo Fisichella, Carlos Sainz (Senior), and his old sparring partner Steve Warson – in a series of eight events around the world, curiously titled Ultima Speedfight, to decide who is the greatest pilot of them all. Or perhaps the largest.

The result is unlikely to be a surprise to Vaillant fans. As was predicted in the Le Mans pit lane after Vaillant's first appearance in 1957: "Ce galopin finira champion du monde!" – This urchin will end up champion of the world!

A few years ago, there was an attempt to have a round of the World Formula 1 Championship in Paris. It was never likely to happen while the capital city had a Socialist mayor – and even less likely under a Socialist President.

It will probably never happen now. The cost and disruption would be enormous. If the idea is revived, it will almost certainly be something like the Formula E 1 race, all enclosed in metal cages, in which case, for the television viewer, apart from a few aerial shots, it might just as well be on the Moon.

As mentioned, there was once a Grand Prix de Paris, on paper at least, involving Michel Vaillant. The circuit was roughly 4.5 miles long. The pits complex was located at the south-eastern end of the Champs-Elysées. The cars then set off along 'the world's most famous avenue,' negotiating three chicanes before a drift challenge around the

Arc de Triomphe. Then it was back down the Champs-Elysées for a short distance before hanging a right into the Avenue George V, followed by a 90-degree left at the Virage de l'Alma, above the infamous tunnel[2].

After this, it was onto the Cours Albert I along the right bank of the Seine, then right, over the Pont Alexandre III, left onto the Quai d'Orsay, left again to re-cross the river via the Pont de la Concorde, arriving back at the start/finish line via a series of chicanes in the Place de la Concorde. One can imagine huge crowds and all the atmosphere of Monaco but with some overtaking possibilities.

And who won this Paris Grand Prix? Surprise, surprise … it was our hero Michel Vaillant. Despite starting 11th on the grid, he took the lead by outbraking Alain Prost's Renault on the last lap. Didier Pironi's Ferrari finished third. On the podium, with a glum-faced Jean-Marie Balestre[3] in the background, Vaillant is congratulated by the suave-looking, sleek-haired Mayor of Paris, Jacques Chirac, who later became President of the Republic, but who failed to defy the passage of time as successfully as Michel Vaillant.

[1] That's E for Electric, allegedly green and clean but not really.
[2] This cannot be taken 'flat' in a Mercedes S-Class, even in the absence of small white Fiats.
[3] Then the President of the Fédération Internationale de l'Automobile (See Chapter 3).

86 Telegraph times

I WAS SADDENED WHEN the *Motoring* section of *The Daily Telegraph* ceased to be a separate supplement at the end of 2016, collapsing back into the Weekend supplement. I had been there at the beginning, and, in fact, began contributing to the newspaper before the Motoring section was launched in 1995.

The Conrad Black era of ownership (1986-2004) of *The Daily Telegraph* is now looked upon in retrospect by those who have survived the thousand cuts since then, and by former employees and contributors, as a golden era. Most of us think that Baron Black of Crossroads, the former jailbird, did more far good than harm to *The Telegraph* newspapers and that he would probably not have got into so much trouble if he had married a woman without a shoe-collecting habit. But that is none of our business. What is undeniable is that *The Telegraph* has been in steady decline ever since.

In *The Oldie* magazine some years ago, columnist 'Enfield Senior' (Edward, father of Harry) wrote perceptively, "We do not take *The Daily Telegraph* in this house any more. It has become a tabloid, in everything but format."

Soon after the weird Barclay twins acquired the newspaper group, journalists and readers began to ask the question, "Why has *The Daily Telegraph* become so much like *The Daily Mail*?" The answer was extraordinarily simple: *The Telegraph*, having fired many of its most respected journalists, hired hacks from *The Daily Mail* to replace them. And, to be fair, some of them were not very nice people.

One journalist who, with characteristic contrariness, moved in the opposite direction was Eric Bailey. He had a somewhat morbid fear of *The Telegraph*'s newsroom, which he called "The snake pit," but he worked his way around it to his own advantage. He was a very good journalist, but also a consummate manipulator with a sharp understanding of office politics. This was essential for long-term survival in what was still called 'Fleet Street' and still is by some people, even though there are no longer any newspapers based there[1].

It was through Eric that I first had work published in *The Telegraph*. The first feature was about the Saturn Car Company (see Chapter 79), and it was Eric who invited me to supply a regular column in the new Saturday *Motoring* section which began in 1995. Before that, *Motoring* had been within the Weekend supplement of the Saturday edition of the newspaper. It was Eric who had persuaded the newspaper's senior managers to embark upon this bold venture, with him at the helm.

Over the years, I contributed pieces to other sections of the *Telegraph*, as well as my regular stuff in *Motoring*. On three or four occasions, I even made it to the front page ... but always under the byline 'Eric Bailey, Motoring Editor'! Eric explained that it was essential for him to maintain a high profile. He always made sure that I was well paid for those pieces.

The *Motoring* section flourished and was highly regarded by readers and the industry. And Eric introduced some interesting innovations, hiring the eccentric used-car dealer Peter Lorimer with a pork-pie hat, who became famous as 'Honest John' the motoring agony aunt. By an odd coincidence, Andrew English became the newspaper's highly-respected *Motoring* Correspondent and Peter Hall was hired as Bailey's deputy, taking over as *Motoring* Editor when Eric jumped ship to become a senior executive at *The Daily Mail* group. He has since retired.

Andrew English had been Deputy Editor of *Fast Lane* and he succeeded me as Editor. Peter Hall had been the magazine's Deputy Art Editor and was among many *Telegraph* employees who were shabbily treated during the ownership of the dim-witted Barclay Twins. Other former *Fast Lane* people also contributed to *Motoring*, such as Mark Hales and Simon Arron.

[1] Will there be any based anywhere in future? Alas, I doubt it.

87 V for Vette

AS I HAVE MENTIONED elsewhere, I have never had much time for American cars, which, in the old music hall phrase, have mostly been designed, like traditional sopranos, 'for comfort, not for speed.'

The first Corvette I drove, in about 1980, merely reinforced this view. It was a fine-looking car and I was quite amazed, burbling through central London on a sunny summer day, that so many young women stopped and stared. Many of them waved. Well, I was young and handsome. Oddly, a few days later, I was driving an MG Metro through central London over the same route, on an equally blue-sky day, and I did not have the same effect. At a red traffic light, I checked myself in the rear-view mirror and I was just as bloody handsome as I had been when driving the Corvette. Perhaps it was a trick of the light: the Metro's windscreen glass may have been tinted.

That Corvette, which had been fitted with decent tyres instead of the gripless indestructibles then supplied as original equipment on the other side of the Atlantic, was not bad to drive in most respects, but it was pathetically slow compared with contemporary European sports cars. Despite its 5.7-litre V8 engine, it had roughly the same performance as a four-cylinder MGB, which, in unmodified form, was a slug on wheels. Its maximum speed was only 115mph. The American manufacturers had at that point been saddled with severe emissions regulations, but had not yet discovered the complex technical solutions that would allow decent performance to be retained.

A few years later, when I was Editor of *Fast Lane*, we had a Corvette C4 as one of our long-term cars. Things had changed by then and now the performance was decent by any standards (0-60mph in around six seconds and a top speed of just over 150mph) and it was very good value for money. The principal downside for UK buyers was that it had left-hand drive[1]. It also had an annoying system in it that forced you to go from first to third gear, bypassing second, unless you smoked it ostentatiously off the line with lots of revs[2].

I really enjoyed that car, and especially recall driving it down to the south of France for a summer holiday, zapping past all the little Renaults and Peugeots and Citroëns on the Route Napoleon. But then it started to rain quite hard and, like all big, powerful cars on big, fat tyres (even if they are good), it was fairly hopeless on wet surfaces. I had to back off to avoid aquaplaning and several of the more spiritedly-driven little Renaults and Peugeots and Citroëns came zapping back past me, their drivers no doubt enjoying a good laugh.

The Corvette is unfairly considered 'an old man's car' in its home territory, and some European journalists sneer at its relative crudity compared with Ferraris and Porsches and so on. I always enjoyed driving them.

I tested various Corvettes over the years. The two that I liked most were very quick versions, first the ZR1 in 1989, and then the Z06 about 15 years later. I drove each of these in the south of France.

The ZR1 was developed with considerable input from Lotus Engineering and the most surprising aspect of it was that the engine was manufactured by Mercury Marine.

The launch was unusual, in that we spent two nights away. The usual routine, even then, was to fly out of Britain first thing in the morning and arrive back on the afternoon of the next day. I came to the conclusion that this extended event was not designed to give us more information about the car, but for GM people to quiz European journalists on how to tackle the market. Perhaps the information and opinions we gave them were not up to standard, or perhaps they ignored what they were told. In any case, it seems not to have done the corporation much good in the long run.

We flew to Montpellier, west of Marseille. From there, we were transported by bus to a hotel in Carcassonne, arriving early in the evening. As usual there was a press presentation before dinner. During this we were informed that we would each be accompanied by a Corvette representative for the test drive.

The next morning, I found myself in the driver's seat, with a stocky American named Jim Ingle sitting beside me. I had not previously met him, but I knew that he was the famous Corvette Chief Test Engineer[3].

We set off and trundled around for a while in early morning traffic and then for a short while on an autoroute. I have no idea where we went from there, except it was initially to the north, probably towards Albi, and then, I think, to the west[4]. It was an excellent route, with a lot of medium and high speed S-bends and plenty of elevation change. Mr Ingle would occasionally make a remark about a junction that we were approaching.

The reason why I can recall nothing in detail of the route is that the red mist had descended as soon as we peeled off the autoroute onto those fabulous, almost traffic-free roads … At one point during the previous evening's dinner, I had heard Mr Ingle, who had been at an adjacent table, remark that, if he had been following in a standard C4 Corvette, he could have kept up with any of the hacks he had sat beside during the exercise so far. So I was on a mission.

We charged around for roughly an hour and stopped somewhere for a scheduled coffee halt, though alas the coffee was American-style, simultaneously weak and bitter. Then we hacked on for another hour or so. After that there was another autoroute section, lasting about 20 miles. It was always useful to have that on a test route, to listen to various noises – tyre, wind, engine, transmission – at different speeds.

I had noticed when we entered the autoroute that the fuel gauge needle was getting close to zero. I mentioned this to Jim Ingle and eased off, cruising in the very high sixth gear at around the advised autoroute limit of 130km/h, the engine turning over at less than 2000rpm. Despite this, it soon began to miss a beat and it was obvious that we were running out of fuel, so I switched off the ignition and eased onto the hard shoulder.

This was before the days of mobile phones, but Ingle had a walkie-talkie (or, as the French perversely insist on calling it, a talkie-walkie). He called for assistance from the following backup team.

It took them almost half an hour to arrive, during which time all the other ZR1s cruised past. I asked, "Tell me, Jim, if you had been in a standard C4, do you think you could have kept up with me?" He looked at me with a fierce stare and then laughed. He said, "No fucking way!"

[1] All Corvettes leaving the factory in Bowling Green, Kentucky have been left-hand drive since the first came off the line in 1953. It was not possible to convert them, either, because the car's driveline was asymmetrically installed, so the passenger footwell was considerably narrower than the driver's side. On more recent models, however, this is not the case and a right-hand drive version of the latest model has been available for British buyers since 2016 – but it almost doubles the price of a new C7.
[2] It was quite simple to have this annoying device detached.
[3] Jim Ingle was the main man responsible for developing Corvettes from the mid-1970s until 1997 when he moved on to other roles within GM. He retired in 2006 after 43 years working for GM.
[4] It is one of my regrets that I did not keep detailed notes of the routes of all the car launches I attended. That might have made a book on its own.

218

88 The ghost of Mika Häkkinen

IN 1998 THE MCLAREN Group launched, at vast expense, an ultra-high-quality glossy magazine called *Racing Line*[1]. This was the brainchild of Rocket Ron Dennis, who turned McLaren into a major force a few years after the tragic death of its founder, successfully introducing the concept of manic-obsessive anal retention to the management of Formula 1 teams.

I had been commissioned to produce an unusual feature for this new monthly publication. On Tuesday, 19 May 1998 I drove to Monaco, the paradoxical city state on the French Riviera which combines possibly the world's highest percentage concentration of criminals among its population with an almost flat-lining crime rate, apart from a thriving trade in the theft and export of expensive cars.

The three major characters I met that day were not criminals, as far as I know. In order of appearance, one was a photographer, another a racing driver and the third an hereditary prince (albeit descended in the paternal line from Italian pirates).

It was a fine azure morning, so I left my BMW in the multi-storey car park near the start/finish line and walked from there through Ste Devote and up the hill to Massenet, the operatic left-hander that leads into Casino Square. Those who have seen Monaco only via television coverage of the Grand Prix are always astounded, when they arrive in the Principality for the first time, by the severity of the elevation changes, especially downwards from Casino Square to Mirabeau Haute, through the Crap Hotel Bend[2], then the first right-hander, Mirabeau Bas, and the second one called Portier, the name of which relates to low-level Catholic students who used to attend a college near there[3].

Even more astounding than the steep up-and-down stuff is that the drivers arrive at the braking point for Massenet at something close to 170mph, and that they shed only about 70mph of that to get through the blind corner between the Hotel de Paris and the Casino. And then there is the tunnel and the Chicane, and so on. The race is usually rather boring after the first lap, but when you have walked around the circuit you can only be in awe of the skills of the drivers.

I met the photographer at the appointed time in a café at the back of Casino Square. We had a chat about what we were going to do while downing espressos, and then walked around the corner to an ordinary-looking modern apartment block not much different from those that might be found in a suburb of Birmingham, apart from two elements: the view across the Mediterranean, and a reception desk. We announced ourselves and a few minutes later we met our racing driver, Mr Häkkinen, who was with his rather scary wife.

Having kissed his wife goodbye for the day, Mika drove us in his crap A-Class Mercedes through the tunnel and the Chicane and Tabac (where there is no longer a tobacconist) and then through Rascasse (where there is no longer a gasometer). From there, instead of continuing to the right onto the start/finish straight, we turned sharp left and headed up the hill to the historic pirates' palace, which, with its parade of guards in bizarre uniforms, is the closest thing you will see to Ruritania without watching a preposterous film starring Ronald Colman or Stewart Granger.

We had a pass to park the crap A-class and we then entered the palace. We were expected, so there was no strip search or anything degrading of that kind. Very soon, we were guided to the private apartment of Prince Albert Alexandre Louis Pierre Grimaldi, who was at that time the heir apparent of Rainier III, and who has since become Son Altesse Sérénissime Albert II.

The idea was that Mika would interview Albert about his sporting exploits (he had been an Olympic tobogganist and had participated in numerous sports. He had also competed in the 1985 Paris-Dakar Rally, but his Mitsubishi broke down). And then they could discuss the forthcoming Grand Prix.

Very soon, I realized that I was in the company of two rather shy men, so it was just as well that I had considered that as a probability and prepared carefully for this rather surreal event. Ideally, I would have interviewed them and asked them questions in turn. But in theory, I was not really there at all. It was Mika who was supposed to be interviewing the Prince. I was merely The Ghost. I had asked Mika casually when we first met at his apartment if he had a set of questions to ask Prince Albert. If he had not already been Finnish, the colour would have drained from his cheeks. He looked worried and said that he did not, so I had said, "Well, let's do it this way ..."

He listened carefully to my suggestion about the way we should get through the ordeal and seemed relieved, but he was still visibly nervous when we put it into operation. He was not yet the relaxed, polished performer he later became in front of camera and without notes. His English was already fluent, if strongly accented, but at that stage could not have conducted an interview to save his life, even, I should think, in his native tongue.

I gave him a clipboard with a set of questions on it that we had rapidly gone through beforehand. He held a pen and pretended to make notes, for the benefit of the photographer. I turned on my tape recorder and we got started.

Every now and then I had to prod him, prompt him, and step in and ask the questions whenever he 'dried up,' which happened a couple of times. And I asked a few supplementaries. Prince Albert seemed amused by all that. He gave the impression of a quiet, modest man. I thought that, in his restrained way, he was quite impressive and reasonably quick-witted. I did not envy him his strange life at all.

After the interview, we stepped out onto the Prince's terrace. The view from there, high above the town and the harbour, even with all the modern buildings, with the Alps in the background to the left and the Med to the right, was quite breathtaking. I asked Mika if, supposing he did not know it, someone told him that a grand prix would be held down there that weekend, what his reaction would be. "I vood say zay vere crazee," he replied.

I said on impulse that I was sure that he would win the race the following Sunday. To my surprise, he seemed surprised. "Do you think so?" he asked. I should have put money on it.

Five days later, Mika scored his first and only win in the Monaco Grand Prix[4], and in convincing style: he had his McLaren-Mercedes team-mate Coulthard well under control from the start, and the rest pulverized. In one sense he was lucky: with 30 laps of the race remaining, a violent storm arrived from the east over my house (only 40 miles west of Monaco), starting with five minutes of hailstones and ending with about 15 minutes of torrential rain. That could have turned the race into a lottery; anything could have happened, even a win for Eddie Bigmouth Irvine, who had suggested prior to the race that all current Grand Prix drivers apart from Michael Schumacher were Number Two drivers, which must have made him, at best, a Number Three.

Anyone who can merely qualify for a Grand Prix has to be pretty good, therefore Irvine was pretty good. However, he was evidently not in the same class as the leading drivers, such as Häkkinen (whom I rated more highly than Schumacher) and at least half

220

a dozen other chaps in fireproof rompers of that era. He should have kept his mouth shut a bit more often, but he is Irish, for one thing.

In *Racing Line*, the photographer received a credit, but, of course, I did not. Such is the lot of a ghost. My copy was printed exactly as delivered, but an introduction had been added, suggesting that Mika Häkkinen was as accomplished with a reporter's notebook as he was in the cockpit of a Formula 1 car. I laughed and then took it as a sort of compliment. And I was paid, which is always the most important thing.

[1] *Racing Line* survived for 141 issues, the last appearing towards the end of 2009. Production quality set new standards and the cost of it must have been eye-watering. Early issues at least had some exceptionally expensive silver print on every page.
[2] The hairpin once known as Le Virage de la Gare.
[3] If Windsor had a Grand Prix circuit, the corner closest to Eton College might be named 'Fag.'
[4] This was the fifth of Häkkinen's 20 Grand Prix victories, and the fourth of that year, on the way to the first of his two consecutive World Championships.

89 "What's the best car you have driven?"

A BLOGGER HAS SUGGESTED that a motoring journalist who does not actually own a car is not qualified to pass judgment on any car. To put it mildly, this is the most utter rot[1].

Before 1976 when I joined *Motor* I owned various cars and was obliged, and, in the end, rather pleased, to resume the expensive hobby after 1991 when I was biffed out into freelance mode. In the intervening 15 years, I had a succession of company cars, in addition to driving about 100 other cars per year. It made no sense to own a car during that period. I always had a mental list of mildly mental cars that I would *like* to own, but then thought, what is the point? It was more a question of time than of economy.

Some of the long-term cars were loaned by manufacturers, others bought and sold by IPC. They were an undeniable perk, especially with the IPC plastic card that covered all running costs, at least until the Inland Revenue decided that they were, indeed, an undeniable perk.

Running a long-term car was also part of the toad named Work, but not something that one complained about. It was necessary to keep a detailed log-book listing faults and failures, servicing costs, likes and dislikes. Fellow owners would sometimes write in with their own experiences, which was often useful, and one picked up information from other sources, such as service engineers. With the internet, gathering such knowledge is easier these days, though caution is required.

In the case of cars bought by IPC, personnel at manufacturers' agents did not always know at first that I was a journalist, though they usually found out after a while, one way or another. Anyway, one got a fairly good idea of what it would be like to run the car on one's own account as an ordinary motorist.

At *Motor*, I had quite a mix of long-term cars. My first was a Fiat 131 Mirafiori, which in most respects was nearly quite nice, but I detested it. I could have put up with the garish lime green paint, but excessive brake servo assistance made it nearly impossible to drive smoothly. Apparently this was the consequence of a clumsy engineering conversion to right-hand-drive. I was astounded that someone, in fact at least two people (one Italian and another British), had signed it off as acceptable for sale. They perhaps did not drive it, in which case they were negligent. If they did drive it, they were incompetent or something at least as bad.

Next, I had an Alfasud 1.3ti, which was wonderful. The flat-four engine, the driveline and the brakes were all splendid. But it was the handling and above all the steering that were standard-setting, transforming my opinion of front-wheel drive. It also had comfortable seats and an outstanding driving position, though the interior finish was appallingly shoddy.

My Sud proved to be a useful benchmark: few road-test cars were as enjoyable to drive. I still do not like front-driven cars much, despite the obvious practical benefits. The only one that I have driven that exceeded that early Sud's finesse was the M100 Elan of the 1990s, a disaster for Lotus but a triumph of engineering skill.

My Sud was perfectly reliable and there was no sign of rust anywhere when I reluctantly relinquished the keys. At the time, this was attributed to the then-new and allegedly magical 'Zincrometal' treatment, which alas merely concealed and perhaps delayed the rot of the low-grade steel that it covered.

Having learned a useful lesson from the Fiat and the Alfsud – that you hate a car despite its virtues, or like it despite its faults, I became keeper of a Datsun Sunny 120Y Coupé; I wondered what unforgivable sin I had committed and tried quite hard, without much success, to find some virtues, and often thought on Fridays, "Oh shit! I have the bloody Datsun for the weekend." Thus the early joy of free motoring was soon overridden by one's critical faculties[2].

After that, I was promoted and had more of a say in which long-term cars I should run. Among these were a Mazda RX-7 and an Audi Quattro, both mentioned elsewhere in this book, and a Ford Sierra XR4i, of which I expected much and was mostly disappointed, not only because of the ventilation mentioned in Chapter 81.

After leaving *Motor* in 1983 to set up *Fast Lane*, which was launched the following year, I was then in charge of the new magazine's long-term car operation. I based my policy on what I had experienced, because it seemed to work well. We ran cars for about the same period as on *Motor* – a bit more than a year usually. In a couple of cases, notably the Porsche 944 and the Lancia Delta integrale, I very much wanted to hang onto them.

The advantage of running long-term cars from a work point of view, apart from the fact that everyone on the staff always had a car to get to and from work, was that one found out all sorts of things that would not show up from a normal test, in which one drives the model for just a few hundred miles.

An example of this involved tyres and the Porsche 944. Racing driver Jonathan Palmer[3] and I each took delivery of a 944 in 1984. A few months later, we compared notes. Jonathan liked his car in most respects, but complained that he was constantly locking up the front wheels. I was amazed, because I was experiencing mild brake fade when I drove hard.

It turned out that while both cars were on Pirellis, Palmer's was supplied with CN36, while mine was on the far more grippy P6. Black, round and mysterious, tyres are, and they can transform a car's behaviour.

Porsche's recommended pressures for the 944 also seemed weirdly unsuitable, causing excessive understeer, but that was easily resolved. Brilliantly developed from the mediocre 924, it was a marvellous car. Its successor, the 968, was even better, but alas it failed in the end because of the reputation of those whiz-kid City types who bought them. You can pick up a 944 or 968 for not much money at the time of writing, but perhaps they will soon be recognized as 'classics.'

A question that every motoring journalist hates being asked is, "What's the best car you have ever driven?" Well, I know I do. Just in case you read this book and subsequently meet me, I shall answer it here and then you can ask me something else.

The trouble is that there is no easy answer. There is obviously no such thing as 'the best car in the world,' for example, and there never has been. It depends upon what you are looking for.

All right, here goes. Yes, I have enjoyed over the years driving Ferraris, Lamborghinis, Porsches, and so on, though some of each have been deeply disappointing. But I rather lost interest in 'supercars' years ago. Their huge tyres have so much grip on dry surfaces that you have to be travelling at speeds far beyond what is reasonable on public roads, to get anywhere near their limits. On slippery surfaces, the limits are so low that those 'supercars' are practically undriveable.

Therefore, the cars that linger in my memory for positive reasons are not among the most powerful that I have driven. They include some of those mentioned in this chapter, the BMW E36 3-series, the first saloon with the multi-link Z-axle. I liked its successor the E46 even more; and then the malign styling influence of Mr Bangle arrived[4]. Above all, again demonstrating that one likes certain cars despite their flaws, I cherish the memory of the Alfa 75 Twin Spark. Yes, really, that is my answer[5]. So now we move on to an easier question, with the same answer.

[1] For books, the situation is arguably different. Owning a Morgan 3 Wheeler gave me insights that were useful when I wrote my book about the model.

[2] At that stage, I had not driven a Skoda Estelle, which in original form was a dreadful car. However, considering the brilliant development by which Porsche engineers transformed the Skoda, I am sure that a suspension guru could have turned the 120Y into a fun car.

[3] See Chapter 45.

[4] See Chapters 74 and 74.

[5] And, if you meet me, tell me how much you enjoyed this book, and then ask, "What's the best car you have ever driven?" there's going to be trouble.

90 "What's the best car you have owned?"

WHEN I BECAME FREELANCE (perforce as The Bard would say), embedded in my imagination was the specification of the car that I wanted. Because I wanted rear-wheel drive and relatively modest external dimensions, it did not take long to narrow down the options and the bargain, low-mileage, secondhand buy at the time was the Alfa 75.

It was essentially a very good car, the first Alfa to leave the factory not already rusting, yet its value fell off a cliff as soon as the first owner drove out of the showroom. This tended not to happen with BMWs and Mercedes-Benzes.

There was an old joke about the Milanese marquee: when you bought an Alfa, you were buying only the engine; the rest of the car was thrown in for no extra cost. You soon found out why, even with the 75.

British buyers of the 75 had a choice of two splendid engines – the 1962cc Twin Spark or the 3-litre V6. The latter gave more vigorous performance, and melodious intake and exhaust music, but the Twin Spark, the latest in Alfa's long and continuous development of four-cylinder motors with double overhead camshafts, was the better choice. The V6 made the front end of the 75 far too heavy and consumed a lot more fuel, necessitating a larger tank which substantially reduced boot capacity.

As for the rest of the 75, it had possibly the most ridiculous interior design of any car I have driven, and the finish was not much less shoddy than that of my Alfasud a couple of decades earlier. The warning lights cried 'Wolf!' when there were no wolves around. The most annoying warning light was 2in square and bright red and did not relate to wolves, real or imaginary: it flashed infuriatingly, incessantly and needlessly when the absurd U-shaped handbrake, resembling the control lever of an aircraft but operating only in the vertical plane, was applied. Job #1 was to cover that warning square with black tank tape, because the fuse also operated something useful, I forget what. For no obvious reason, switches for the electric windows were set into the roof lining.

The cheaply-upholstered seats were surprisingly comfortable, but the pedals in right-hand-drive models caused discomfort. They were fine on a short drive, but if you travelled for any distance, you had to spend five minutes learning to walk again. It was all to do with the angle of the throttle pedal. It was possible to improve this marginally by raising the front of the driver's seat, using various bits and pieces and a Meccano mentality.

With all this in mind, apart from the nice engine, why would anyone in his right mind have bought a 75 TS? The giveaway prices obviously helped – you got that car salesman's cliché, 'a lot of car for the money.' Apart from the novelty of a rust-free bodyshell, it was actually rather a well-built car in most respects. But so far, I have not presented a compelling justification for purchase. I shall try my best.

Most people considered the 75's four-door body ugly. It grew on me, but perhaps this was because I enjoyed driving the car so much. The engineering beneath that angular shell was fascinating, eccentric and pure Alfa, a developed version of the Alfetta and GTV (introduced in 1972).

The front suspension was conventional in one respect – unequal-length double wishbones and hydraulic dampers – but unusual in the use of torsion bars rather than coil springs. At the rear was a de Dion setup with inboard disc brakes, as in Aston Martins of that period, but with the added complication of a transaxle, in search of 50/50 front/rear weight ratio. Alfa's engineers perhaps went a step too far with the brake location (the perceived advantage being a reduction in unsprung weight).

Even without modifications, the handling was far superior to that of the equivalent BMW 3-series, at that time the E30 (with semi-trailing arm rear suspension), and the assisted rack-and-pinion steering was outstandingly communicative. However, I was convinced that the car could be considerably improved by some modifications, as it understeered too much, leaning excessively on the loaded front wheel when cornered hard.

I looked around for various remedies and homed in on Rhoddy Harvey-Bailey, renowned suspension guru, Alfa specialist and successful former racer. He converted quite a few 75s with a simple but clever kit consisting of a substantially stiffer front anti-roll bar and stiffer rear springs.

Rhoddy confirmed that I had made the right choice of engine. He reckoned that the 75 V6 with his kit was better than a standard TS, but that putting the kit on the TS handed back the advantage to the four-cylinder model. Later, I added adjustable front Bilstein dampers, which I set towards the softer end of the scale.

With these alterations, the ride and handling of the 75 TS was a match even for the Z-axled E36 3-series mentioned in the previous chapter, and from me, that's high praise.

The gearbox was undoubtedly the 75's weakest link and the pun is unfortunately apt. Alfa struggled for years trying to sort out the gearchange of its transaxle road cars, starting with the Alfetta and GTV in 1972, of which the 75 was the last. In fact, the company's transaxle experience went back even further, to the classic 158 Grand Prix car.

A transaxle delivers the weight distribution benefit already mentioned, but it has two disadvantages. First, without the assistance of engine heat, the gearbox oil takes much longer to reach optimum operating temperature; on cold mornings, my car was reluctant to engage gears, especially second for some reason, so I would usually go from first to third for the first few miles.

The other problem is that the gear lever is remote from the gearbox. Alfa Romeo, unlike Porsche with the 924/944/968 and the 928, never sorted the system perfectly on its road cars. It tried two different methods, which it called 'isostatic' and 'isolastic.'

Explaining the difference, an Alfa engineer made an analogy: think of a running man, he said. In the first case, he is wearing jockey briefs, and in the second he is not; this works slightly better if spoken with an Italian accent. The isostatic version's linkage was held firmly in place by several rubber-bushed mountings, while the isolastic solution did not. The analogy sounded like absolute bollocks to me, and alas, neither system worked very well, though I rather liked the gearchange, once the oil warmed up. It was precise, but it felt delicate … and it was.

Due to an inherent design flaw, the 75's gearbox rarely lasted more than about 50,000 miles without needing a major rebuild. When I sold my car, it had covered nearly that distance and it was beginning to whine, a sure sign that it was on its way out. This demolished my optimistic theory that my practice of always double de-clutching for downward changes would make it last forever.

That was not the reason I sold it, and I regret that I did so. If I had kept it, I would have bought half a dozen gearboxes and kept them in storage. Despite all its numerous faults, I consider this to have been the best car I have ever owned, or even run at someone else's expense. Yes, really[1].

[1] Even though, logically, my Honda Civic is a far better car.

91 Retromania

THE CRAZE FOR AUTOMOTIVE retro began long ago, possibly when Britain's Vintage and Sports Car Club was created and its founders arbitrarily decreed that everything manufactured before 1918 was somewhat passé and everything after 1930 a bit, well, *common*. I exaggerate, but not much.

The originator, if that is not a contradiction in terms, of the modern retro trend among mainstream manufacturers is wrongly considered by many to have been Volkswagen with the New Beetle.

This came about by accident. Realizing that it had nothing new to display at the 1994 North American International Auto Show in Detroit, yet desirous to get some publicity, Volkswagen sanctioned the construction of a show car, called Concept One, which looked like a modern VW Beetle, but otherwise had nothing whatever to do with Mr Hitler's obnoxious little car for the people.

The objective of gaining publicity was a resounding success. However, VW then found itself under pressure to put the damn thing into production. This was a major problem, because, during the planning stage, that had not been a consideration.

Broadly speaking, there are three types of concept car. First, there are those which closely illustrate what the fully-developed production model will look like next year. This is little more than an inexpensive form of advertising.

Second, there are those that incorporate design and engineering elements that are likely to appear in future production models, though the manufacturers always make clear that there is no possibility of anything exactly like the show concept ending up in showrooms. These are nearly always the most interesting, to me anyway.

Finally, there are the concepts that say, "Hey, look what our brilliant designers can do! We are not going to build this or anything like it, but, now you are here, why not buy one our jolly good cars with almost unbelievable emissions figures?" Concept One was emphatically in this final category, which is more usually the province of French car makers.

Mechanically, the show car was a lash-up on a Polo platform, and there were numerous details of its design that, for various reasons, mostly connected with compliance to regulations, were entirely unsuitable.

Thus Volkswagen became the first major car manufacturer to be ensnared into creating a volume-production retro car. A huge amount of design and engineering work was required for that to be possible. Inevitably, the end result was less aesthetically admirable than the show car.

The New Beetle was an instant success, so, of course, everyone else started banging out retro stuff, BMW with the new Mini in 2001 and Fiat 500 2007. The Americans jumped on the bandwagon with the Plymouth Prowler, the Chrysler PT Kerbcrawler, the Ford Shelby GT500 and the Ford GT. Mercedes-Benz joined in with the SLS AMG. The whole lot are utterly pointless to my eyes, except that they have made money for their makers, and that of course is the point.

The kind of retro that I admire most is more conceptual than visual. For example, if BMW had avoided pastiche and instead developed the Mini Spiritual concepts that were created by Rover's engineers and designers, I would have been impressed. They were strikingly innovative, just like the original Mini 40 years earlier, and completely unlike the BMW Mini. But the Munich design studio wanted the job and got it.

If the Beetle was not the first of these retro machines, which manufacturer started the trend? It was Nissan, with its 'pike cars.' They were certainly the weirdest, and they differed from most of those previously mentioned (the Chrysler and the Plymouth excepted) in not being visually based on anything specific. Why 'pike'? I have no idea. Perhaps because 'halibut' is difficult for the Japanese to pronounce. I cannot tell you, either, why one of the pike cars was called Figaro. I doubt that it was a clever Nippon joke about hairdressers' cars.

There were four pike cars, the first and most subtle of which was the Be-1, first shown at the 1985 Tokyo Motor Show. Designed as a fashionable urban runabout, it had a vaguely retro look without any specific clues to its inspiration.

Next came the Figaro and Pao, both shown at the 1987 Tokyo Motor Show. The Pao was vaguely reminiscent of the Renault 4L, with shades of Fiat. More than 51,000 were made in two years of production. I shall return to the Figaro ...

At the following year's show, Nissan displayed the S-Cargo, clearly derived from the Citroën 2CV Fourgonnette (light van). This is the rarest of pikes (8000 sold).

The pike cars sprang from the vivid imagination of freelance 'conceptor' Naoki Sakai[1], who personally eschewed anything as banal as drawing designs. Instead, he communicated his ideas about "feelings and desires" to his designers – all women or male homosexuals – at his Water Studio in Tokyo. Nissan and later Toyota hired him because his speciality was creating products that enhanced corporate identity.

Some of his pronouncements on Design, The meaning of Life and – his specialist subject – his own exalted genius could have been created specifically for *Private Eye*'s Pseuds Corner. However, these little cars were all highly successful.

Demand for the Figaro was so high that buyers were selected, as for the Be-1, by lottery. There were nearly 400,000 applications for the 20,000 Figaros. As with the Be-1, it is difficult to pin down the cars of the past that went into the mix that became the Figaro, but the latter gives far more than a figurative nod to the past.

Although the pike cars were specifically marketed for sale solely in Japan, a few of them were bought by specialist importers, which is how I found myself behind the wheel of a Figaro in 1992.

Considering its styling, I noted that it had hints of early Pininfarina from the era when that was two words, in particular of the Peugeot 403. There were also suggestions of Austin, and even of the ghastly Nash Metropolitan. It was a clever pastiche, with some neat detailing.

I found that it did nothing particularly well and nothing noticeably badly, except that it was badly let down by a definitively unpleasant three-speed automatic gearbox (the five-speed manual was far more popular among Japanese buyers, which does not surprise me). It was sluggish and dull to drive, but the people at whom such vehicles are aimed would probably not be aware of that. It's a 'Look at me' car.

In many practical respects, when one checked it out thoroughly, the Figaro was not at all like the product of a major manufacturer such as Nissan, any more than it was like a car from the 1950s. Sometimes the expression, 'You win some, you lose some' seems to miss the target. The Figaro's luggage space was negligible, under the bonnet was a tangled spaghetti mess of wires, and so on.

As for the interior finish, the seats were covered in a sort of *cowish* material from that hinterland where you wonder if it is an extraordinarily clever type of plastic imitating leather, or what Anthony Hussey of Connolly Leather[2] used to describe as "leather-backed paint." I wondered if it might have been dolphin hide.

Objectively, from a practical point of view, the New Beetle is rubbish in every respect compared with a Golf. The Figaro is the 1950s in a blivet, whereas the Micra on which it

228

was based was an honest, if not very imaginative attempt to be a car of its time. Well, car purchase is not always rational. Some people love these Retro cars, but they are not for me, and that's fine as far as I am concerned.

It depresses me when car manufacturers slide into that negative trend. "But," you may point out, "You have a Morgan 4/4." Indeed I do. It is not a Retro car. It is a Retro experience, which is not at all the same thing. And my other car is a Honda Civic.

[1] The designs of the Pao and Figaro are mainly attributed by some people to Shoji Takahashi. Discussions and arguments, which are of no interest whatever to me, rumble on about who did what.
[2] His favourite family joke was "My mother was a Connolly and my father was a Hussey, which is probably better than the other way round."

92 Why I hate concours d'élégance

FOR ME, SOME APPARENTLY simple questions beginning with "Do you like …?" do not have simple, succinct answers. This is so in relation to dogs and children, and likewise concerning old cars. I find that it is impossible to generalize.

As touched upon elsewhere in this rambling tome, I have driven some old (and also new) cars that I have enjoyed enormously, some that have disappointed me, and others that I have simply detested.

If I had stacks of money, I would have a large garage, but I would try to restrict its contents to a total of five cars, none of which would be brand-new. I would probably keep my 2011 Honda Civic, because it is a very practical everyday machine and I would definitely keep my Morgan 4/4, for reasons that I explain elsewhere.

The other three cars would be: an early drophead 4.2-litre E-type Jaguar; a large, elegant saloon from the 1980s or 1990s, perhaps a Jaguar XJ12 MkIII or a BMW 7-series (E38); and a sports car from the 1920s or 1930s, probably an Alfa Romeo, a Bugatti, or an Amilcar.

I would also have a chauffeur/mechanic, whose wife would be an excellent cook … But I ramble. Back to questions. Here is one to which I can give a very short and definitive answer: "Do you like concours d'élégance?" The answer is NO.

I like the Goodwood Revival and Members' Meeting, and the Silverstone Classic, and other such events, though I always worry when watching them that valuable, and in some cases unique, classic racing cars may be severely damaged. But they were built to be raced rather than stuck away in a museum and therefore they should be raced, with all the risks that that entails.

A concours d'élégance is quite a different matter. These are events where a lot of highly-polished, pretty and pretty expensive cars are gathered together at some attractive location with champagne and canapés, and so forth, served to those attending, who for the most part are highly-polished, pretty and pretty expensive.

It was perhaps because of my antipathy to this kind of thing that *The Daily Telegraph* commissioned me to report on the ninth Louis Vuitton Classic in 1996. This is the Henley or Ascot of static classic car meetings, and, as at those other events, many of the people attending are there to been seen rather than to see. There was a sprinkling of minor royalty and numerous thespians. I resisted an unwise impulse when I crossed the path of Gerard Depardieu to ask, "Who do you think you are staring at, Big Nose?"

I wandered among the crowds milling about a selection of extraordinary motor cars arrayed in the late summer sunshine in the grounds of La Bagatelle. This exquisite little house was built in 1777 for the Comte d'Artois, later Charles X, the last Bourbon king of France, during the period in which he arranged for the French State to pick up the tab for his world-class extravagance.

But back to the cars. Among those gathered, I spotted several candidates for my fantasy garage, most of them Alfa Romeos.

The classic car fraternity resembles the antiques trade with its mix of plausible rogues, charlatans, insufferable snobs, fanatical enthusiasts and exceptional craftsmen. Unless you are a true connoisseur of classic cars, which I am not, you can easily be misled.

For example, one of the Alfas that caught my eye was, apparently, entirely unrestored, though in what is described by vendors as 'excellent running condition.' However, a knowledgeable classic car journalist told me that its attractive 'patina' had been diligently applied by a chap who specializes in such work. Conversely, some other 60-year-old cars with Lexus-like shut lines looked as if they had been built recently, which may have been the case. Again, this is reminiscent of the antiques trade, with its constant tension between 'originality' and restoration. Not to mention clever fakes with paperwork that seems to confirm provenance.

Most of the cars had been delivered by trailer, but at least the Louis Vuitton organizers eschew the Pebble Beach Tendency. Pebble Beach, in Monterey, California, hosts the biggest annual international classic car show, where the prissiest of anal-retentive owners drain all the fluids from their classic cars to avoid leaks that might prejudice the equally anal-retentive judges. An American classic car owner once observed of his fellow exhibitors: "Most of these guys wanted to marry a virgin. The way they treat their cars is a kind of compensation."

Robert Cumberford, one of the Louis Vuitton judges, a car designer and journalist, told me that the first requirement was that the cars must be in running order. "Otherwise they won't be able to drive around to the front of the house for the awards ceremony. If it doesn't start straight away, we wander off and look at other cars, then come back."

Along with Cumberford, the other judges at La Bagatelle formed an interesting bunch. There was Luigi Colani, a famously eccentric German designer of Kurdish descent, creator of one-off cars and Canon cameras. He once produced a prototype lorry cab among whose many extraordinary features was an ejector seat for the driver. To date, no truck manufacturer has adopted this innovation.

Leading designers of a more conventional bent included Walter da Silva, then at Alfa Romeo, and who later held senior posts at SEAT, Audi and then Volkswagen; Uwe Bahnsen, who had been head of design for Ford of Europe; Patrick le Quément, at that time Renault's design chief (he did not have to travel far from Renault's design offices at Boulogne-Billancourt); Fabrizio Giugiaro (son of Giorgetto). Other judges included my friend Anthony Hussey of Connolly Leather[1], Alain de Cadenet[2] and Paul Frère[3].

One car whose owner comprehensively eschewed the Pebble Beach Tendency was a 1934 Mercedes-Benz 500K Roadster. It had been driven to La Bagatelle from England. I was pleased that it won the Prix Connolly, its well-worn leather seats reflecting the view of Anthony Hussey that leather should look as if it came from an animal rather than an industrial process.

Well, it was an excellent lunch and a pleasant day out, but it did nothing to alter my opinions concerning concours d'élégance.

[1] See previous chapter.
[2] Alain de Cadenet, television presenter and racing driver mainly of classic cars, most notably his splendid Alfa Romeo P3. He also competed, as driver and entrant, in endurance racing, finishing third at Le Mans in 1976 with his top-class team mate Chris Craft.
[3] Paul Frère (1917-2008), Belgian racing driver, journalist and author. He took part in 11 Grands Prix, finishing second at Spa-Francorchamps in 1956 in a Lancia-Ferrari D50. His most notable racing success was victory in the 1960 Le Mans 24 Hours, sharing a Ferrari 250 Testa Rossa with fellow-countryman Olivier Gendebien.

93 Stop the world ...

I HAVE MET SEVERAL brilliant people over the years, some of whom have been mentioned in these pages. They have all seemed to me at least slightly mad[1]. Mind you, it is sometimes hard to judge. If the theory of phlogiston had turned out to be true, Johann Joakim Becher and Georg Ernst Stahl might be considered on the same level as Isaac Newton rather than as a pair of half-baked fruitcakes.

One very clever man of my acquaintance is Rod Paris, a research chemist who had made a fortune in his second career, creating a business that developed and supplied plastics and composite materials to the motor industry. He had a very low boredom threshold and was actively trying to sell the company even though it seemed to me to be almost a licence to print money. I thought at the time that he might have become exasperated by 'plaster of Paris' jokes.

He reasoned that he had done the interesting bit, which was to set up the business and to prove convincingly that it was a viable idea. Also, it was quite obvious that he had already made a lot of money from it and would make far more by selling it and passing on the risk and hassle of running it to someone else. Then he could move on to new adventures, which he did. I used to play chess with him in his office during working hours.

He bought a Morgan Plus 8, but was soon bored with it, which surprised me. I could understand a Morgan owner being exasperated, but *bored* seemed unlikely. I thought that the Plus 8 in standard form already had rather more power than its chassis could happily cope with, but Rod had other ideas. He proved conclusively that substantial increases in power and torque would shred various components in the transmission.

He had the Rover engine turbocharged. In those days, before Saab and Porsche built a bandwagon for all the rest to jump onto, this was unusual. That mad Mog was stupendously quick, but it was also absolutely terrifying. Press the throttle and, after a brief period of turbo lag, the rear tyres would light up. This caused problems when accelerating out of bends. In fact, never mind the bends – steering correction was frequently required when attempting to drive in a straight line. Although the Morgan Plus 8 was not an especially wide car, the public highway often appeared to be rather too narrow to accommodate this one.

At the time that I drove it, Rod's Plus 8 consumed fuel at the rate of 4mpg, though that could perhaps be improved to 6 or even 7 by more prudent application of the throttle. When we discussed all this, he replied with memorable understatement, "I don't think we've quite got it sorted yet." He did get it to work a bit more efficiently, and he competed in the car in a few drag races "as punishment for bad behaviour."

This bad behaviour had included serious problems with the driveline. Several clutches were consumed, and when that was beefed up, the problems moved downstream. The gearbox turned out to be the next weak link. That was solved by replacing the standard unit with a bombproof ZF five-speed (from an Aston Martin DB5). The next victim was the limited-slip differential, which failed when I was in the passenger seat as Rod was driving up Richmond Hill.

The car proved two things. First, that the Rover-Buick V8 was exceptionally tough, and second, that if you planned to increase its power and torque significantly in a Morgan you had to re-engineer everything between it and the rear wheels.

When Rod and his family and the Plus 8 emigrated to Papua, New Guinea for a few years, he wisely removed the turbocharger. In the end, he sold the car, with over 100,000 miles on the odometer, for three times the price he had paid for it new from the factory.

After driving this car, it took me many years to shake off my antipathy towards Morgans, and, when I bought a 'trad,' I chose the 4/4 not only for cost reasons, which I explain in detail in Chapter 95.

Seeking something to do with his time and with some of the stacks of money that kept pouring in, Rod became involved in motor racing as a sponsor. He even bought a disused garage in Chiswick with a rolling road. With barely any discernible effort on his part, he turned this into a profitable enterprise that was widely used by racing teams.

One day when, playing the black pieces, I unexpectedly beat him at chess, he made an enigmatic remark: "You must come and see my world-stopping machine."

We drove the couple of miles to his garage, where, in a basement room, lurked a weird-looking device. A vertical shaft from a small diesel-powered generator rotated a horizontal, nine-foot steel pole, at one end of which there was a small battery driven propeller, at the other a balance weight.

The theory, as I recall, was that when the tips of the pole attained 900mph, you could switch on the little propeller, switch off the diesel generator and then gyroscopic effects would make the pole continue to spin without a reduction in speed until the little battery ran out. By then, sufficient energy would have been generated not only to recharge the battery but to provide all the energy needs of an average house.

Here was a highly intelligent and apparently sane man implying that he had discovered a means of creating perpetual motion. Had I been wearing boots with straps, I might have stuck my index fingers through them and attempted to lift myself off the floor.

"I've sent the papers to London University and they can't fault the theory," he said. "But I can't get it to work yet. The differential speed between the pole and the propeller seems to be crucial."

He mentioned two further potential problems that had not yet been addressed. The lesser of these, when the pole was rotating at maximum speed, was that a mechanical breakage might wreck the entire building.

"There goes the neighbourhood," I remarked.

When the ends of the arm exceeded the sound barrier, he was obliged to abandon his experiments because of some pettifogging municipal legal restraints. Also, at about the same time, he found out about the law of conservation of angular momentum. I read about this at some length, after which it was necessary to lie down in a darkened room for half an hour.

Several decades later, Rod remarks, "Even though it couldn't work, none of the physicists who poured scorn on it could give a reason *why* it wouldn't, apart from contravening the said law[2]."

The greater potential problem, supposing it were possible by some means to slip past the law of conservation of angular momentum and put such a device on the market, was a side-effect rather than a potential local accident … and it was literally global in its significance. Rod calculated that, if every household in the world had one of these, the rotation of the Earth would slow down by something like one millionth of a second per year.

Mulling this over in the 1970s, without the expertise to arrive at a meaningful conclusion, I wondered if he had gone barking mad. On the other hand, I thought exactly the same about a chap I had lunch with around the same time, who told me with feverish enthusiasm that he was going to break the World Land Speed Record with a jet-engined vehicle that would exceed 600mph. He showed me some photographs of his test vehicle, a low-loader Bedford lorry with a jet engine bolted onto it. That man was Richard Noble.

[1] On the other hand, not all the mad people I have met have been brilliant.
[2] By this, he means the law of angular momentum rather than bylaws in Chiswick which prohibit the tips of nine-foot long poles from breaking the sound barrier.

94 Back to basics

THE FIRST CAR I owned[1] was an Austin Seven, essentially similar to the first car I drove[2], but built in 1932 rather than 1934. It provided just about the most basic motoring imaginable, or at least I thought so until I bought a new Morgan 3 Wheeler in 2013[3].

One reason for this rash purchase was that I have lived for some years a short distance from some of the greatest driving roads in the world, and it seemed a wasted opportunity that I used them so rarely, mostly when sampling new cars for *The Daily Telegraph* on launches based in the Var, the Alpes-Martimes, or the Bouches du Rhône.

The Austin had all sorts of things that my 3 Wheeler (which, although a featherweight compared with most motor vehicles, seemed, at around 550kg/1200lb, a bit of a heffalump in comparison) did not have: a windscreen (with a wiper), two doors, windows all-round, weather protection, and, of course, four wheels (five, including the spare).

The Seven, like the M3W, did not have a factory-fitted heater, but an ingenious previous owner, using old vacuum cleaner components and baling wire, had rigged up a system that drew warm air from the radiator to the cabin. It was reasonably effective; the 'on/off switch' was a cork. This was not possible with the Morgan, since there is no radiator. However, as I always wore a helmet and dressed up in cold weather rather like a polar explorer, I never felt seriously chilled.

On the other hand, unlike the Morgan, the Austin had no seat belts, and neither a fuel gauge nor a fuel pump: the tank was ahead of the bulkhead and petrol arrived at the carburettor thanks to gravity. One had to regularly check the fuel level with a dipstick. Actually, I rather wished the M3W had this crude but accurate measuring system rather than its hopeless gauge that reported that the tank was empty when it was still a quarter full.

I am not sure what the top speed of the Austin was. It is the only car that has ever caused me to back off the throttle through sheer terror on a clear, straight, dry road. I had got up to about 45mph, I suppose, but it felt like far more than that. In fact, it felt as if one were venturing beyond the parameters ever considered by the Austin Motor Company's engineering team. I kept below forty after that. In retrospect, I think that a thorough suspension overhaul would have cured the problem, more or less.

After an engine rebuild masterminded by my more mechanically skilled brother, the Seven was astonishingly reliable throughout a harsh winter. With its skinny tyres (on 3.5in wide, or one might say narrow, rims[4]) it could get up slippery hills that defeated more modern cars (and which would leave the M3W helplessly spinning its wider rear wheel).

In fact, on packed snow, the Seven really came into its own, and could be cornered in hilarious, low-speed four-wheel drifts, whereas on a dry surface the tyres gripped too much and the body moved sideways instead, making alarming creaking noises.

If I had had one of those annoying stickers on the back of the 3 Wheeler, it might have read 'MY OTHER CAR IS A HONDA CIVIC.' It did not have such a sticker, nor that other one about being slow, paid for and ahead of you, favoured by smug occupiers of the lowest shelf of the middle class, if such a class still exists, driving the sort of car that people win on television game shows. In fact, there were no stickers on it at all except one proclaiming 'HOT' on the top of the engine, warning idiots to keep their hands off.

I removed that, but occasionally had to shout at idiots just after I had parked. It did, indeed, get HOT.

At the time of writing, I still have the Civic. It has all the equipment I need, at the very least, as I do not wish to fly in it or for it to be amphibious. It has all sorts of rather clever things, apart from the number of wheels and seats, that the M3W lacked: anti-lock brakes, electronic 'stability control,' heating, air conditioning, beep-beep reversing sensors, central locking (an utterly useless idea if you have no doors), electrically-operated windows (ditto with no windows), a radio/CD player (about which, younger readers may already be asking, "Dad, what was a CD player, for fuck's sake?").

The first thing that a lot of people asked when looking at my 3 Wheeler was often, "Isn't it unstable?" It is a good question with a rather complex answer. The Morgan tends to slide its front wheels when pushed hard on a dry surface and then needs to be neutralized by a slight lift of the throttle. On slippery roads, you can get a bit of power oversteer, but it is wise not to play around with that too much. The big danger is if, like Tiff Needell on the telly, who went from tarmac to grass and back to tarmac, you suddenly then have more grip than is desirable and the machine can, indeed, roll. Luckily for Tiff, who was not wearing a helmet, that did not quite happen.

However, with two steered wheels at the front and one driven rear wheel, the M3W is far more stable than the Bond Bug, for example ...

Mike Kimberley had been working at Lotus for a few months. He and his wife were renting an old vicarage in Ketteringham. He used to drive home from Hethel for lunch. One day a Bond Bug, the first off the line, arrived on a low loader.

Kimberley chose it for his lunchtime drive, but rolled after a few bends and had a huge accident, cart-wheeling and barrel-rolling. He came to inside a steaming wreck, soaked in petrol and with some broken bones. He was taken off to hospital.

Half an hour later, Colin Chapman arrived on the scene. Traffic was by now being directed by Lotus' head of security. Chapman asked who had crashed the Bug and was told, "Kimberley, the new man from Jaguar." Without hesitation, Chapman said, "Right, he's fired."

But then Lotus' sales and marketing director got hold of another Bond Bug and insisted that Chapman should drive it. He hacked around his private drive – and soon put it on its side. Kimberley was immediately unfired, and he has carefully avoided vehicles with a single front wheel ever since.

Let's return to the more sensible side of my garage. My Honda can also, thanks to its so-called 'magic' rear seats (a very clever piece of design and engineering) carry a large dog in greater comfort, especially with regard to entry and exit, than is possible in far bigger vehicles.

One can evidently raise the Honda's specification to an even higher level, as there was a blank switch on the fascia of mine. I have not the faintest idea what that might be for, but I found it intellectually and aesthetically displeasing, so I carefully copied the size and typeface used for the other switches and it now proclaims itself as the 'EJECT' button.

It does not actually function like the ejector seat in the Aston Martin DB5 of James Bond, as portrayed by that annoying Scotchman, alas, but perhaps it keeps passengers on their best behaviour, or at any rate silent, which often amounts to the same thing as far as I am concerned.

In France, they actually market cars as 'Suréquipée' (literally, over-equipped). This is 'Non-stop nonsense'[5] on wheels. But the French spend an increasing amount of their time abusing their own language without apparently realizing it.

236

1 No, I did not buy it new.
2 See Chapter 62.
3 For full details of this, read my M3W book.
4 Exactly the same size as the modern Morgan 3 Wheeler's front wheels.
5 See Chapter 50.

95 From 3 to 4/4

BUYING THE MORGAN 3 Wheeler leaped straight into my list of *The Ten Most Irresponsible Things I Have Ever Done*; I forget which act of foolhardiness it displaced. The M3W had gone on sale in 2012 and I was fascinated by the concept. Some people have suggested that I bought mine as a penitential gesture of solidarity with other M3W buyers, because I had played a small role in its creation. However, I think that subconsciously I wished to disprove the popular description of Hondas, 'last purchase before the check-out desk.'

The background to all this is explained in my book[1].

I liked the idea of light weight combined with a powerful engine, though it turned out that the production vehicle was both considerably heavier and less powerful than Charles Morgan had predicted that it would be when launching the car at the 2011 Geneva Motor Show[2]. The fanciful claim that it could do 0-60mph in 4.5 seconds was repeated parrot-fashion in numerous publications. Nevertheless, it was still a hoot to drive, and my mild disappointment with the acceleration was not the reason why I sold it. It still felt pretty quick, quick enough to start being demanding to drive, even a bit scary, at relatively modest speeds. But that was not why I sold it, either.

My 3 Wheeler was off the road for two of the 18 months that I owned it, after the bolt that holds the crankshaft pulley in place had leapt forward and punched through the timing case, ripping the sturdy timing belt to shreds. Since the S & S vee-twin is of the 'non-interference' type (ie in such circumstances, the valves and pistons do not come into contact), no internal damage was done.

Nevertheless, it was inconvenient, to put it mildly. However, this gave me time to re-read a chapter of my book, entitled "Are you a Morgan 3 Wheeler type?" In this, I asked several pertinent questions. The first of these was: "Am I a bit mad?" I suggested that anyone answering "No. I am not mad," was evidently completely barking and therefore might be a potential Morgan 3 Wheeler owner.

Having confidently answered "No" to Question 1, I moved on. The other suggested qualifications for ownership were more problematical. I had recommended that a buyer should be a skilled mechanic and ideally should live within an hour of the nearest Morgan dealer. I failed on both counts. I can fiddle around with cars a bit, but not much, and my nearest Morgan dealer is five hours' drive away, though there is a sub-agent within an hour and a half from home.

The warranty was due to run out and I decided to sell. An Italian banker took the car away on a trailer and the next day I placed an order for a 4/4. This has become quite a trend: for most 3 Wheeler buyers, it is their first Morgan. Many then exchange it for a 4/4 or Plus 4.

The 4/4 was introduced in 1936. If you place an early model alongside the latest you can see certain similarities but also considerable differences. They have the same wheelbase and both have a simple steel ladder chassis, which has evolved somewhat over the years. The older car is noticeably higher. Above the chassis is a frame made of ash, to which the body panels are attached. A lot of people without any engineering knowledge believe that Morgans actually have wooden chassis.

Until the turn of the century (20th to 21st), the panels, rolled not pressed, as Mr Bond might say, were made of steel, with aluminium as an extra-cost option, but since then the lighter metal has been standard on all 4/4s and Plus 4s; the latter is essentially the same car, but with a more powerful engine, and wider wings to accommodate large wheels and tyres. I might start detailing all Morgan's other models here, but I shall refrain from doing so.

The specification of my car was clear in my mind for several months before I placed the order. I wanted it to be as close to basic as possible, since even the base price is sufficiently high, but I had a few essential extras in mind. Foremost of these were three suspension mods, two of which were inexpensive: I wanted brake reaction rods, which stop the front axle twisting during heavy braking, and, at the rear, I wanted a Panhard rod, a crude but effective device that prevents lateral movement of the rear axle in relation to the chassis. The more costly item was Suplex/Bilstein front dampers.

There are several alternative suspension options for the 4/4, including a new coil spring system instead of the semi-elliptic leaf springs that have been used at the rear since 1936. I think I have ended up with a very good compromise for road use, though I would probably opt at least for stiffer damping if I wished to use the car for track days[3].

Another reason for buying the 3 Wheeler, and then the 4/4, was that my journalistic career had more or less stopped and I had time on my hands.

[1] Go to http://www.veloce.co.uk for details
[2] Since then, Charles has been ousted from his executive role at the family company, though he remains a major shareholder. Had he followed his great-grandfather and great-great-grandfather into The Church, Charles might have become a loose canon.
[3] But if I wanted a track day car, I would not buy a Morgan 4/4.

96 Career advice

SO YOU WANT TO be a motoring journalist? My advice is: DON'T. Choose a different career. You will have gathered from this book that I had a lot of fun, among all the hassle, during decades of driving and writing about cars. I also managed to make a reasonably good living from it.

Today, however, it is mostly not fun, and only a tiny minority of those involved in this odd profession manage to earn decent money. There are plenty of other jobs where you can get paid proper money for not having much fun. Choose one of them instead, and have fun outside working hours.

In any case, apart from the poor pay and the severely reduced fun quota, motoring journalism is another of those jobs[1] that flourished in the 20th century, but which are now fading away. What will be the point of a specialist motoring writer in a world of autonomous cars? The party's over. It is probable that the world's last-ever motoring journalist has already been born; I shall return to this in my final chapter, with further predictions of a morose nature.

Even worse than all the above is that it is almost certain that print journalism is on its way out. National newspapers are fading fast, and their motoring sections have degenerated, with rare exceptions, into advertorial.

Most of the specialist motoring magazines that remain at the time of writing will disappear within the next decade. A few may stagger on a while longer. I can imagine the excellent *Motor Sport* as the last British survivor. Then what? Demand for information and entertainment will obviously persist, but it is doubtful that the long-term loyalty that people have displayed in the past to their favourite magazines will be transferred to websites. Also, the business model of websites is far from clear: it is very difficult to make a profit from them.

Supposing you rashly ignore my wise advice and go ahead and become a motoring journalist, I wish the very best of luck to you. The only useful suggestion I can offer is that you should select a *nom de plume*, in order to make casual encounters outside working hours less stressful. Your byline could be a subtle variation of your real name.

For example, if you happen to have the good fortune to have been born with an excellent moniker such as Henry Felix Catchpole, you could style yourself for professional purposes as 'Felix Catchpole' when writing articles in EVO magazine and then you would be able to relax as Henry Catchpole in everyday life. Felix Catchpole did this the other way around, styling himself as 'Henry.'

Inevitably, at dinner parties, people would ask, "Henry, are you related to Felix Catchpole, the chap who writes for EVO magazine?" You assume a puzzled expression in response to this wide-mouthed frog question and reply, "No. Never heard of him. Is he any good?" Then you pretend to be a debt collector, or a rat catcher, and change the subject, even though it is suggested that you look very much like Catchpole the famous motoring hack.

The main advantage of this stratagem is that it saves you from the inevitable follow up questions, such as, "I am considering buying a New Beetle. What do you think?" This is one of those "Does my bum look big in this?" inquiries, and it is better to mumble something non-committal and change the subject, because it is usually not a question at all, but a demand for unconditional approval.

It will almost certainly turn out that your questioner is not weighing up whether to place an order for a New Beetle or whatever the car mentioned may be: the deposit has already been paid. If you laugh scornfully and say that the New Beetle is bought by poseurs without the wit to see that the Golf is much better in every respect, including looks, and add that if you buy a Golf nobody will laugh at you derisively, and so on and so forth, you may find yourself in a mildly embarrassing situation for the remainder of the dinner party. I know this from experience.

The same thing occurred to a colleague who was with a group of motoring journalists in Club Class on the way to a launch. This was in 1980, not long after the MIRA incident described in Chapter 44. Someone asked, "What do you think of the Fuego?" One or two hacks expressed mildly critical opinions.

Someone asked my colleague what he thought of it. He replied gruffly, "It's just a hairdresser's car." This was his standard dismissive expression for cars that he did not like, especially those that posed as sporty cars, but which were, in reality, cruisers.

To his surprise, the well-known lady hack who had sought his opinion went into a hissy fit and said, "Well that's put me in my place!" How was he to know that she had recently married a hairdresser and that they had bought themselves a Fuego?

Another question that might be asked is "What is the best car you have ever driven?" The trouble with this one, for me, is that the answer is long and complicated, and I'd prefer to discuss something else over dinner. Ask me something about ships or shoes or sealing wax. Or rats. However, if you have been paying attention, you will recall that I have answered the question in Chapter 89, so please do not ask again.

Sometimes the announcement that one worked as a motoring journalist provoked a sarcastic and/or aggressive reaction, in the form of an insinuation of varying directness, that all motoring journalists are corrupt and in the pockets of the manufacturers. I always found this intensely irritating, but easy to deal with.

"Have you read anything I have written?" I would ask. The answer would always be negative, and then I would make a disdainful remark, and change the subject to my questioner's glittering career, which I would proceed to decorticate, or talk to someone else.

On the topic of alleged corruption, as readers who has been paying attention will have inferred, hospitality for a car hack means that on a car launch you live like a zillionaire for 24 hours or so before dropping back into a more humdrum existence, or at least it did when I was in the business. But that does not per se imply corruption. Yes, one ate very well and the wines were usually excellent. And yes, after dinner, in the days of plenty, one usually spent an hour or so in the bar, where one could choose from a range of Havana cigars to accompany one's 30-year-old Armagnac. And no, I did not ever snaffle half a dozen of Montecristo's finest and stuff them into my jacket pocket.

All the serious hacks enjoyed this convivial atmosphere, but would then write exactly what they thought of the car that was being evaluated – even if that meant hurling a few brickbats. Industry PR men took no offence when a car was fairly criticized – and they would often privately agree with the criticisms. They would not let an error pass without comment, however, and quite rightly so.

Reading this, you may think we were a bunch of piss artists. Well, we did have some laughs, but, in all of this, we would be sitting at dinner or standing at the bar with engineers, designers, managers, PR people, and finding out the background story in a relaxed atmosphere. It was rare that one came away from one of these events without an extra story, as well as the main event, appraisal of the new car.

Now we live in a more puritanical era, and I understand that on car launches, most hacks eat their dinner rapidly, purely for the purpose of topping up energy levels, and then disappear to their rooms to bash words into their portable electronic typing machines. There is a perceived requirement to get the basic info out as fast as possible. Never mind the quality – see the speed. While meeting this requirement, these hacks inevitably miss out on the supplementary story.

A lot of people who have never done the job think that road testing cars is easy. You need only read a few test reports here and there, in the national press, local newspapers and even in some specialized magazines, to become aware that it is not. In many cases, Oscar Wilde's work ethic is followed: "If a job's worth doing well, it's worth doing badly." A lot of those who do the job badly probably think that they do it well. They seem unaware of their shoddy/execrable grammar and erratic spelling; or perhaps they do not care. This is usually combined with tired clichés and florid similes, which these people consider to be 'fine writing,' I suppose.

There is one well-known journalist, who appears to pride himself on not checking his copy. He writes a 'blog' which usually contains at least one literal in every four or five lines; I would write 'in every paragraph' but he has an aversion to paragraphs. At least he usually checks his facts, and the nuggets of the story are to be found within his garbling. Some other hacks often fail even on this basic requirement.

In road test writing, the most jarring and surprising fault of all is the failure to address the most vital questions, even though they are in most instances glaringly obvious and in every instance what every reader seeks to know. At whom is this car aimed? How well does it supply what potential buyers want? How does it compare with rivals? I wonder why all this bothers me so much, especially when the job is on its way out.

I repeat that, if you manage to become a motoring writer, good luck and enjoy it while it lasts, as far as that remains possible, because, as I have suggested, it will not last long. The era of being permitted to control motor vehicles on public highways, which has lasted a little more than a century, is rapidly drawing to a close. The car companies have been working on this for decades, but it was only recently that technological advances have rendered it practically feasible, at least in the minds of those pushing for it. Some of us retain considerable doubts, not only for technical reasons.

---

[1] Such as petrol pump attendant, switchboard operator, shorthand typist, etc.

97 Crossing the finishing line

IF FORMULA 1 TEAMS were set the task of creating a driverless Grand Prix car that otherwise conformed to current regulations, it would take them only a short time to set it up so that it could turn the perfect lap, every lap. Just as with chess, and the complex Chinese game of Go, no human being, no matter how skilled, could match it.

A clever Formula 1 engineer, which is to say someone more clever than 99.9999-recurring per cent of the population, is probably working on this idea already. The 'driver' would just sit there, lightly holding the steering wheel (which might not be connected in any way to the front wheels), in reality only a passenger. Spectators would be none the wiser.

This could be taken a stage further, with a walking, talking robot instead of a human being. After crossing the finishing line he would shout in a squeaky voice, "Wahoo! Thanks, guys! You did a brilliant job!" and then climb awkwardly out of the car and stand on it, violently punching the air or rudely raising an index finger. Nobody observing the post-race interviews would spot the difference.

In fact, something of the sort has already been created. At the time of writing, there are several autonomous racing series under development. However, these big toys are not closely derived from Formula 1 cars, or even from the Formula E electric racers, so no direct comparisons are possible.

What is the point of that? The only plausible explanation that comes to mind, apart from 'Because we can,' is that it is a sinister plot, indirectly funded by governments, designed to hasten the headlong rush towards autonomous vehicles. It certainly cannot be for entertainment value.

It does however, raise the question: what is the point of motor racing? And that is a tricky one. There is no point really, but one could say that about all sporting activities – cricket, football and golf, to name but three. Especially golf. And indeed, the same is true of many human activities, such as writing books.

Formula 1 engineers scan and deconstruct every sentence of the rule book in search of the tiniest loophole that might yield an advantage. Grand Prix racing has always been a battle of technology as well as a contest between drivers, and it has always been essential for those who govern the sport to prevent it from going too far in one direction or another. As Lao Tzu remarked about 2400 years ago, there is no freedom without limits.

For example, when those ludicrous, enormously tall wings appeared in the late 1960s, they were soon banned, but only after structural failures had led to serious accidents. It is a pity that the opportunity was not seized to ban wings altogether; I shall come back to that.

Peter Gethin scored BRM's last-ever Grand Prix win at Monza in 1971, with four other cars within 0.61 seconds of him as he crossed the finish line after 78 minutes of non-stop slipstreaming. His average speed was 150.755mph, which stood as the record Grand Prix race speed until 2003, when Michael Schumacher's winning Ferrari averaged 153.875mph, again at Monza, without the assistance of slipstreaming.

It should be noted that during the four decades between Gethin's and Schumacher's victories, the circuit had been made substantially slower by the installation of three chicanes. Also, Schumacher made two pit stops for fuel and fresh tyres, while Gethin ran non-stop. Despite all that, if they had completed the same number of laps (the 1971 race was over 55, the 2003 race 53), the German would have finished about a minute ahead of the Englishman – and with a much wider gap, if they both drove on the same circuit. Most of the gains were derived from cornering speeds rather than engine performance.

If there had been no restrictions in the regulations and no changes to the circuit, Formula 1 cars might today be hitting 300mph or more on the approach to the Curva Grande, and the average race speed could be over 200mph.

Obviously, regulations are essential, primarily for the safety of spectators, but also for drivers. The difficulty is finding agreement about what those regulations should be. Two major things that have changed since Gethin took the chequered flag in 1971 are aerodynamics and electronics.

Formula 1 was once, and is still supposed to be, the pinnacle of high-tech motor racing engineering. At the same time, it is intended that it should produce exciting and close racing. These two aims are incompatible. There is no doubt that most of the best racing drivers in the world are in F1, but, in recent years, their talents have been wasted, because they spend too much of their time managing complex technical systems, in consultation with huge teams of engineers both at the track and back at the factory, rather than actually racing.

If something like Formula 5000 as it was in the early 1970s were introduced as a replacement, with low-cost grunty V8s, big fat tyres and limited downforce, it would produce really good, close racing, which would be superb for both drivers and spectators, as well as substantially less expensive.

That is not going to happen, but some limits need to be applied if Formula 1 is to survive, such as banning electronic systems that can be monitored from outside the car, and placing strict limits on aerodynamic appendages. These two measures would immediately cut costs, unfortunately making a large number of clever people redundant.

In recent years, those in charge of Formula 1 have fiddled around with the technical regulations, which have become ever more detailed, to the point that even specialists cannot always follow what is going on.

Overtaking has become difficult for two reasons. First, downforce aerodynamics make it difficult to follow another car closely, so there are no more slipstreaming battles such as happened at Monza in the old days. Second, carbon fibre discs have drastically shortened braking distances. Instead of tackling the root causes, the FIA introduced DRS (Drag Reduction System). This opens a flap in the rear wing and gives the following car a dramatic speed boost of up to 15mph on designated straights. This can be used only when a driver is within one second of the car ahead and the driver being followed is not permitted to respond by using his DRS (unless there happens to be another car ahead of him).

In addition, each car is obliged to use more than one grade of tyre during a race, so while it sometimes looks to the untrained eye as if Driver A has pulled off a superb pass on Driver B, it usually means only that Driver A's car is on the more grippy compound and is able to use his DRS. As a result of this, there is quite a lot of passing in modern Grand Prix racing, but not much real overtaking in the traditional sense. I can hear the voice of Herbert Hartge: "Non-stop nonsense!"

Mainly for cost reasons, the German Grand Prix can never return to the full Nürburgring. Nevertheless, Formula 1 cars should be designed so as to be able to do a lap of the Nordschleife without becoming uncontrollably airborne, which has not been possible for many decades.

The first measure to achieve this should be to ban front wings, and restrict the width and design of the bodywork ahead of the front axle line. When the teams object that this would lead to excessive rear downforce, they should be told that the rear wing is optional. When they object that the rear wing is a lucrative advertising site, they should be told that they can keep the wing, but make it neutral, like the silly optional rear wing on the Lamborghini Countach. Standard-issue steel brake discs should be compulsory.

Other problems are the entire business plan and the ineffective administration. It is bizarre that the teams and the major circuits have ignored their potential power. The failure to act jointly in their own interests has been ruthlessly exploited over many years.

Suppose they had all – teams and circuits – got together, summoned Messrs Ecclestone and Todt (for what he is worth) to a meeting and said, "We have a ten-point agenda. Point Number 1 is: FUCK YOU! Now, gentlemen, do you have anything to say in response to that before leaving the room?"

Ecclestone is now out of the frame, and the new regime seems to be addressing the major problems of Formula 1, without any obviously devious agendas. There are at least some mildly encouraging signs.

But how will motor racing fit into a world in which nobody drives any more? Probably not at all. Already, it seems like a 20th century activity that has outlived its purpose, if it ever had one. It's such an anti-social, unpleasantly masculine activity, is it not? An occupation pursued by narcissists with a death wish. Well, that is probably the view of a lot of young people in the new age of no-platforming Puritanism. It was fun while it lasted. So was driving on the road.

98 The trouble with Uncle Harry

ONE OF MY EARLIEST foreign press trips for *Motor* magazine in the late 1970s was a Peugeot[1] launch, during which we visited the Belchamp test track at Sochaux. We were taken to the perimeter fence and instructed to watch carefully.

Half a dozen Peugeots approached in convoy. Each braked and changed down two gears for a hairpin bend, then accelerated away; one could hear that they had automatic transmission. The only odd thing was that the cars were driverless. This was in the late 1970s, and the test cars, full of bulky 'state-of-the-art' computerized control systems, weighed perhaps twice as much as showroom equivalents. Even so, I remember thinking, "Oh shit! *That's* the future."

Peugeot was, for once, ahead of the game. Happily, though, there existed at that time a group of engineers committed to making the company's cars fun to drive. They achieved that objective admirably for several years, especially with the 205, but nothing is forever, and those in charge of the company decided that such things were of minor importance.

Also, at the time, there was not space in the cars for all the control systems as well as people and luggage. But it was obvious that miniaturization and technical progress would eventually solve that, as it has done far more rapidly than anyone in the late 1970s imagined possible.

And now, almost every car maker is working frantically on driverless car systems. Why? Because governments are forcing them towards this, and they have calculated that they must comply or collapse. Don't ask me why governments are forcing this agenda[2].

In the 1980s, an Oriental student at the Royal College of Art's renowned Vehicle Design Course proposed a sort of driverless living room on wheels[3]. In the 1990s General Motors, via its Hughes Aerospace division[4], came up with an idea called 'platooning' in which groups of driverless vehicles, full no doubt of passengers indulging in all sorts of activities not involving concentration on the road ahead, would be transported from A to B.

An element of this concept that attracted my attention was that its authors considered it perfectly safe for a convoy of cars without any human influence to travel at 100mph or more, whereas the law in most countries has ruled that it is dangerous for any car with a human being at the wheel to exceed 70 or 80mph[5] on an empty motorway in perfect weather conditions. But I digress …

I had an interesting conversation with that RCA student. "What," I asked, "if a pedestrian or a dog crossed the road in front of it?"

"Oh, they would be killed," he replied casually, though he indignantly denied this remark after I had reported it, claiming that I had misrepresented him. Well, whatever, as they say. I must admit that, although he was an annoying twat, he had the clearer vision of the future.

In the transitional stage towards this Brave New World in which motorists will progressively be rendered extinct, and everyone will live in a state of Government-imposed diminished responsibility, the vital question is this: What about Uncle Harry? And his dog, of course.

Late at night, after enjoying well-lubricated dinners, the inhabitants of this future world whiz around weird futuristic cities in millions of these passenger cells, some of which are privately-owned or leased, and others, it is suggested, driverless taxis ordered via mobile phones, though I have serious doubts about that concept, as I shall explain in the next chapter.

But there is another problem while autonomous and non-autonomous vehicles share public highways ... Uncle Harry is a piss artist. He wears a trilby, but that is possibly irrelevant. In scenario A, he has had nine cans of Special Brew and an unspecified number of whisky chasers. He steps off the pavement without looking. So does his dog, who is equally irresponsible, without the excuse of the Special Brew and the chasers. Harry and his dog are fresh road kill.

In scenario B, Harry is stone-cold sober. He is smoking his pipe, though that is illegal even outside a motor car, chugging along in his dilapidated Volvo, using his normal method of blending into motorway traffic from the slip road: approach broken white line at unnecessarily reduced speed, virtually stop, glance over right shoulder to check that the way is clear, pull out regardless. A platoon of 20 vehicles, inches apart, is approaching at 120mph, which the authorities have decided is perfectly safe, provided there is no on-board driver.

The laws of physics override the sophisticated electronic systems which do not have sufficient time to react, the platoon ploughs into the Volvo and, once again, Harry is cold meat[6]. Happily, he left his dog at home on this occasion, but who will feed it this evening (or tomorrow)?

The motorway in Scenario B is now blocked by debris, with pieces of Uncle Harry and his Volvo here and there. Several other deaths occur, because one of the 20 vehicles was a 40-tonne truck. Journalists arrive on the scene in their pilotless passenger cells at the same time as police cars, ambulances and fire engines, the public-service vehicles still with real drivers who are licensed to assume control of their vehicles when necessary, being considered the only people capable of doing that without unacceptable risk.

Of course, the above scenario will not happen exactly like that, and it is improbable that there will be such large-scale pile-ups during the long transitional period before full autonomy is imposed, except in fog, because the platooning concept will not yet have been introduced. Nevertheless, that transitional period will be extremely dangerous.

Looking on the bright side, even when things go pear-shaped, turn turtle and fall off their perches, it's nearly always good news for someone; in this case, as ever, it's good news for the legal profession. Taxi drivers would say, "There you are, I told you so, squire!" However, there are no more taxi drivers in our Brave New World, so they won't be saying that, or anything.

Determining liability and insurance consequences in the case of an accident involving several vehicles, some under autonomous control, and others not, will provide great financial gains for our 'learned friends.'

The world-renowned manufacturer of high-quality pepper mills.
If you do, I shall get very cross.
My living room is not on wheels but it shares with this concept vehicle the absence of a steering wheel.
Founded by Howard Hughes (1905-1976), the megalomaniac/tycoon/aviator/engineer/film producer/aerial starlet shagger/bearded weirdo recluse/etc.
Or some other arbitrary figure thought up by a bicycling or chauffeur-driven bureaucrat.
So not markedly different from the average commuter.

99 Last hominid at the wheel

YOU MAY THINK THAT my predictions in the last few chapters are exaggeratedly pessimistic and that I am joking. I do not think so and I am not ...

Why, you may be asking, did I suggest that the world's last motoring hack has already left the womb? My answer is simply that the job will no longer exist, because cars as we know them will no longer exist. How can you test drive something that you are not driving?

While I am in predictive mode, in my opinion it is probable that the last civilians who will be permitted to drive motor vehicles on public roads in Europe or the USA have already been born, and other countries will follow the trend within a relatively brief period. In the first few decades of the 22nd century, the dwindling survivors of this heroic group will be sought after by interviewers to recall how strange and difficult and frightfully dangerous that must have been – actually being in full control of a moving motor vehicle on a public highway.

Perhaps that sounds fanciful, not to mention stupid, but I am fairly convinced that it is going to happen. In the late 1990s, I was convinced that European governments would see sense at the last moment and back down from introducing the euro. I was also certain that Bush Junior and Blair were calling Saddam Hussein's bluff and that they would not actually be sufficiently stupid to send troops into Iraq. And so on. Well, what do I know? So I am pessimistic about the introduction of autonomous cars: I am sure it is going to happen.

Already, as this book is prepared for publication, on-road trials have been officially authorized and are being conducted in various countries. All the major car companies are investing fortunes to prepare autonomous vehicles for production, though Porsche has stated that it is not interested. This is wise, because companies like Porsche, Ferrari, Lamborghini and Aston Martin have no long-term future, so investing in such technology would be throwing money away.

What would be the point of a 'supercar' if you cannot actually drive it, and the speeds of all road vehicles are under electronic control? Luxury manufacturers, on the other hand, will be able to thrive.

Obviously, also, it will be the end of the motorcycle industry, because you could not have bikers mixing in with unmanned vehicles. Now there is a major problem: what about parcel delivery services and those farty little pizza mopeds? How will that be done?

If track driving days continue into the post-operator road vehicle era, there may be scope for some specialist manufacturers to survive, though it is difficult to imagine that the current volumes of such companies, while relatively small, could be maintained.

Nissan has already tested its semi-autonomous system extensively on public roads in Japan. A prototype Audi A7 travelled autonomously (with a test driver ready to take over, if necessary) the 550 miles from San Francisco to Las Vegas for the 2015 Consumer Electronics Show. In Britain, if you are driving around the Coventry area, cars from the Jaguar Land Rover group with which you share the road may be taking part in 'UK-CITE' (UK Connected Intelligent Transport Environment) research project. These trials will continue for several years while the technology is developed.

In the next stage, semi-autonomous vehicles will be available for leasing to the public. The drivers of these will, at any time, be able to override the system and take control, and will be obliged to do so in areas that do not yet have the infrastructure installed.

One of those think-tank/'business strategy' companies predicts that, by 2025, approximately 13 per cent of vehicles on the road will have autonomous features of one kind or another, that this will rise to 25 per cent by 2035, and then expand exponentially thereafter.

Thus, it will begin with permission to use a semi-autonomous vehicle on public roads where the infrastructure has been installed, mixing in with other vehicles actually being driven by those sitting behind the steering wheel. Next, fully-autonomous will be permitted. Finally, it will be compulsory. The only steering wheels after that will be attached to classic cars in museums.

It is unlikely that it will be possible to actually buy an autonomous vehicle. All must be under centralized control, and here we run into a wide range of other unpalatable but inevitable societal shifts involving further erosion of freedom. The gap between rich and poor will widen still further.

The FBI has already expressed its concern about autonomous vehicles, which, for terrorists, will provide the most sophisticated, yet also the simplest, bomb-delivery system so far devised. Apart from that, the whole network will be vulnerable to a massive cyber attack that would leave millions of people stranded at the roadside.

In any case, where will you be going in your autonomous vehicle? It will have been constructed by robots in a factory with very few human employees, and it will be controlled by on-board robotics interacting with roadside signals. But you will not have a job to go to, because that will have been taken over by robots as well. Nobody seems to have spotted the obvious flaws in this Utopian vision, or to have asked the obvious questions about its sustainability[1].

Then there is the taxi question. The traditional London cabbie will certainly not last long. 'The Knowledge'[2] has become progressively more pointless with improvements in satnav systems.

It is widely imagined by transport wonks in governmental employment and in the motor industry that the driverless taxi will be a part of this Brave New World. A pilot scheme has already begun in Japan. It is easy to see why this has captured the imagination, and it sounds so obvious.

You need to get, for example, from point A in London to point B. You call a cab using your mobile phone, the cab arrives, you insert your plastic card into a slot or swipe it, tap in or utter your desired destination and the taxi takes you there by the shortest/quickest possible route, without conversation, though a bowdlerized, apolitical chatting electronic cabbie might be an optional extra. You arrive at your destination, remove your card and leave. Simple and easy ...

There are several problems with this. In particular, some passengers will undoubtedly feel free to do all sorts of things in a driverless cab that they would never dare to do in the presence of a jabbering cab-owning driver ... all those things that people do in a 24-hour period, some of which necessitate cleaning up afterwards. Among the less problematic of these activities for subsequent users of the cab in question might be eating or having sex.

I suppose that this system could work in Japan, where the population has, by and large, maintained a tradition of politeness, respect for other people, and a collective sense of what is acceptable behaviour and what is not. But that is not the case elsewhere.

It is more likely that camera surveillance in cabs will be compulsory. A voice, ideally like that of the late Joyce Grenfell, will tell occupants, 'Don't do that!' and, if the occupants ignore the command, the module could be redirected to the nearest police station, with doors locked. However, as Stanley Baldwin remarked, "The bomber will always get through" and the security implications of the driverless taxi are nightmarish.

Some of the major technical problems afflicting autonomous cars (those I have mentioned, plus several others, such as poor performance in bad visibility, and difficulties of access to motorways at times of high density) can be overcome. However, some others, especially the possibility of grid failure, which could have numerous causes, are more difficult to resolve and could have catastrophic consequences. And by no means all the problems are technical. As often at crucial moments in human history, there is a blind rush towards an uncertain future.

Decisions on vital matters that are likely to blight the lives of future generations are being made today by mad people who will not personally be around either to endure, or to be held responsible, for the economic and social consequences. There is much talk, for example, of the possible introduction of a guaranteed minimum income. Those of the Dr Pangloss persuasion, who believe this to be a good idea, have evidently not considered the consequences, which would be far worse than the imagined dystopia of George Orwell, Aldous Huxley and Kurt Vonnegut. In such a scheme, The State would be even more The Master than it is now. It would be the reintroduction of serfdom, but in a far more controlled form than ever before. Everyone, from birth to death, would effectively be the property of the government.

Happily, along with the ragbag of unprincipled villains, lunatic visionaries and naive idiots in favour of these ideas which will make the lives of their descendants miserable, I will have checked out long before all this happens, in the fond hope that reincarnation is as false a theory as phlogiston. Thank you and best wishes.

[1] I shall not bother to ask them here, because they are too bloody obvious.
[2] The system by which prospective licenced drivers of 'black cabs' learn all the routes, highways and byways, by riding around on mopeds with clipboards mounted on the handlebars and then have to pass a rigorous exam.

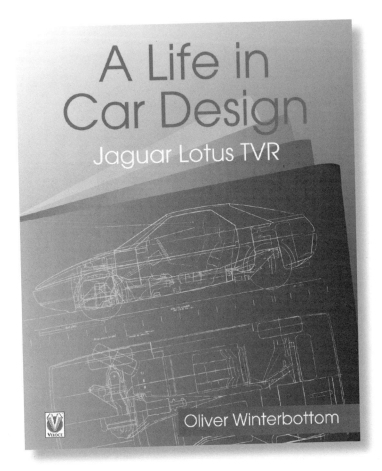

A Life in
Car Design
Jaguar Lotus TVR

Oliver Winterbottom

This book gives a unique insight into design and project work for a number of companies in the motor industry. It is aimed at both automobile enthusiasts and to encourage upcoming generations to consider a career in the creative field.
Written in historical order, it traces the changes in the car design process over nearly 50 years.

ISBN: 978-1-787110-35-9
Hardback • 25x20.7cm • 176 pages • 200 pictures

For more information and price details, visit our website at www.veloce.co.uk
• email: info@veloce.co.uk • Tel: +44(0)1305 260068

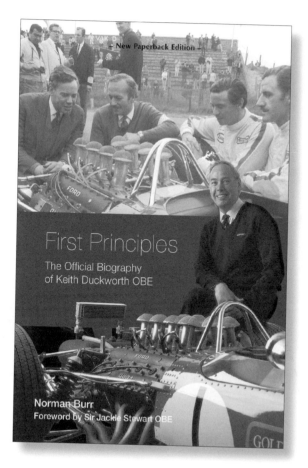

First Principles

The Official Biography
of Keith Duckworth OBE

Norman Burr
Foreword by Sir Jackie Stewart OBE

This book chronicles the life of Keith Duckworth OBE, the remarkable engineer, co-founder of Cosworth Engineering and creator of the most successful F1 engine of all time, the DFV. This is a rounded look at the life and work of the man – work which included significant contributions to aviation, motorcycling, and powerboating.

ISBN: 978-1-787111-03-5
Paperback • 23.2x15.5cm • 352 pages • 200 pictures

For more information and price details, visit our website at www.veloce.co.uk
• email: info@veloce.co.uk • Tel: +44(0)1305 260068

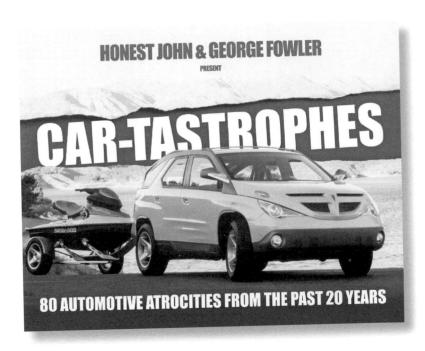

HONEST JOHN & GEORGE FOWLER
PRESENT

CAR-TASTROPHES

80 AUTOMOTIVE ATROCITIES FROM THE PAST 20 YEARS

Automakers are as prone to turn out clunkers as politicians are to lie. Their cars may be ugly, misconceived, badly built, diabolical to drive, ridiculously thirsty, or just plain unreliable. So which were the worst of the past 20 years?

ISBN: 978-1-845849-33-7
Hardback • 15x19.8cm • 168 pages • 165 pictures

For more information and price details, visit our website at www.veloce.co.uk
• email: info@veloce.co.uk • Tel: +44(0)1305 260068

Index